STRUGGLE and FULFILLMENT

STRUGGLE and FULFILLMENT

The Inner Dynamics of
Religion and Morality

Donald Evans

FORTRESS PRESS   **PHILADELPHIA**

First published in Great Britain by William Collins Publishers, Inc., in 1980. First Fortress Press edition 1981

Library of Congress Cataloging in Publication Data

Evans, Donald D
Struggle and fulfillment.

Bibliography: p.
Includes indexes.
1. Ethics. 2. Religion. I. Title.
[BJ1012.E9 1981] 241 80-8050
ISBN 0-8006-1426-7

8294J80 Printed in the United States of America 1-1426

Contents

Preface

This book was begun in 1970. Its completion was made possible by a Killam Senior Research Scholarship granted by the Canada Council for 1975–77.

Earlier drafts of various sections have benefited by criticisms or suggestions from Marcus Adeny, Gregory Baum, Don Browning, Stephen Harris, Thomas Langan, Gene Outka, Philip McKenna, Yu Jin Pak, Austin Repath, Richard Rubinstein, Michael Stark, Jack Stevenson, and Richard Weisman. Loren Lind and Robin Smith provided very pertinent and detailed editorial comments on both style and substance. An extensive reflective response from Giles Milhaven was specially stimulating and helpful.

I have been inspired and influenced by many writers, but noticeably by Gregory Baum, Martin Buber, Erik Erikson, James Gustafson, Sam Keen, William Lynch, H. Richard Niebuhr, Gabriel Marcel, and Paul Tillich. More recently, Wilhelm Reich has become important for me.

I am deeply indebted to Therafields, a therapeutic community in Toronto, for what I have learned there about myself and other human beings. Without my experience in Therafields this book would not have been possible. I dedicate it to my therapists, Adam Crabtree, James Healy, and Marion Plotnik, and to my teacher, Lea Hindley-Smith.

Introduction

Deep within myself I find conflicting tendencies. Some lead me to affirm life, others to deny it. Each day there is a struggle The issue is which tendencies will prevail. It is up to me whether I call upon the life-affirming tendencies or ignore them, whether I resist the life-denying tendencies or acquiesce in them. In other people I see a similar struggle. Each of us is moved by creative and destructive forces which we can aid or hinder. These forces are expressed in basic stances which pervade us as persons, stances such as trust and distrust, self-acceptance and self-rejection, concern and self-preoccupation. Our fulfillment as human beings depends on which kind of stance predominates.

This book is not an autobiography, but it has arisen from firsthand experience of the struggle which it depicts. My account of the basic stances is based mainly on my own experience and the experience of people whom I have known at a deep level in their profound struggle towards a life of love.[1] I am convinced that the more profoundly a person experiences this struggle the more he or she comes into conscious contact with universal characteristics of human beings. Depth brings breadth. So the crucial test of what I say is whether it illuminates the deeper experiences of reflective readers. I also hope that as a philosopher I have a distinctive contribution to make by shedding new light on the underlying structure of the struggle. I am presenting a systematic study rather than a collection of illustrative episodes.

In this book I not only describe the human struggle, but also show how this description provides a new view of religion and morality in which we focus on their inner dynamics and their essential unity. When I began work on the book a decade ago I conceived it as a theoretical investigation of religion and morality and their interrelation. I gradually became convinced, however, that it is a mistake to focus mainly on the theoretical structures of religion and morality. These need to be understood in relation to certain life-affirming stances such as trust which are the core of both authentic religious faith and genuine moral

1

character. And since our fulfillment as human beings depends on the extent to which these life-affirming stances prevail over their opposites, religion and morality and human fulfillment all have a common core.

The most crucial personal struggle in religion, morality, and life is between trust and distrust. A large portion of this book is an exploration of these two pervasive ways of being and behaving in the world. Here I will provide only an introductory sketch. The trust to which I refer is sometimes called "basic trust" to distinguish it from particular trustful stances towards particular people. In everyday life we trust a person in some respects and distrust him in others. We find some people trustworthy in most respects and others in few. Basic trust is not the same as any of these particular stances though it affects all of them. Indeed, it affects our particular distrustful stances as well, for it pervades the whole personality and it is brought to every individual whom one encounters. It is an overall mode of existing in the world, a dynamic trust-readiness:[2] one is creatively responsive to whatever trustworthy elements are actually or potentially present in each individual; if there are few, one acts accordingly. But the initial assumption, prior to the particular facts of each new encounter, is that something positive may emerge. Such trust is not naïve or self-deceptive concerning evil. A man of trust such as Jesus accurately discerns the precise way in which this or that person cannot be trusted: the secret treachery of Judas, or the hidden hostility of a questioning scribe. A contemporary Jew who has basic trust will see through the superficial friendliness of some Christians and challenge their hidden anti-Semitism. Basic trust is not a matter of trusting many people rather than few, for the number of people in one's environment that one can realistically trust is an external variable. Basic trust is an inner stance which one brings to each situation, whether this is an ideal community or a concentration camp. It is an initial openness to whatever is life-affirming in nature and other people and oneself. Sometimes a great deal is immediately accessible, sometimes little. What counts is the active acceptance of whatever is available. This trust-readiness towards particulars is an expression of an assurance that our human life has significance in a cosmos which is fundamentally for us rather than against us. Such a cosmic confidence is maintained in spite of many specific occasions for realistic distrust and in spite of our tendency to treat these as symbols of a cosmos which is against us.

Peter Berger[3] describes how a cosmic trustworthiness can be symbolized by a particular person, a "face of reassuring love, bending over our terror." A child wakes in the night, alone and frightened. Mother comes, and her presence somehow conveys the message, "Everything is all right." For Berger this common parental reassurance has such cosmic scope ("not just this particular anxiety, not just this particular pain—but *everything* is all right") that it can be translated as "have trust in being." Such pervasive, cosmic trust is conveyed to the child by the mother only to the extent that it is present within her already. It is a confidence that life is worth living, since it has already been provided with reality and meaning. Sometimes, however, basic trust can continue even though a man can find no particular persons whom he can trust, and even though what seem to be his deepest needs are being frustrated and no one seems able or willing to help. Though father and mother and all his friends forsake him, "Underneath are the everlasting arms" (Deut. 33:27; RSV). Wittgenstein described a similar attitude when he spoke of "the experience of feeling absolutely safe . . . the state of mind in which one is inclined to say, 'I am safe, nothing can injure me whatever happens'."[4]

The opposite of basic trust is basic distrust. This is an overall stance of the personality towards anything and everything in one's experience. Peter Berger's story about a child waking in the night, alone and frightened, could go on quite differently. The child waits and waits, but no one comes. Each flickering light or sudden sound increases his terror and somehow conveys the message, "Everything is all wrong." Each colic pain reinforces his sense of total helplessness and abandonment. His absent mother symbolizes a totally loveless universe. If mother finally does come, she may be too late. The child may have become wary and hostile, or almost paralyzed with despair. He is no longer open to receive the reassurance which he so deeply craved. Instead, he is ready to distrust whatever comes his way, at least for a while. If he is disappointed too deeply and too often, distrust can come to dominate his life.

Such pervasive distrust-readiness is not confined to infants. Every adult has it, to some extent. In so far as I bring this stance of basic distrust to each situation, I select real and imaginary evils as the main focus my attention and I see them as typical of my environment as a whole. Any suffering which comes my way becomes for me a symbol of total helplessness and abandonment. And if I am rejected by someone for whom I yearn, this is a symbol of a totally loveless universe. On the other hand, I tend to ignore any good, or if I do not notice it I see it as an aberration. So instead of responding creatively to whatever trustworthy elements there may be in each person I meet, I tend to weaken these elements by the wariness or despair which I bring to my encounter with that person. In general, basic distrust moves me to reject whatever there is in me and in others that promotes life, and to occupy myself with whatever undermines it. Basic distrust is a commitment to life-denying forces as the dominant pervasive reality in me and my environment. Basic trust is a similarly pervasive commitment to life-affirming forces. The stark choice between these two commitments is crucial in the human struggle.

As we consider this struggle we will see that trust is both a religious attitude and a moral virtue. On the one hand, it is focused on whatever trustworthy reality pervades and unifies our environment. Trust in that reality is expressed in worship, and trust is the context in which religious beliefs authentically arise. On the other hand, trust is focused on other human beings. It is expressed in conduct which affirms life in ourselves and others, and it is the context in which moral beliefs authentically arise, for example, the conviction that life is worth living.

Since basic trust is both a religious attitude and a moral virtue, I shall call it an "attitude-virtue." I shall call its opposite, basic distrust, an "attitude-vice."

In this book I propose that basic trust and seven other attitude-virtues are the main constituents of both religion and morality. The relation between religion and morality can thus be depicted in the following diagram:

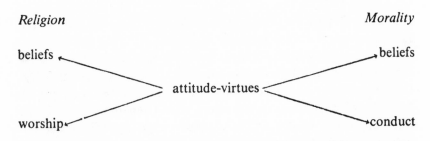

Religion   *Morality*

beliefs   beliefs

                                        attitude-virtues

worship   conduct

In making such a proposal I am presupposing that religion is primarily a set of attitudes and that morality is primarily a set of virtues. I am also claiming that the eight attitude-virtues are the main constituents of human fulfillment. So I am not only providing a new interpretation of religion and morality, but I am also proposing a view of human nature and a way of life which goes along with this view. I depict human life as a conflict between the attitude-virtues and the attitude-vices and I challenge myself and the reader to nurture the former and resist the latter. Human fulfillment consists of a steady predominance of the attitude-virtues over the attitude-vices, a victory in which a person is able to love freely and spontaneously, in harmony with himself, other people, and the ultimate reality which pervades the universe.

I do not give equal attention to all the attitude-virtues. Part One of this book is a detailed description of the struggle between trust and distrust. Part Two, shorter in length, is a brief description of the struggles between the other seven attitude-virtues and their opposites and a discussion of all eight together. This disparity in length of treatment does not mean that there is a corresponding disparity in importance. The other seven attitude-virtues are very important. They are all integral parts of human fulfillment, and the last three can even be viewed as the most important goals in human life. I hope to write at length about all seven elsewhere. The structure of this book arises from limitations of space. It would be possible to write solely on trust and distrust, but this would give a misleadingly narrow picture of what religion, morality, and life in general are about. A more comprehensive context is needed. Indeed, here in the Introduction I am now going to give a preview of Part Two, listing and sketching the other seven attitude-virtues and their opposites:

Humility is a realistic, unashamed acceptance and exercise of the limited powers and the finite freedom which I have as a human being. One opposite is pride, which is a self-deceptive attempt to act out my infantile fantasies of infinitude, of unlimited strength and status. The other opposite is self-humiliation, which is a self-deceptive attempt to ignore my real though modest powers and achievements, preferring instead to wallow helplessly in shame.

Self-acceptance and its opposite, self-rejection, have to do with guilt—not realistic guilt concerning specific harms done, but pervasive, undiscriminating guilt which terrorizes and paralyzes me. The issue here is whether my energies are released for creative involvement in the world as I accept someone's acceptance of me, or whether my energies are directed inwards in destructive self-punishment.

Responsibility is the stance of a person who can be counted on to do a good job of tasks assigned to him or undertaken by him, including the overall task of living as an effective and worthwhile human being. A responsible person is conscientious and competent. He is a disciplined disciple, learning and applying the traditional rules of his community; and he is an innovative individual, providing new initiatives and new methods when the situation requires such. The opposite is irresponsibility: each specific task is unstarted or botched or unfinished, and life as a whole is a mess.

Self-commitment is a stance which integrates my personality and gives me a sense of personal identity. I commit myself to a reliable vision of nature and human history and human community and of my place in relation to them, trying to be true to myself and to my experience of the world. The opposite is an alienated dissipation of my personal substance and energy, scattering myself in all directions.

Friendliness is a stance of readiness and willingness to enter intimate "I-Thou" relations of love, giving and receiving at a deep personal level. It includes confirmation, confrontation, celebration, devotion, respect, and affection towards other persons. Some of the elements in friendliness are only appropriate towards friends, but others are also appropriate towards anyone whom I encounter. The opposite of friendliness is self-isolation, either in solitude or in impersonal role playing among people.

Concern is a stance of readiness and willingness to help others in response to their needs, especially those who cannot reciprocate in the same way: infants and children, the sick and the helpless, the underprivileged and the oppressed. There are two kinds of concern: "pastoral" (direct, face-to-face helping) and "prophetic" (political action against oppressive power structures in society). The opposite of concern is self-indulgence, which is a sentimentalized pastoral concern for myself as my own "infant and pet" and a comfortable acceptance of affluence and influence which depend on my favorable position in an unjust society.

Contemplation is the stance of a person who profoundly appreciates the reality and uniqueness of each particular in the universe, including himself. It is fostered by various forms of meditation which discipline his attention, cleanse his vision, and open his heart. Gradually he is liberated from the self-preoccupation and self-consciousness which distort and subjectivize our usual perception of reality. He also becomes aware of a still center within himself which somehow participates in a reality which is ultimate, and from this vantage point he can see that all things similarly participate.

The eight attitude-virtues are connected in various ways. Friendliness and concern are each species of love, and together they create a context for contemplation, which is also a species of love. The combination of all three is the supreme goal in human life, though the emphasis in this combination differs from person to person. The other five attitude-virtues are prerequisites for these three. Only in so far as we have a firm grasp on ourselves can we let go of ourselves in love.

My choice of eight attitude-virtues is not arbitrary. At the end of Part Two I will not only justify my selection but also show that the eight can be ordered in a pattern of priorities. The selection and the pattern are based on the way in which human beings naturally develop. Each of us is unique, but we share a common human nature. Each of us has a distinctive struggle towards fulfillment, but in that struggle there are common prerequisites and common goals. The eight attitude-virtues provide a framework within which each of us can shape a style of life which is both individually appropriate and essentially human. And the most fundamental attitude-virtue is trust.

In relation to each attitude-virtue there is a twofold struggle. First, and foremost, there is the struggle to be open: to accept life-affirming forces into one's own life so that the virtues may grow. This sounds easy, but actually most people find it difficult. Second, there is the struggle to resist forces of destruction which otherwise would take over one's life in the form of one of the attitude-vices. In this twofold struggle the issue is whether the attitude-virtues or the corresponding attitude-vice will predominate. In each case the outcome is never completely certain. Often an attitude-vice wins out, at least for a while. Indeed, only a few people come close to human fulfillment, which is a steady predominance of all the attitude-virtues in their most mature forms. For nearly everyone, however, some growth towards fulfillment is possible. The main requirement is a sincere attempt to be honest and persistent in the struggle, trying to turn towards life. This is what matters most, rather than how near or how far we are from fulfillment. We vary greatly in our personalities and our situations. What counts for each of us is the direction of our movement from where we are now.

In all this we can be heartened by two things. First, none of us need be alone in the struggle. We are all in it together, and the overall process is a movement out of self-isolation and self-preoccupation into genuine community. And second, there is a realistic basis for believing that the destructive, life-denying forces at work within us and among us, though immensely powerful, are derivative distortions of a fundamental drive towards life and love. Many human beings are rotten in many ways, but human nature is not rotten at the core.

The struggle between the eight attitude-virtues and their opposites is publicly expressed in our daily life. The center of the struggle, however, is private and internal: deep decisions for or against life take place in the hidden recesses of the human heart. For many people, however, the most immediate struggle is *external*. Those who are poor struggle for sheer survival and those who are powerless struggle against economic and political oppression. Others who are more fortunate sometimes identify themselves with their cause. The focus in this external struggle is on public results rather than private decisions, on social justice rather than individual fulfillment. There is a tension between the two kinds of struggle, a tension which is only partially eased by the fact that prophetic concern is both an essential ingredient in individual fulfillment and an important factor in the external struggle. In *Faith, Authenticity and Morality* (see Bibliography A) I have discussed this tension and the primary question which arises: "Which should have priority, personal liberation or political liberation?" In this book, however, I focus on the internal struggle. I am aware, however, that the freedom to focus mainly on the internal struggle, though not a dispensable luxury, is a privilege which many people do not share. Also, I am aware that those of us who have this privilege must seriously ask whether we *should* focus mainly on the internal struggle, for the poor and the powerless need our help in their external struggle. I am convinced, however, that the internal struggle is ultimately the most important for every person.

Another limitation on my account of the human struggle is that not only my focusing on the internal struggle but also what I actually say about it will reveal some of the biases of privilege: specifically, those of a white Protestant middle-class North American intellectual male. In general, though I am keenly aware of psychological influences on my perspective, I am less aware of sociological influences. I have not wrestled as much with the relativism and bias which my societal origins and status bring to my thought, so I suspect that these may cause considerable distortion. Also, in my account of the origins of attitude-virtues and attitude-vices in people generally, I have paid more attention to psychological influences than to sociological influences. A more adequate account of, say, trust would not only refer to early experiences in the family but also say more than I do concerning the impact of society.

All any of us can do, however, is try to detect and transcend the various limitations of our own life experience as historical beings and the various self-deceptions which Freud and Marx can help us to uncover. The more we try, to the limited best of our ability, and the more we are open to correct and supplement our own vision by what others see from their perspectives, the closer we may come to some universal truths concerning what it means to be human.

These truths, if genuinely universal, apply as much to women as to men. In the past, books which generalize concerning human nature have traditionally been written in the masculine gender only. This stylistic simplication is understandable, but it excludes one half of the human race from explicit mention. The representative human being is always referred to as "he." The representative human characteristics, whether virtuous or vicious, belong to "him." Such stylistic sexism reinforces real-life sexism: men still tend to be regarded as the primary paradigms of human nature. How is one to avoid this reinforcement? To speak of "he or she" and "him or her" on every occasion is awkward and cumbersome; some passages would become grotesque in their complexity. In this book I have decided, instead, to describe human beings from time to time in the feminine gender: I refer to "someone" or "a person" and then go on to use the pronoun "she." This will jar some readers at first. We have all been conditioned to expect "he." But this is not a matter of good grammar or felicitous style; it is merely a sexist convention.

When I describe an attitude-virtue or an attitude-vice in one gender rather than another this does not mean that those of that gender are more likely to have it. Throughout the book I describe human qualities which I regard as equally male or female. I have tried to counteract a male bias by reflecting what women say concerning their deepest experiences of human nature. In this book I have tried to present the crucial struggle which goes on within every human being.

Although I am making sweeping claims concerning human nature, I realize that what I present is a personal perspective which is limited by the influences and the sources which have shaped it, not only the biases of privilege which I have mentioned, but also three other factors. *First*, I have gained many insights from various books on religion, morality, and psychology. The most influential sources are listed in Bibliography A. Obviously if I were working in a different intellectual context my account would be very different. *Second*, Christian tradition has influenced me in many ways beyond the conscious derivation of ideas from academic books on theology. I do not appeal to Christian tradition as an authority, but it is the religious context within which I live and think. I am convinced that what I have written is generally compatible with much in Christian tradition, but I do not try to prove that this is so; that would require a different kind of book, a theological work. Nor do I expect that compatibility with Christian tradition would be an argument in favor of the book for a reader who rejects that tradition; rather, it may be a reason for suspicion. The primary test for such a reader is whether or not what I say jibes with his or her own experience as a non-Christian, but it would be pointless to try to hide the influence of Christian tradition on my own experience. *Third*, as I have already noted, the book is influenced by my own experience of the struggle which it depicts. My account of human nature has been pervasively affected by my own psychological history, both past and present. I am aware of this in great detail because much of what I have written came directly out of experiences while involved in deep psychoanalytic work. But the more aware I become of psychological influences which may distort and limit my vision, the more likely it is that my findings will apply to other human beings, especially if I am also relying on the experiences of others who are trying to be honest with themselves. Such a critical self-awareness means that a personal perspective is not purely subjective if the personal probings have been profound and sustained. But the extent to which my findings have universal validity is something each reader can decide.

Although this is a philosophical book it is not a book of technical philosophy — or technical theology or technical psychology, for that matter. I have tried to write about common human experiences in a language which links together morality, religion, and psychotherapy. I thereby *show* that there can be a unity of these three rather than *argue* that there might be. But many technical philosophical questions arise from what I say, especially concerning the ways in which religious beliefs depend on religious attitudes. Originally I had planned to discuss these questions in the book as an ongoing commentary on my account of the human struggle. Certainly I have been aware of the questions as I wrote, but I was also aware that I was not writing primarily for professional philosophers. So I have decided to place technical commentary in footnotes where it will not distract or intimidate the general reader. (The most significant notes for philosophers are probably those related to the last section of Part Two.)

My presentation is more of a showing than an argument, but it depends on a crucial assumption which I shall now explain at some length. I hope that readers who are keen to plunge into the experiential material concerning trust and distrust will bear with me for a few pages as I consider this assumption, for it provides the basic framework for the whole book. My assumption is that religion is primarily a set of attitudes and morality primarily a set of virtues. In contrast with this, many thinkers regard religion and morality as mainly matters of *belief*. For them the core of religion is a set of beliefs concerning ultimate reality, so that religious attitudes are secondary and are justified by reference to the beliefs. And for them the core of morality is a set of beliefs concerning what kinds of actions ought or ought not to be performed, so that moral virtues are secondary and are justified by reference to the beliefs. Philosophers who hold this view look at statements which express religious and moral beliefs and ask whether these statements are logically connected.[5] But since I hold that beliefs are actually secondary and derivative in religion and morality, I do not think that a study of statements will get to the heart of the matter. Indeed, I think that to confine ourselves to such a study would be a gross intellectualist error. The statements need to be understood in relation to the inner dynamics of religion and morality, which give them their meaning. I agree with Martin Buber:[6]

> The essence of the relationship between the ethical and the religious cannot be determined by comparing the teachings of ethics and religion.

Religious faith is for me primarily a set of attitudes such as basic trust. Whether or not people render these attitudes explicit in religious beliefs is a secondary matter. The attitudes are "religious" in that they are both *pervasive* and *unifying*. An attitude can be pervasive in two different ways: internally and externally. It is internally pervasive if it influences the person in all the dimensions of his personality, however we distinguish these: as thought, will and feeling, as observable behavior and private experience, or as conscious and unconscious processes. It is externally pervasive if it is brought to any and every situation, influencing the person's dealings with everything he actually has contact with, and ready to influence his dealings with anything else; its scope is unrestricted, universal. When I describe an attitude as "pervasive" I usually mean that it is both internally pervasive and externally pervasive. The attitude is a fundamental way in which the self relates to the environment, an active perspective on the world as a whole.

The world may seem to one person to be a universe, a unified cosmos. To another person it may seem to be an unintegrated multiverse, perhaps even a chaos. I maintain that this is because the one person is integrated and whole whereas the other is divided and fragmented. The unity or disunity of the perceived environment is a mirror of one's own personal unity or disunity. Some pervasive attitudes help to unify the personality by bringing all its dimensions into a kind of harmony, whereas other pervasive attitudes tend to divide the personality. Where an attitude is internally unifying it is also externally unifying, and vice versa. That is, if the attitude unifies the person, it both *promotes* a recognition of a pervasive unity in his environment and is *reinforced* by such a recognition. The attitude is focused on whatever pervasive reality unifies the environment and the person is thereby enabled to deal with the environment in a unified way. Basic trust, for example, is focused on a pervasive, unifying reality which is trustworthy. The conviction concerning the cosmos depends on the attitude which we bring to the cosmos.

If a pervasive attitude is internally divisive it is also externally divisive, and vice versa. A divided self discovers what seems to be a divided world and this discovery reinforces its internal disunity. In general, convictions concerning the unity or disunity of the world, and concerning the *kind* of unity or disunity, are reflections of differing pervasive attitudes. What I am saying here is very abstract, but it will become clear when we examine various attitudes in a concrete way. We will see that each attitude is an overall way of being in the world, a way of viewing everything and dealing with everything. But if each attitude provides its own perspective, how can we tell which one provides a true perspective? Which attitude enables us to see what is really out there rather than what we project out there? There is no simple way to settle this question. I shall maintain, however, that distrust distorts our vision and trust enables us to discern what is really there. And when we view the world from a stance of trust there is a conviction, perhaps implicit rather than explicit, that a trustworthy reality pervades and unifies our environment.

The attitudes which we will consider have a *moral* significance as well as a religious relevance. They are moral virtues. A moral virtue is a pervasive, unifying stance which is an integral part of a person's fulfillment as a human being, and which influences his actions in each and every situation, especially his dealings with other human beings, where it helps to promote their fulfillment. A moral vice is a pervasive stance which frustrates human fulfillment in oneself and others. Both a virtue and a vice shape a person's conduct. The virtue gives it a distinctive life-affirming tone, whereas the vice gives it a characteristic life-denying tone.

As I wrote this book I wondered whether to use the terms "virtue" and "vice" at all, for they are so commonly associated with prim self-righteousness and harsh self-condemnation. What I mean will gradually become clear as I give examples, but I must immediately dissociate my meaning from the narrowly moralistic meaning which the words often have in everyday life. It seems better to me to reinstate these terms in continuity with their historical meaning (which goes back to the Greeks) rather than to discard them because this meaning has been distorted. For me, at any rate, a virtue such as trust is an ability or strength, but it is not an occasion for smug self-satisfaction, for it is not a private achievement or a private possession.[7] Rather, it is a strength which emerges and continues in interpersonal relations of giving and receiving, and it is not discerned in competitive comparison with other people but in mutual encounter with them. Nor are the vices, which are the opposites of the virtues, appropriate occasions for a punitive, moralistic condemnation which evokes paralyzing guilt. The fact that I have a vice such as basic distrust is not a reason for rejecting myself. Having vices is part of the human condition. People have them in varying degrees and forms, but they are to some extent inescapable. What I need from myself and others is not blame for having the vice, but encouragement and challenge to struggle against being dominated by it. I need to accept myself as I now am, a mixture of wheat and tares, trust and distrust; otherwise, in a vain attempt to eliminate the weedy tares, I will uproot everything. Although I need to expose and resist my distrust in a firm way, I also need to tolerate it. And my main focus should be on cultivating whatever trust I have, opening myself to whatever nourishes it. (As I write this I remember an occasion when I was struggling, in my own severely serious way, to emerge from the depths of depression. A wise counselor said, "Struggle doesn't just mean trying hard in spite of your despair. What are you doing that you really enjoy, that means life for you?")

I should also note that what I mean by a "virtue" or a "vice" is not a disposition to behave in such-and-such external ways in such-and-such kinds of situation.[8] Such a view of virtue and vice fits in with a conception of morality as a set of rules devised to regulate social behavior so as to reduce conflict and foster cooperation.[9] A moral virtue is then simply a disposition to behave in accordance with one of the rules, and a moral vice is a disposition to behave in violation of one of the rules. But in the kind of morality which I am describing, a moral virtue and a moral vice are not merely behavioral dispositions. Each does influence external behavior, but each is also revealed in the "style" or "timbre" of a person's behavior, its inner spirit of life-affirmation or life-denial, and its origins in the depths of the personality. And since a virtue or vice is an internally pervasive stance, its scope is not restricted to certain kinds of behavior which most clearly express and exemplify it; it influences all behavior to some extent.[10] Moreover, as an externally pervasive stance it brings its own cosmic perspective to each particular situation. In general it is not so much a way of behaving as a way of being in the world.

It is true that much of what is usually called "morality" consists of rules and dispositions to follow rules. It is a guide to behavior. Such a morality is sometimes attacked by people who advocate a "situational" morality, which stresses the decision of the individual in each situation rather than rules. Both moralities, however, are primarily concerned with behavior: "What actions or kinds of actions ought I to perform? What ought I to *do*?" Obviously this is important. I maintain, however, that there is a prior question which is more important: "What kind of person ought I to *be*?" An "ethic of being" precedes an "ethic of doing." More specifically, the primary question is, "What pervasive stances, what virtues, should be dominant in my life?" I advocate an ethic of being which is an ethic of virtue, an ethic of ways-of-being-in-the-world.

I also maintain the moral virtues are religious attitudes. They are attitude-virtues, that is, ways of being in the world which have both a religious and a moral dimension.

Although I am proposing my own account of religion and morality rather than simply describing other people's accounts, I am not being merely a maverick. The primacy of attitudes in religion is stressed in a great deal of contemporary Protestant theology,[11] and the primacy of virtues in morality is a perennial claim which is being made again in contemporary philosophical ethics[12] and Christian ethics.[13] Where my account differs from most is that I do not merely connect certain religious attitudes with certain moral virtues. Rather, I claim concerning certain pervasive stances that each is both a religious attitude and a moral virtue. Yet even here I am not alone. Paul Tillich's "courage"[14] can be construed as being both a religious attitude and a moral virtue, and so can Martin Buber's "I-Thou attitude," [15] Gabriel Marcel's "hope,"[16] and Erik Erikson's "trust."[17] Indeed, I am indebted to all these thinkers, though my own proposal includes a range of attitude-virtues which is wider and more comprehensive.[18]

I do not give equal attention to all the attitude-virtues. Part One of this book is a detailed description of the struggle between trust and distrust.

Part **ONE**

The Struggle Between Trust and Distrust

Chapter 1

The Constituents
of Trust and Distrust

One of the most familiar expressions of trust is Psalm 23:

> The Lord is my shepherd; I shall want nothing.
> He makes me lie down in green pastures,
> and leads me beside the waters of peace;
> he renews life within me,
> and for his name's sake guides me in the right path.
> Even though I walk through a valley dark as death
> I fear no evil, for thou art with me,
> thy staff and thy crook are my comfort.
>
> Thou spreadest a table for me in the sight of my enemies;
> thou has richly bathed my head with oil,
> and my cup runs over.
> Goodness and love unfailing, these will follow me
> all the days of my life,
> and I shall dwell in the house of the Lord
> my whole life long. (NEB)

Here some of the main elements in trust can be seen in implicit contrast
with corresponding elements in distrust. First, there is an *assurance* that

the essentials for life are already being given to us: the means to satisfy our basic bodily needs ("green pastures") and the presence ("Thou art with me") which reassures us that we are accepted and cherished as we are, that life has ultimate meaning already, that we can depend on ultimate reality. This assurance is in contrast with the pervasive *anxiety* which is also part of human life. Second, there is *receptivity*, a grateful acknowledgment and enjoyment of the generous abundance which is being provided. This is expressed or implied in the whole second paragraph of the psalm, which contains no hint of the cosmic *wariness* which is the enemy of receptivity. Instead of being resentful, hostile, and miserly in his overall stance, the psalmist is actively responsive to the divine generosity. One expects him to be generous rather than bitter and begrudging towards other men. A third element in trust is *fidelity*, a faithful commitment to the source of the essentials for life. Rather than turning away from the green pastures and the reassuring presence, *idolatrously* craving some substitute-good at the end of a different path, we steadfastly recognize and receive the good which is already at hand in the path where we find ourselves. Fourth, there is a *hope* that even in the "valley dark as death" the renewal of life and the unfailing love which we have received in the past will continue into the future. The psalmist does not succumb to a crippling and cowardly *despair*; he walks on.

Psalm 23 is a classic, but it needs to be supplemented by the first two lines of Psalm 22, which express another element of trust, one which at first sight seems to conflict with the assurance, receptivity, fidelity, and hope of Psalm 23:

> My God, my God, why hast thou forsaken me
> and art so far from saving me, from
> heeding my groans? (NEB)

Trust involves *passion*: allowing oneself to feel and to express one's most profound and intense feeelings, rather than deceiving oneself that these do not exist and falling into *apathy*. Among the feelings which we are most tempted to repress are those which arise when we seem to be forsaken. When a person feels totally abandoned, he has agonizing feelings of loneliness and grief and helpless yearning which may be too terrible to acknowledge. On a slightly less profound level he has distrustful feelings such as angry resentment which are also difficult to acknowledge. In Psalm 22 the passionate distrust can be felt and expressed because at some deep level the psalmist is confident that this will not drive God away or make him hostile. A cry of dereliction is expressed to a God who is still *there*, though not near. If a man has trust, he has an assurance that he is accepted as he is, his whole self. What Psalm 23 fails to indicate is that this whole self which is accepted includes his distrust as well as his trust. Distrust does not disappear entirely, even in the most trustful of men; but it need not be hidden from himself and from God. It can be felt and expressed even in the worst crises of life; then, indeed, it may emerge most strongly. Trust enables distrust to come out into the open. And the most fundamental struggle within each human being is between the two.

The struggle between trust and distrust goes on in various ways. Each of the five constituents of trust has an opposite, as we have seen:

Trust	*Distrust*
Assurance	Anxiety
Receptivity	Wariness
Fidelity	Idolatry
Hope	Despair
Passion	Apathy

In the following chapters we will consider each pair in turn. Almost all the constituents of trust and distrust have subordinate elements which can be distinguished and discussed, so eventually we will have quite a complex conceptual map of trust and distrust. This might suggest that the struggle between them can be adequately understood by standing at a safe distance away from it and constructing a tidy and comprehensive framework of concepts concerning it. This is not true. The struggle is personally experienced as a disorderly daily scrimmage between forces which usually do not identify themselves until there is a temporary truce and the dust of battle has settled for a while. My account of trust and distrust has been gradually written during times of temporary truce when the memory of the struggle is still vivid. What I say has no pretensions of finality, even though my conceptual map may suggest that everything has been nicely sorted out. What I hope is that I can do two things: I want to express the urgency and intensity of the struggle in ways which resonate with some of the reader's most profound experiences, and I want to articulate some of the main outlines of the struggle in ways which illuminate those dark depths.

Chapter **2**

Assurance and Anxiety

The most fundamental constituent in trust is the assurance that life is worth living because its essentials have already been provided. Assurance has two components, which I shall call "reality-assurance" and "satisfaction-assurance." Reality-assurance is primary, so I shall consider it first, and most extensively.

Reality-assurance is the assurance that life is worth living because it has already received the meaning and reality which are necessary for human fulfillment. This formal definition is only useful to the extent that I can convey to the reader what I mean by "meaning" and "reality" as essentials for this life. This is difficult, for both my own understanding and that of the reader depend mainly on the extent to which each of us already has reality-assurance. Moreover, much of what is being conveyed is both prior to the learning of language and beyond the limits of language. It began when we were infants and it transcends our ability to plumb and express our own depths.

Concerning "meaning," I first quote Martin Buber:[1]

> There is the inexpressible confirmation of meaning. Meaning is assured. Nothing can any longer be meaningless. The question about the meaning of life is no longer there. But were it there, it would not have to be answered. You do not know how to exhibit

and define the meaning of life, you have no formula or picture for it, and yet it has more certitude for you than the perceptions of your senses.

Someone who lacks this assurance that life is meaningful is perpetually anxious lest the little meanings which she seems to find in her life are concoctions which hide an ultimate pointlessness and absurdity. All her involvements in petty projects or grandiose schemes have as their background the dreadful possibility that life is a tale told by an idiot, signifying nothing. All her responses to the disappointments and tragedies of life, whether she be weak-kneed or heroic, may be in vain. An assurance that life is meaningful is crucial for human life. The need begins in infancy. As Erik Erikson points out, there are few frustrations which a young child cannot endure if parents are "able to represent to the child a deep, an almost somatic conviction that there is a meaning to what they are doing."[2] If parents have an assurance of meaning they can pass it along to their children. Meaning is something one receives. It comes first from one's parents and then pervasively from others in one's environment and then from one's inner depths. It comes *from* these but also *through* them, for meaning seems to come ultimately from a reality which is revealed through the meaningful presence of particular people and through the interior texture of one's own life. This meaning is received as a gift, and the gift comes as something to be lived. One's fundamental life task is to express this meaning by living it in one's own particular way. One's life then has many particular meanings, most of which can be articulated and specified, and all of which are partly created by oneself. But the ultimate meaning is assured because it is not a goal which must be achieved but a gift which has been received.

   Closely related to the assurance of meaning is the assurance of reality. The two are so intimately connected that I have referred to them together as "reality-assurance." But the reality element can be distinguished. It is described, for example, in R. D. Laing's account of what he calls "ontological security":[3]

   A basically *ontologically* secure person will encounter all the hazards of life . . . from a centrally firm sense of his own and other people's reality and identity . . . a sense of his integral selfhood and personal identity, of the permanency of things, of the reliability of natural processes, of the substantiality of natural processes, of the substantiality of others . . . The individual, then, may experience his own being as real, alive, whole; . . . as having an inner consistency, substantiality, genuineness and worth; as spatially coextensive with the body.

The ontologically insecure person is preoccupied with preserving rather than gratifying himself . . . If the individual cannot take the realness, aliveness, autonomy and identity of himself and others for granted, then he has to become absorbed in contriving ways of trying to be real, of keeping himself or others alive, of preserving his identity, in efforts, as he will often put it, to prevent himself losing his self.

Laing's account of ontological security and insecurity is excellent, except that it does not say enough about the importance of bodily awareness. The ontologically secure person is not only aware that she is "spatially coextensive" with her body. She is also intimately aware of her body as a unity which is firmly and securely grounded and established on the earth, and as a participant in life energies which pervade her physical environment. Assurance of reality is not only a mental or psychical state. It is also a physical or bodily state which can be felt from inside or observed from outside. A person feels in her feet and her guts and her heart that she has been confirmed in her existence, and others can detect her reality-assurance in the firm way her feet meet the ground.[4]

Sam Keen combines the elements of "meaning" and "reality" in the following passage (which is the key paragraph in his analysis of what it means to say "God is" with the "total self"):[5]

The ultimate significance, meaning, security, value, dignity of my life is not dependent upon anything I can do, make or accomplish. Therefore, my action may spring out of what I am rather than arising out of a desperate need to establish myself. I am already founded, rooted, grounded in (depth metaphors) or contexted and encompassed by (metaphors of inclusion) that which guarantees my integrity.

In so far as I have reality-assurance, I am confident that my life has meaning and reality because these have already been provided; they come with life itself. They are gifts to be recognized and received, not goals towards which I anxiously strive, or unreachable benefits which I forlornly crave. They are gifts from an ultimate meaningful context, an ultimate ground of being, gifts to me and to all the beings I encounter. As recipients of meaning and reality, we are confirmed, accepted, and valued. In spite of all the evil in me, I am "good" in the sense of being valuable: it is good that I exist. And the same is true of the world as a whole.

This sense of being valuable is a necessary condition for having an assurance. Life does not seem significant and solid unless I am confident that I matter. An infant cannot receive into his own life the assurance which his parents have that life has meaning and reality unless they confirm him and accept him and value him and he assumes this gift as a given within himself. Similarly an adult cannot receive the essentials for life unless he accepts his own value in the cosmos as a gift which is a given.

Although the assurance of meaning and reality and value is the fundamental constituent of basic trust, there is something more basic. The crucial *condition* for reality-assurance is *acceptance*[6] of meaning, reality, and value. I am assured of them only to the extent that I actively accept them into my personal existence. Such acceptance is the basic condition not only for reality-assurance and trust but also for human fulfillment, which has trust as its basic condition and constituent. Human fulfillment is thus remote from people whose life is a matter of willful striving and determined self-assertion. Although there is a legitimate place for striving and self-assertion, these should rest on a relaxed stance of responsiveness to essentials for life which are already being provided. Often we need to struggle vigorously against destructive forces, but the most important struggle occurs in actively accepting rather than rejecting the good, the creative force, which is already being provided. It is strange that we need to struggle to accept, but this is because we not only long for abundant life but also fear it. When we do accept, however, there is a time free from all struggle, a time in which we can enjoy the resources which are actually available, relaxing and rejoicing as we receive and share. The time may be brief or it may be prolonged, but after a while new challenges will emerge and new struggles will become necessary. In all of this the most fundamental inner decision is between acceptance and nonacceptance. Acceptance means being open to life energies, cherishing their many manifestations, welcoming into one's inmost being the myriad forms of love and joy, beauty and creativity, harmony and radiance, mystery and presence, meaning and passion. For those who are in touch with their bodies, the life energies are experienced as intensely pleasurable "streaming" sensations of a vital current which moves from the base of the pelvis to the ground under one's feet, to the crown of one's head and to the space beyond one's finger tips. The current is intimately associated with deep and relaxed breathing. Thus reality-assurance is, in part, an awareness of a tangible reality. (We will consider this further in the chapter on trust as passion.)

There are two ways to reality-assurance. One is positive and one is negative.[7] In the first stage of the positive way, I take some person to be symbolic and representative of whatever it is that pervades my total environment. The person's presence conveys a meaning and reality and life energy which, though limited, seem to participate in an utterly dependable meaning and reality and life energy which pervade the cosmos. Like the child in Berger's story, I am assured that somehow everything is all right since I am grounded and surrounded and confirmed by an all-inclusive benevolence. In a more mature version of the positive way, I do not focus solely on one person. The realization gradually dawns that in many different individuals there is a cosmic source of trustworthiness at work. And in a still more mature version, a third step in the positive way, I do not focus solely on other persons. I begin to view the creative, life-affirming elements within myself as also being symbolic and representative of the cosmic reality. This is not megalomania, but its opposite: a sense of participating with countless others in a reality and meaning and life energy which pervade the universe.

A very specific, autobiographical example of the positive way is provided by Sam Keen.[8] When he was a child, his father made a promise to him and yet never kept it, though what was promised meant the world to Keen. Years later, visiting his dying father, Keen brought himself to say, "In all that is important you have never failed me. With one exception, you kept the promises you made to me—you never carved me that peach-seed monkey." Two weeks before the death of his father, Keen received the monkey in the mail:

> For me, a peach-seed monkey has become a symbol of all the promises which were made to me and the energy and care which nourished and created me as a human being. And, even more fundamentally, it is a symbol of that which is the foundation of all human personality and dignity. Each of us is redeemed from a shallow and hostile life only by the sacrificial love and civility which we have gratuitously received. As Erik Erikson has pointed out in *Identity and the Life Cycle*, a secure and healthy identity is founded upon a sense of *basic trust* which is first mediated to a child by the trustworthiness of his parents. Identity has its roots in the dependability, orderliness, and nurturing responsiveness of the world of primal experience. . . . I uncover the promises made and kept which are the hidden root of my sense of the basic trustworthiness of the world.

Keen's peach-seed monkey is mainly an example of the first, relatively immature, version of the positive way towards reality-assurance, though Keen also moves into the second stage as well. In the first stage an adult draws on experiences of positive parenting during infancy as he looks on some contemporary as a symbol of cosmic trustworthiness. The contemporary might be a parent, now much older of course; or it might be a surrogate parent such as a senior friend or a therapist or a spiritual director or a guru. More frequently, however, the adult who treasures this contemporary's presence is finding some reality and meaning and confirmation which were *not* received during infancy. Unlike Keen, the person is moved by experiences of an early parenting which were negative rather than positive in impact. This focus on a person who gives something precious which one missed during infancy, something which one has always desperately longed for, can be dangerous. Later I will describe how it may degenerate into a destructive and obsessive idolatry. Here I want to describe how it can lead into a more mature form of reality-assurance. Instead of relying on one "face of reassuring love, bending over our terror," some individual who reassures me as mother once did (or as mother never did, however much I wanted her to), I begin to see a life-affirming presence in *many* people. These are people who have the attitude-virtue which in this book is called "friendliness," that is, a readiness to confirm others, celebrating their strengths and respecting their freedom. I begin to see that they convey their strong sense of the significance and substantiality of life not only to me but also to many others, not only to those who are weak and wistful but also to those who are already strong in reality-assurance, with whom they have a mutual relation of giving and receiving. The third version of the positive way is a further step beyond this: I find that I can include myself among the many who participate in the meaning and reality and acceptance which pervade the universe. Then the basis for assurance is no longer entirely outside myself, in other people; it is also revealed within myself. And at this stage I am no longer preoccupied with a self-centered concern as to whether the universe is for or against *me*. Self-preoccupation is replaced by *appreciation* of everyone and everything, including myself, for we all participate in the same reality.

This final, contemplative stage of reality-assurance is the goal of the positive way. We will consider it more carefully in Part Two. The crucial stage, however, is often the first, when we see some particular as symbol of a cosmic Good Mother rather than Bad Mother. (Since mothers are usually the dominant influence in very early infancy, the image is usually maternal rather than paternal in our unconscious mind.) The first stage involves a decision, partly unconscious, to select something benevolent rather than malevolent as symbol or representative of whatever reality is common to my whole environment. This primitive, fundamental choice is not made, and cannot be made, on the basis of a statistical survey of the relative quantities of good and evil in the universe. Nor is it a matter of deciding between rival speculative hypotheses with reference to their intellectual adequacy as overall explanations of the cosmos. It is a profoundly practical choice between fundamental stances of the whole personality, pervasive attitudes which shape the way in which I view the world and the way in which I live in the world. The decision to accept someone as representative of Good

Mother rather than to fear someone as representative of Bad Mother is a primitive version of a fundamental choice: I accept or I reject the meaning and reality and life-affirming strength which are available for me. The choice is between participation in life and participation in death, for resistance to life involves acquiescence in the destructive forces which are at work in the world and within myself. More mature versions of this choice occur in the second and third stages of the positive way, but the first stage is crucial.

Some people seem to evade the choice by seeing the world as neither benevolent nor malevolent but *neutral*.[9] The word "neutral" here can have two different meanings. On the one hand, I may see the world as neutral in the sense of callously indifferent. Though it is not hostile, it does not seem friendly to my needs and aspirations. I had expected a world which is caring and comforting, but instead it turns away from me. So I feel disappointed and forlorn and resentful. I see the world as Indifferent Mother, which is merely a species of Bad Mother. My anthropomorphic projection is obvious. It is an expression of a kind of distrust which we will consider in the chapter on "wariness."

In the second meaning of "neutral" the projection is hidden. A neutral world may mean a world devoid of value, a world from which it would be irrational to expect any positive (or negative) relation to my needs and aspirations. It simply has no connection with these. The world is neither kind nor hostile nor uncaring. Just as any particular thing seems detached and disconnected from me when I view it as a detached, disconnected observer, so does the world as a whole. When I bring to the world a passionless perspective it seems unrelated to my passions. It is a cosmic mirror-image of my own neutrality and impersonality. If I am emotionally out of touch with my deepest desires and if I am thereby closed to the life energies within myself, I can discern no dynamic depths in the world outside. I will not have a vital, embodied reality-assurance. This lack, however, will be hidden from me, for my sense of self will have been reduced to an abstract intellect and a manipulative will, and my sense of external reality will be correspondingly superficial: abstract structures and manipulative powers. My neutrality will not be obviously a form of basic distrust, for I will neither warily resist intrusions from a hostile world nor bitterly resent a cosmic cold shoulder. But, as we will see later in the section on "apathy," such neutrality can be the subtlest way to resist reality, the most devious kind of distrust. This will become clear when we eventually contrast it with its opposite: a trustful, passionate participation in reality.

The most obvious choice, however, is not between apathy and passion, but between symbols of Good Mother and Bad Mother. Sometimes this choice is focused on things in nature rather than on persons. And sometimes one and the same item can be seen alternatively as a positive and a negative symbol. Virginia Woolf[10] reveals some of her own deep inner struggle in her description of ocean waves falling on an island beach:

> The monotonous fall of the waves on the beach, which for the most part beat a measured and soothing tattoo to her thoughts and seemed consolingly to repeat over and over again as she sat with the children the words of some old cradle song, murmured by nature, "I am guarding you—I am your support", but at other times suddenly and unexpectedly, especially when her mind raised itself slightly from the task actually in hand, had no such kindly meaning, but like a ghostly roll of drums remorselessly beat the measure of life, made one think of the destruction of the island and its engulfment in the sea, and warned her whose day had slipped past in one quick doing after another that it was all ephemeral as the rainbow.

The most primitive choice in the positive way is between the cradle song murmured by nature and the ghostly roll of drums. The choice is not like a decision made at a crossroads to take road *A* rather than road *B*, knowing that I will thereafter never see *B* again. Distrust cannot be simply willed away. A distrustful vision of the world, set aside today, may return to color my consciousness tomorrow. But I can choose whether to consent to it or resist it. The choice is expressed in the way I live my daily life. I can struggle to accept whatever is life-affirming within me and around me. I can struggle to withdraw my support from whatever is life-denying. As I struggle, trust can gradually come to predominate over distrust. Indeed, trust itself changes its character. Instead of regarding the waves as a symbol of a cosmic Mother who is Good rather than Bad (malevolent or indifferent), and instead of regarding them as a mirror image of my own neutrality and thus as not participating in life energy, I begin to contemplate them as they really are. Instead of transferring infantile hopes or fears from mother to various particulars and asking "Is the world-Mother for me or against me?", I move beyond both kinds of self-preoccupied projection so as to appreciate each particular as it is, and the world as it is. And instead of detaching myself from movements of life in my body and my environment, I passionately perceive them. In such a contemplative stance I can see specific evil and ugliness, but this occurs in a world which is saturated with good and beauty, light and life. What I then discern in the waves is not a cradle song or a ghostly roll of drums or an object for scientific scrutiny but rather an expression of a glorious life energy which flows through the whole cosmos and which floods my own embodied being.

As I have said before, such a contemplative vision, based on mature trust, is the goal of the positive way to reality-assurance. Occasional glimpses of it can encourage us as we struggle at a more rudimentary level. But the more primitive Good-Mother kind of trust is not to be despised. It is for all of us the indispensable foundation on which the higher vantage point of disinterested, ecstatic contemplation is built. It is the primary positive way to reality-assurance.

The *negative way* to reality-assurance is the opposite. Its route to the ultimate is not *via* a presence but *via* an absence. A person exposes himself to the terrifying experience of the void. Meaning and reality disappear completely from one's consciousness. There is a total absence of any reassuring presence. Neither outside oneself nor inside oneself can one find any significance or substance to provide security. The fall into the void occurs when a person lets go of his cravings and his striving for a kind of meaning and reality which he can possess and control. If he already has any such bogus meaning and reality, perhaps in some achievements as a "self-made" man, he abandons the consolation which this has brought. As he lets go of the false self and the world it has created for survival and security, he feels that reality has let go of him, abandoning him to a drifting and desolate existence. As he stops clinging to his own concoctions, he falls helplessly through the void, frightened and forlorn, lost in an endless emptiness. But although it seems that his drop has no destination, eventually he lands gently and firmly on solid ground, with an assurance of meaning and reality which is firmer than anything he has ever experienced. At the bottom of the void is the ultimate in confirmation and security.

Sam Keen provides a vivid, personal account of the negative way, in a passage which deserves to become a classic:[11]

> It was as if my interior space had been hollowed out and boredom, anxiety, despair, impotence, erratic willfulness, and shameful self-consciousness were dumped in and agitated like clothes in a washer. These demons whirled around my inner emptiness, their harsh screams reverberating and blending into painful cacophony in the vacuum. I was possessed by vertigo. No way to stop the swirl. No solid ground. No place to rest. No power to discover or cling to what was satisfying.
>
> Only once the vertigo disappeared. *The* phone call came. My father was dying . . . For a time my emptiness was filled with grief, my vaccuum transformed into a wound.
>
> But the vertigo returned. When death took my father it also challenged my last authority. Nothing abides, nothing resists the acids of change and decay. I had once sought grounding in the history of Israel and in the certainties of the Christian community. That had failed me. My father had failed me by dying, he had disappointed my illusory hope—Fathers do not die. In my disappointment the question that shaped my quest was, "What can I do to give my life meaning, dignity, density?" In back of this question, no doubt, was the old Christian query, "What can I do to be saved? To be healed?"
>
> My answer came suddenly jumping up and down in my mind with the force of an obvious fact long denied. I woke one night in Manhattan with the words, "Nothing, nothing" on my lips. As I started to laugh at the comedy of my own seriousness my vertigo began to subside. I saw that I had been obsessed with the wrong question. In the face of the uncertainty of life and the certainty of death no human act or project could render existence meaningful or secure. Nothing I could *do* would result in my being saved, ontologically grounded against tragedy and death. Either dignity and meaningfulness come with the territory or they must forever be absent. Sanctity is given with being. It is not earned.

In the first paragraph Keen is partly into the void, partly struggling to stay out. He can stay out by experiencing painful but less terrible feelings which, because of their familiarity, provide some sense of security. Even anxiety is more tolerable than the void. By the third paragraph he is well into the void, experiencing the absence of meaning and reality—not only in his father, now dead, but also in the cosmos which his father had symbolized; but he is clinging to the illusion that he can and must *do* something to provide the missing meaning and reality. In the last paragraph the breakthrough to reality-assurance comes: there is nothing that he can do to create meaning and reality—all his cravings and strivings are useless; but somehow the experience of the worst (nothing he *can* do) enables him to experience the best (nothing he *must* do). The assurance comes that there is no need to do anything to get out of the void. What is needed is a not-doing, a letting go of the cravings and strivings and whatever consolations have been within his control. When he lets go, he recognizes and receives the reality and meaning which are at hand, already given, both within him and outside him. Sanctity (that is, reality and meaning) is given with being.

Both the positive and negative ways are required for deep reality-assurance. On the one hand, the negative way paradoxically requires a substantial base of positive assurance within a man. Otherwise he does not dare to let go of his strivings and cravings, which provide a kind of security, a substitute-meaning and substitute-reality, a defense against the raw experience of the void, with its terrifying feelings of radical abandonment, desolation, and emptiness. Unless, at some time in his life, a person has had some strong positive experience of accepting a meaning and reality conveyed by others, he cannot enter the void. When he does so, and is not *conscious* of any meaning and reality, some reality-assurance persists at an unconscious level. If this were not so, he would not be able to give up every conscious basis for feeling secure. (The fact that reality-assurance has both conscious and unconscious dimensions will also turn out to be important when we consider other constituents of trust.)

Although the positive way is needed if someone is to be able to follow the negative way, the negative way is needed to remedy defects in the positive way. First, other people die, and then one's assurance has to be adequate to face their absence as sources of meaning and reality. Although Keen's positive experience of his father was important in enabling him to move into the negative way, the death of his father made the negative way necessary. More mature versions of the positive way are less vulnerable, however, to the tragic contingencies of life; the death of one person does not destroy one's reality-assurance if it is based on what one has discerned through many persons, including oneself. There is a more fundamental reason why the negative way is needed in addition to the positive way: the *void*. I am convinced that the void is common to all mankind and that everyone tries to evade it by strivings and cravings and substitute-miseries. Unless the evasions stop and the void is experienced, the positive way cannot bring deep reality-assurance, for the constant repression of the void subtly and secretly weakens the assurance, poisoning it with anxiety.

My conviction that the void is common to all mankind is impossible either to verify or to falsify in any decisive way. Nevertheless there is converging testimony from many diverse sources that there is a way to a kind of reality-assurance which is *via* a terrifying experience of a state which people try to hide from themselves in their daily lives, a state aptly called "the void." Testimony can be cited from Roman Catholic mysticism (e.g. St. John of the Cross' "dark night of the soul,"[12] existentialism (e.g. Tillich's "anxiety of meaninglessness,"[13] Protestant religious experience (e.g. Luther's "as if already in hell),"[14] and psychotherapy (e.g. Janov's "primal pain,"[15] Laing's "experience of negation,"[16] and Erikson's "abysmal alienations . . . which are the human lot"[17]). There are serious difficulties in any attempt to show that what all these thinkers refer to (and what Eastern writers concerning the void refer to) is essentially the same void. The experiential routes and the descriptions and the explanations all differ in important ways.[18] But where the converging testimony is reinforced by personal experience it seems to me reasonable to believe that the void—in some form or other—is common to all mankind.[19]

If someone is to experience the void, she needs a special kind of acceptance—not the acceptance of whatever meaning and reality are available, but an acceptance of a situation where there is *no* meaning and reality. This means that she is not only open to "being" but also open to "nonbeing." Instead of trusting only when and because the essentials for life are available, she can also trust when they are absent. Instead of trusting only when and because God is present, she can also trust when God is absent. Instead of trusting only when and because her self is being confirmed, she can also trust when her self is being lost: "Though he slay me, yet will I trust in him" (Job 13:15; KJV). Only such unconditional acceptance can bring an assurance which is beyond any possible undermining.

Degrees of assurance. It seems undeniable, however, that some people do gain a moderate degree of reality-assurance without having experienced the void, though perhaps for others this is not possible. Reality-assurance does differ in degree, and this fact has important implications for morality and religion. There is a continuum of assurance, from minimal to maximal. At the lowest level there is a minimal assurance without which a person dies or becomes irretrievably psychotic. Without minimal assurance I literally cannot take a step lest the earth cave in under my weight. I must have confidence that there is a minimal reality and regularity in my environment, even if most of what is provided seems to be unsubstantial and meaningless. A slightly stronger assurance is perhaps required for suicide, where this is a deliberate act based on a decision; there must be at least enough meaning for it to matter whether or not one kills oneself—which is, of course, not much meaning. Such minimal levels of assurance are necessary for morality and religion in that they are necessary for *any* kind of living and acting. If there is no point at all in any living and acting, there is no point in living and acting in the special ways which we call "moral" and "religious."

Higher levels of reality-assurance are relevant to morality and religion in a very different way. When Sam Keen talks about "being redeemed from shallow and hostile life"[20] in relation to the basic trustworthiness of the world, and when he talks about the "sanctity" which is "given with being,"[21] such a reality-assurance is not necessary for sheer survival or nonsuicide; one can get by and make do with much less. A high-level assurance is not relevant to morality and religion in the same indirect way as a low-level assurance. It is more directly relevant. Concerning morality, high-level assurance is relevant in two ways. First, a strong reality-assurance is a necessary condition and constituent of a human life which is fully and authentically human, an instance of human "flourishing" or "fulfillment". Second, a strong reality-assurance radically affects the way in which a man deals with others, for it enables him to see them in a disinterested, realistic way and to treat them as ends in themselves. Otherwise, he tends to see them and to treat them as means or obstacles or disappointments in subordination to his own inescapable, overwhelming needs. That is, what dominates his dealings with others is a relentless search for something which will remedy his lack of assurance, or for some way by which he can reduce or evade the painful anxiety which (as we shall see) accompanies the lack of assurance.

Concerning religion, variations in strength of reality-assurance are also important. We have seen that it is plausible to claim that a minimal assurance is a necessary condition for a minimal human existence. In this case, if any cosmic belief is implied, it too is minimal. The belief is merely that there is some cosmic reality which provides sufficient meaning to go on living rather than dying or disappearing into psychosis or committing suicide. It seems to me misleading to use the term "God" to refer to such a minimal cosmic reality,[22] or to describe such a minimal assurance as "religious," for what is meant is remote from what the terms usually mean. But when the reality-assurance is strong, as in the case of Sam Keen, it is far more than what is needed for a minimal human existence; and if a belief is implied it is a religious belief, a belief in God. God is here conceived as the Provider and Guarantor of what Keen calls "sanctity": the profound meaning, reality, dignity, integrity, and value of his life. Here is what Keen himself says:[23]

> Theology, making use of the rich emotive language of love, trust, mercy and grace, affirms that the source out of which life comes and into which it disappears intends the fulfillment rather than the frustration of those values we hold to be fundamental for human dignity . . . For the religious man, God-language functions to affirm that the ultimate context into which human existence is inserted is trustworthy.

Let us return to the brief description of assurance with which I began: "the assurance that life is worth living, because its essentials have already been provided." Note how the moral relevance and the religious relevance—and the possible variations in these—are indicated in that description. Life is *worth* living: how much worth has it, enough for survival or enough to build on towards one's fulfillment and enough to free one to seek the fulfillment of others? The essentials have been *provided*: does the Provider provide essentials for survival or essentials for fulfillment?

Satisfaction-assurance. When I began with the brief description of assurance, I said that assurance has two components—reality-assurance and satisfaction-assurance. It is time we considered the latter, which can be illustrated by the following passage from Matthew 6:25-27 in the Sermon on the Mount:

> I bid you put away anxious thoughts about food and drink to keep you alive, and clothes to cover your body . . . Look at the birds of the air; they do not sow or reap and store in barns, yet your heavenly Father feeds them. You are worth more than the birds! (NEB)

This passage can be interpreted in two radically different directions:

> a) There is no need to be anxious about food and clothes because, in one way or another, God will provide them. You will not be hungry or cold. Your bodily needs will be satisfied. God takes care of you, like a good shepherd or a loving parent.

> b) Don't be anxious about food and clothing. It's all right to sow seed and to weave cloth, but don't worry about the outcome. Even if it should turn out that you are hungry and cold, what matters is the assurance of worth (and reality and meaning) which you have from God. You are absolutely safe in that reality-assurance, whatever happens to your body.

If we have to choose between (a) and (b), it seems to me that (a) is the more plausible exegesis of the text, yet it is untenable as a life-stance. Not only is it contradicted by the facts of life as experienced by millions of people who have starved to death; it is also contrary to other New Testament teachings concerning the bodily privations which Christians, like Jesus on the Cross, may well have to endure. It seems to me that a more tenable and typical religious assurance—and perhaps a more plausible exegesis of the text—is expressed in words which combine elements from (a) and (b):

> c) There is no need to be anxious about food and clothing. It's all right to sow seed and to weave cloth, but don't worry about the outcome. You matter to God, and so your bodily needs matter to God. He provides the means to satisfy them, like a good shepherd or a living parent. But *even if* you should turn out to be suffering from hunger and cold, what matters is the assurance of worth (and reality and meaning) which you have from God. You are absolutely safe in that reality-assurance, whatever happens to your body.

Here there is a crucial assymetry between the response to satisfaction and the response to frustration. We are being asked to look on the satisfaction of our bodily needs as a symbol of the care and the acceptance which the ultimate has for us. Thus satisfaction of our bodily needs can reinforce our reality-assurance. But frustration of our bodily needs is not to be taken as a symbol of rejection by the ultimate, though there is a tendency in all of us to interpret it in that way. When satisfaction-assurance is being undermined because we are suffering pain and privation and frustration, we are being asked to fall back on our reality-assurance, not allowing that to be undermined. It is clear that here satisfaction-assurance is subordinate to reality-assurance.

An interesting psychoanalytic parallel to this can be seen in what Erik Erikson says about an infant's trust:[24]

> The amount of trust derived from earliest infantile experience does not seem to depend on absolute quantities of food or demonstrations of love, but rather on the quality of the material relationship . . . sensitive care of the baby's individual needs and a firm sense of personal trustworthiness within the trusted framework of their culture's life style. This forms the basis in the child for a sense of identity which will later combine a sense of being "all right," of being oneself, and of becoming what other people trust one will become. There are, therefore, (within certain limits previously defined as the "musts" of child care) few frustrations in either this or the following stages which the growing child cannot endure if the frustration leads to . . . a final integration of the

individual life cycle with some meaningful wider belongingness. Parents must . . . be able to represent to the child a deep, an almost somatic conviction that there is a meaning to what they are doing. Ultimately, children become neurotic not from frustrations, but from the lack or loss of societal meaning in these frustrations.

This quotation, though specially relevant in a discussion of satisfaction-assurance, obviously also raises a general question concerning infantile trust as an analogy and a source for adult trust. This is a complex and controversial matter, which I will discuss in Part Two. Here I will simply state my two main convictions concerning it. First, adult trust, though extensively similar to infantile trust in form and content, and though deeply influenced by it, is not identical with it. For example, I have already described two later stages of the positive way which are not possible for infants. Second, the adult's psychological need for trust does not undermine the rationality of the religious beliefs which trust involves, but rather supports it. It is rational to have a religious belief if an attitude which is a constituent of human fulfillment involves the belief. This is specially so if there is no *other* way to decide rationally between the belief and its opposite. It is also so if the belief is rationally supported in some other way.

But I have digressed. Let us continue the discussion of satisfaction-assurance. I have noted that when bodily satisfactions are not met, a man has recourse to reality-assurance as the most fundamental kind of assurance. In my discussion of reality-assurance, I noted that the most fundamental decision is whether to accept or reject the meaning and reality which are provided, whether to look on positive or negative particulars as symbolic of the ultimate. This applies to bodily satisfactions and frustrations. But although satisfaction-assurance is subordinate, it is not dispensable. A reality-assurance divorced from bodily needs (as in (b) above) is inadequate. The psyche and the body are too intimately connected for a reality-assurance concerning psychic needs to be all that matters. In the positive way to reality-assurance, when another person who symbolizes the ultimate conveys meaning and reality to me by caring for me, the caring is often expressed in the form of a concern for my bodily needs. If it is never expressed in this form, then what matters to that person and to the ultimate is not me, the whole person, but only my disembodied psyche; I am split, and only part of me has meaning and reality. There is also another way in which satisfaction-assurance is an important ingredient in trust, which we will see when we consider trust as receptivity. An important element in trust as a receptive, grateful, generous stance is an assurance that the necessary means for satisfying one's bodily needs have been provided. The extreme opposite to this is a wary, resentful, begrudging stance toward an environment which seems hostile, frustrating, and stingy in relation to one's bodily needs.

One feature of assurance, then, is that it has both psychic and bodily components; it includes both reality-assurance and satisfaction-assurance. There are other important features: assurance is pervasive, unifying, and relational.

Assurance is pervasive. Assurance is present to some extent in any and every situation, and it influences the whole personality. Some elements in assurance can only be recognized if we consider an extreme case where the element is absent, for example in a mental patient who dares not take a step lest the ground collapse under him. Almost all of us have such an assurance all of the time without noticing it in ourselves or others. Other elements in assurance, however, are very obvious, either in the person's own momentary private experience (Keen waking in Manhattan) or in his momentary behavior, which subtly reveals that he is firmly grounded in meaning and reality. But although assurance can be experienced or observed at times, much of it is unconscious, accessible only to the extent that a person allows the unconscious dimension of his life to open up in some form of deep psychotherapy or profound spiritual pilgrimage. The extent to which one has assurance at the unconscious level is not a matter of simple introspection or observation. At any particular time, one's unconscious assurance may be less or more than what one feels or what others notice. And over long periods of time there may be a great discrepancy between the unconscious level and the level of conscious feelings, explicit beliefs, and external behavior. I remember a preacher who spoke fervently of divine providence who discovered early in his therapy that he was deeply distrustful of self, men, and God. And in contrast with this I have known professed cynics who have discovered an unconscious foundation of solid assurance which they had never acknowledged.

Assurance is unifying. A pervasive stance is not necessarily a unifying one. When I discuss anxiety I will show how it fragments the self and fragments the world. Assurance, however, is unifying. It involves an acceptance of meaning and reality and life energy into the self as a whole. All dimensions of the self are drawn together and grounded and energized by this gift. The gift can come via anything and everything in the environment, and it comes as from a common source. Thus assurance is a unified stance towards a unified world. It involves a conviction, which need not be conscious or explicit, that there is a pervasive source of the essentials for life. Believing that there is such a source is not a matter of giving assent to a speculative hypothesis which is open to scientific or quasi-scientific testing; rather it is a matter of having a conviction which arises from one's basic stance. *And the kind of unity which one believes in depends on the kind of basic stance one has.* Later we will see that each of the various constituents of distrust (except for anxiety) finds a kind of unity in the world. I shall argue that in each case the unity is precarious and partial, for it depends on a unity of the self which is itself precarious and partial.

Assurance is relational. Assurance, in its most fundamental or primitive form, involves a relation between a unified self and a unified world, an encounter between two realities which are intimately associated but nevertheless distinct. H. Richard Niebuhr puts it this way:[25]

> In so far as in (faith) trust I acknowledge that whatever acts upon me, in whatever domain of being, is part of, or participates in, one ultimate action, then though I understand nothing else about the ultimate action, yet I am now one.

> The self as one self among all the systematized reactions in which it engages seems to be the counterpart of a unity that lies beyond, yet expresses itself in, all the manifold systems of actions upon it. In religious language, the soul and God belong together; or otherwise stated, I am one within myself as I encounter the One in all that acts upon me.

The reverse is also true: I encounter the One in all that acts upon me as I am one within myself.

In so far as assurance is associated with encounter, it differs radically from another stance which is unifying but not relational, a stance which I shall call "merging oneness." The contrast between the two stances can perhaps best be seen if we consider two contrasting water metaphors which are used to elucidate the two stances. I once heard a Buddhist monk explaining a state similar to what I call "assurance." He talked about learning how to swim; one has to allow the water to hold oneself up, rather than thrash about desperately for some other security. In this metaphor there is an intimate relation between the swimmer and the water, but they remain distinct. There is a relation, not an identity. A person relies on the reality which provides security, but he does not merge with it. In contrast with this metaphor of a man learning to swim there is the metaphor of the stream merging with a boundless ocean. This latter metaphor depicts a mystical state of merging oneness in which the boundaries of one's body and one's psyche disappear. This "oceanic feeling," as it is sometimes called, is not associated with a belief in a God whom one *encounters* and who is *distinct* from oneself, such as Niebuhr's God. Rather, a conviction typical of the oceanic feeling would be that any person, and any particular entity, is like a momentary concentration of converging ocean currents, a temporary focus of expression for the universal reality.

The two contrasting water metaphors (swimmer and stream) thus help us to distinguish between primitive assurance and merging oneness, and to understand why the associated religious beliefs are so different. The contrast is also clarified if we consider the two contrasting life stages to which psychoanalysis may point when trying to trace origins and to suggest analogies for these states. Concerning primitive assurance, psychoanalysis may point to the infant in intimate relation with the mother: "In the beginning are the generous breast and the eyes that care."[26] Concerning merging oneness, psychoanalysis may point to the foetus in the womb, [27] not yet consciously distinct or separate enough from the mother to be in an active relation of encounter with her.

But although primitive assurance, the most fundamental form of trust, is relational, merging oneness is also an element in trust. In the chapter on trust as passion we will see that, as a participation in life energies, passion involves a kind of merging in a cosmic current. And the importance of merging oneness will also be obvious in the chapter on contemplation, the eighth attitude-virtue, for contemplation depends on a mature form of trust in which the ultimate is revealed as much within oneself as outside oneself. Thus we will see that in so far as trust involves not only primitive assurance but also passion, and in so far as trust matures to facilitate contemplation, we need to think in terms of *both* one-to-one encounter and one-in-One merging, so that both water metaphors become applicable, both psychoanalytic references become relevant, and the associated religious convictions involve both divine transcendence and divine immanence.

I am jumping ahead too far, however. We have been considering the ways in which assurance is pervasive, unifying, and relational. I maintained earlier that the basic constituent of trust is the assurance that life is worth living because the essentials for life have already been provided and accepted. The opposite of assurance, and the basic constituent of distrust, is anxiety. To this we now turn.

Anxiety. The opposite of assurance is a pervasive state of chaotic agitation. If I feel raw anxiety I feel my body being shaken up by conflicting charges of energy and I feel my consciousness being overwhelmed by formless flurries of panic. Anxiety is different from fear. Fear can mobilize my body and mind into a temporary unity to meet some specific threat; it focuses my strength and attention in a particular direction. Anxiety, however, scatters my strength and tears me apart as I respond to a nameless threat which teases and torments me from every direction at once. I lose my grip on myself and the world I live in. It is not a total disappearance of meaning and reality such as occurs in the experience of the void; instead, they are fitful and uncertain. They are like blinding lights which flash on and off through the darkness in a restless, irregular way, providing tantalizing but frightening glimpses of myself and my world. It is as if heaven and earth and my own interior space were kept in perpetual unease by cosmic strobe lights. Anxiety is a chronically unstable state. Like a frightened, injured bird hovering between a mountain ledge and the opening of an abyss, I hover between the solid ground of reality and the endless emptiness of the void.

This is because I am in direct contact with neither reality nor void. Anxiety arises from an inability or refusal to recognize the essentials for life which are actually at hand and from an inability or refusal to recognize and experience the void, which is also actually at hand. In both facets anxiety is paradoxically self-deceptive: in some disguised, indirect way I already acknowledge something which I can not or will not acknowledge openly and directly to myself. Perhaps one should say, "can not *and* will not," for there are elements of both inability and refusal in the stance—a combination which is typical, though paradoxical, wherever there is self-deception. Anxiety is a self-deception concerning both the best and the worst, both the reassuring provision of life energies and the terrifying self-loss in the void.

It is easy to see why we would try to avoid the void, and why whatever reminds us of the void, especially death, tends to make us unconsciously or consciously anxious. But why do we resist the essentials for life? Why do they appear as a nameless threat, an occasion for chaotic agitation and relentless pressure, rather than as a marvelous gift? This is a question concerning the origins of "sin" or "alienation" in human beings, and it is characteristically answered in terms of myths concerning a "fall" from "paradise." Such myths veil as much as they reveal. I know of no intellectually adequate account of the ultimate origin of human self-deception concerning the essentials for life. It seems to me, however, that Wilhelm Reich provides an illuminating perspective on the more immediate origins. According to Reich, anxiety is a distorted experience of life energies. We don't recognize and receive the essentials for life in that we do not open ourselves to life energies which pervade our bodies and our environment. In infancy we are taught to "armor" both body and psyche against the direct experience of these life energies, partly because they are intrinsically connected with sexual pleasure. So, instead, we experience the life energies in a distorted way, not flowing freely through us and our surroundings, but blocked, like steam in a leaky pressure cooker. Though distressing, anxiety is a way of feeling alive, and we become used to it as the fuel for all sorts of compulsive and scattered behavior. In my own therapeutic experience there have been vivid occasions of stark contrast between the two ways of relating to life energy. Within a few seconds there may be a shift from a terrifying, agitating pressure to a reassuring "streaming" sensation of warmth and light and vitality moving through the whole body. Some such change in bodily awareness is usually involved when the shift from anxiety to assurance occurs in ordinary daily life, though it is less starkly obvious. People who are out of touch with their bodies may not notice it at all, but they will be aware of a mental shift from a state of restless worry to one of calm enjoyment, from feeling shaky and driven to feeling secure and effortlessly active.

Anxiety arises as we resist the gift of the essentials for life and as we try to avoid the void. It is so painful that it is rarely experienced in its purity, by itself. Instead of feeling undiluted anxiety, we tend to move into one or other of the following states, which are different kinds of distrust:

Wariness. I concentrate on defending myself against all the evils which seem to beset me. The defences which I build also exclude the good . Either I cannot discern it or I fear to let it in lest some evil also sneak in. And my secret fear of the void is disguised as a fear of a hostile environment, full of enemies; such fear, though painful, is more tolerable.

Idolatry. I crave and strive for some substitute-good ("Life would be worth living if only I possessed x or achieved y") or I become addicted to a substitute-good ("z alone is what makes life worth living for me; without z I could not go on living").

Despair. I give up looking for any meaning and reality in myself or others. I resign myself to a helpless, hopeless, bleak existence. This provides a kind of security and protection against the void because it is all so inescapable, inevitable, and somehow familiar.

Apathy. I convince myself that I don't really care whether or not life is worth living. I do this by repressing my deep feelings, including those which might lead me into wariness, idolatry, or despair, and the anxiety which underlies these. This also deadens feelings of gratitude, hope, or joyful confidence. And I am, of course, remote from assurance and the void. A life of detachment from feeling provides its own kinds of security.

What each of these four states involve will become clearer when we consider them as the opposites of receptivity, fidelity, hope, and passion. A diagram may be useful here, in summing up the discussion of assurance and anxiety:

Trust	*Distrust*
Assurance	Anxiety
Receptivity	Wariness
Fidelity	Idolatry
Hope	Despair
Passion	Apathy

There is one assymetry here. When assurance is strong, it tends to foster *all* the other elements in trust together, though one of these may be somewhat more evident. When anxiety is strong, it tends to foster *one* of the other elements in distrust rather than any of the others. The other elements are not mutually exclusive, and a person may shift from one state to another (for example, from idolatry to despair and back to idolatry); but usually one state predominates at any one time, and the others are then far less operative. Thus the elements in distrust can be thought of as alternative "strategies" for dealing with anxiety, though they are not consciously and deliberately chosen. Or they can be thought of as alternative "symptoms" of the same illness, though the patient is not entirely helpless or ignorant in the matter. Just as anxiety involves self-deception, so also does the move into any of the other forms of distrust.

Anxiety is a part of every human life. Even people who have a high degree of assurance, even people who experience the special assurance which is found at the far side of the void, do not constantly maintain assurance. Anxiety is also at work on occasion. In most people it is always at work. We saw that although undiluted anxiety is rare, anxiety is often repressed from consciousness and then fosters wariness, idolatry, despair, or apathy. But sometimes anxiety is not totally repressed. Instead it is mixed with one of these other elements of distrust, especially wariness, which tends to allow more conscious anxiety than the others. When anxiety is only partially repressed it is felt as a disturbing worry or apprehension which has no specific focus, or which is disproportionate to whatever it is focused on.

It takes *courage* to face anxiety. Courage protects whatever assurance a person has, for repressed anxiety undermines assurance much more powerfully than anxiety which is acknowledged as part of one's being. The assurance which effectively deals with anxiety is a courageous assurance. And each of the other four elements in trust involves courage,[28] for each involves a refusal to repress anxiety in spite of the temptation to do so. Receptivity resists wariness, fidelity resists idolatry, hope resists despair, and passion resists apathy. Let us now consider receptivity and wariness.

Chapter 3

Receptivity and Wariness

What I mean by "receptivity" here is not the acceptance of the essentials of life which is a precondition of all the constituents of trust. Although I might well have used the word "receptivity" to refer to that acceptance, I use it here to refer to one of the constituents of trust. Receptivity is expressed in a syndrome of stances: gratitude, confirmation of others, and generosity. Its opposite is wariness, which is expressed in a corresponding syndrome of opposite stances: resentment, hostility, and miserliness.

Let us consider *wariness* first. Like other constituents of distrust, wariness is a pervasive stance. It is not a realistic, specific stance towards specific intrusions into one's life which would actually be harmful. Rather, it is an overall way of being in the world which subtly and powerfully influences the way in which one views and deals with each and every situation. It is a chronic, undifferentiated defensiveness against intrusions, as if one were a medieval knight who wore his suit of armor not only during battles, but twenty-four hours a day every day of the year. Actually, the real threat is inside oneself, for wariness, is a strategy for avoiding the pain and terror of the void, the frightening agony of finding nothing inside oneself and nothing on which to stand. It is easier to face this in a disguised and diluted form as an external enemy.

49

The wary man concentrates on feelings of being deprived or threatened or begrudged by others, so that the price of survival is eternal vigilance against intruders. If the active attention of his whole personality is thus directed outwards, he need not look within himself. The tense anxiety which he feels is very unpleasant, but he can accept it and even value it as a constant warning signal to be on his guard against malevolent powers. These powers seem to be waiting for any opportunity to deprive the wary man of any meager scraps of spiritual nourishment which are still in his possession, or to undermine his very existence by removing the very ground on which he stands. Against the threat of being deprived, his pervasive stance is bitter resentment. Against the threat of being destroyed, it is hostility. Resentment and hostility are two expressions of wariness.

Resentment has two facets. One facet, which I have already mentioned, is a self-protective resistance against intruders who would try to take away what little inner substance remains: each person whom the resentful man meets seems likely to be a greedy robber, plotting against him; and the whole universe seems to hum ominously with whispered conspiracy against him. The second facet is a readiness to view people and the world as miserly frustrators, coldly and cruelly denying him what he needs for life. Complaining against a callous cosmos which has provided so little, the resentful man sulks in self-pity, like an infant whining querulously for comfort from a mother whose heart is closed. This second facet differs from the first facet in that the "depriving" which he resents is not an action (a theft) but an inaction (a failure to give). Usually both facets of resentment are present. Instead of becoming fully conscious of his inner emptiness, the resentful man locates the source of his pain outside himself in other people who plot to take the essentials of life from him and who refuse to give them to him. Often he focuses on some one person as the twofold depriver. This person is seen as the symbol of the ultimate reality which pervades the universe—the Grand Depriver.

In all this resentment there is great bitterness. Even the little nourishment which he has received tastes bitter to the resentful man. He would like to spit it out. More dramatically, he would like to spit it back into the face of the Grand Depriver. And there is much bitter blaming of others, punishing them by making them feel guilty for his plight. Others are judged to be not merely ungenerous but viciously unjust when they covet his few morsels or when they begrudge him a few morsels from their abundance. The resentful man is what Edmund Bergler [1] calls an "injustice-collector", constantly finding or creating occasions which he can construe as proofs that others are unjustly depriving him of something he needs. Actually, the envious coveting and miserly begrudging which the resentful man finds so pervasively and profoundly in his environment is partly a projection of his own covetousness and miserliness. If some of his close associates are moderately or even strikingly unbegrudging and generous towards him, he cannot recognize it. And if some of them actually are covetous and miserly towards him, he sees them symbolically as the cosmic Grand Depriver, though that is not what they are. This distortion arises partly from a need to disavow his own covetousness and miserliness which, as we shall see, are characteristics of the wary man; he can project it on to others. But the main motive for the distortion lies deeper. Resentment is a strategy for avoiding the pain of the void. As such it is a precarious strategy. Unless it is pursued with obsessive thoroughness, so that his attention never wavers from the task of collecting evidence concerning external deprivers, the awareness of how little there is within his life can move the resentful man into despair. Sometimes such awareness can be the occasion for moving into an experience of the void, but usually despair is the outcome.

Resentment, like other expressions of wariness, is an attempt to unify self and world. But all that is unified in the self is, at best, the defence structure against intrusions. To the resentful man, this character armor sometimes seems to be his whole self, but actually most of the personality has been hidden away underneath. And the world which is unified against him by a malevolent reality is not the whole world; whatever is benevolent and generous has been denied. And since the parts of self and world which have been denied press forward to be acknowledged, both self and world are divided.

Hostility is a second element in wariness. Both resentment and hostility are strategies for avoiding the pain and terror of the void, but whereas resentment mainly tries to avoid the pain, hostility mainly tries to avoid the terror. The hostile man confronts his apparently hostile world with his own bristling, chip-on-the-shoulder hostility. Each is a mirror image of the other, and this similarity between man and pictured world provides a sense of familiarity which is consoling and reassuring.[2] The hostile man is constantly alert to destroy an omnipresent enemy lest that enemy destroy him. Instead of the Golden Rule, the hostile man follows a policy of perpetual pre-emptive strike: "Do unto others what they (maliciously) want to do unto you, and do it first if possible." The policy fits his paranoid picture of the world. His policy is not one of having specific, realistic fears in relation to specific, actual threats. Rather, the policy and the picture of the world form together a pervasive stance of fear towards whatever happens. As Paul Tillich has pointed out,[3] the human mind is a permanent factory not only of idols, but also of fears. Instead of directly facing the fear of the void, a man externalizes and disguises and dilutes that fear by finding or creating enemies who seem bent on his own destruction, enemies against whom he can fight. The destructive hostility which he sees in others is partly a projection of his own destructive hostility, a refusal to acknowledge its full extent in himself by attributing much of it to others. But both the picture of others as hostile and his own destructive hostility have a common origin as mutually reinforcing components of an overall strategy for avoiding the void. In particular, what the hostile man tries to avoid is the terrifying, annihilating *helplessness* which would be felt in the experience of the void, when the ground disappears under one's feet. Against an external threat one is not completely helpless and powerless. Usually one can fight, even if one "goes down fighting." And at the very least one has reason for feeling destructive hostility and thereby one can feel some life and energy within oneself. Anger directed outwards can partly conceal the inner helplessness of the void. Even if one can destroy the enemy only in imagination and not in reality, even if one can only feel destructive hostility and cannot effectively act on it, this is less terrifying than the ultimate helplessness: experiencing a void within oneself which cannot be destroyed in any way. There is no way to annihilate that which is nothing (no thing). There is no way even to imagine oneself annihilating it. The void can be either evaded or experienced; it cannot be destroyed.

Miserliness is a third element in wariness. The resentful man feels that the good which is in his possession is meagre compared with what he needs and deserves. He also feels that this good is likely to be taken away from him unless he protects himself. This meagre, precarious good must therefore be held on to in a miserly, hoarding way, begrudging others any help or gift. The resentful man is miserly. He is like a person who holds on to the air inside his lungs, refusing to exhale it lest no more be available. This prevents him from taking in any fresh air as it does become available. In this state, which might be called "spiritual emphysema," his hoarding impulse overcomes any residual receptivity which may remain. It is a vicious circle: he refuses to give, so he cannot receive, he refuses to receive, so he cannot give. Moreover, when the miserly man compares himself with others who seem to be more fortunate, he is likely to feel envy and covetousness. Their relative abundance reinforces his own sense of being deprived. And if someone else is obviously in a deprived state, any pity which he might feel for the other tends to be used to reinforce his own self-pity. Other people's misery is mainly a reminder of his own misery. The miserly man refuses to give generously to his world because that world has not given generously to him. And even if others now try to give to him, he refuses to make room for these gifts in his life, or he treats them as rations which, though deserved, cannot be relied upon; he does not treat them as reasons for beginning to give of himself.

Wariness is a pervasive stance of the whole personality towards the whole environment. The wary man does not distinguish realistically between situations where specific measures of self-protection are realistic responses to specific depriving or harming intrusions and situations where no such measures are appropriate. The wary man does not distinguish realistically between situations where it makes sense to hold on tenaciously to what he possesses and situations where it does not. Since people's situations vary, there is a variation in the frequency with which self-protective measures are appropriate. If a person is frequently self-protective, this by itself does not show that his pervasive stance is wariness; his life situation may warrant his behavior. Indeed, some people need to learn to trust much of their own distrust. Exploited laborers often need to be more vigorous in defending themselves against being deprived and harmed by their oppressors, who claim to be benevolent. And as R.D. Laing[4] has pointed out, young "schizophrenics" often need to learn *when* to trust their own wary distrust of parents who try to deceive and "devour" them. But in so far as wariness is a pervasive, undiscriminating stance, it is unrealistic and destructive and needs to be resisted. It cannot be eliminated, for it is to some extent a part of every human being, like anxiety and idolatry and despair and apathy. To some extent everyone tends to see a particular, malevolent intrusion into his life as symbolic or representative of a Grand Depriver or a Grand Destroyer.[5] Some people are relatively free of this tendency, but usually some other constituent of distrust is likely to be prominent in them.

In this section I have depicted wariness in its most extreme and blatant forms. Usually it is less extreme and less obvious. Often it is hidden and rationalized behind plausible descriptions of a world which does in fact contain malevolent people who deprive and destroy. Such wariness, disguised for others and for oneself as realism, cannot be resisted until it is exposed. It is easier to see in others than in oneself.

Although the wary person is constantly on guard against malevolent intruders, she is not very realistic in her discernment of evil in people. Much of what she fears is imaginary, and she often cannot recognize the terrible viciousness which actually exists in some people. This would be too disturbing, for she sees so little good elsewhere to compensate and reassure her when she faces real evil. Also, since for her particular evils symbolize and reveal the ultimate character of the cosmos, there are limits to what she can bear to let herself perceive. Few can live with a terrifying vision of cosmic viciousness in which God is an infinite Hitler. Yet Hitler actually existed, his appalling destructiveness unrecognized by most wary people in his own country. A receptive person, however, can bear to see the worst in people, because she feels fundamentally secure and unthreatened and does not view atrocities symbolically, but strictly on their own terms.

Let us now consider *receptivity*. As I said before, I do not mean by "receptivity" the acceptance of the essentials for life which is a common precondition for all the constituents of trust. Receptivity is itself one of these constituents. It differs from acceptance in two ways, each of which makes it more specific. First, the receptive person receives not only the essentials for life but also the *world* (nature, other people, and herself); the essentials for life are seen as being symbolic or representative of the world as a whole which is the context in which these essentials are received. Second, both the essentials and the world, its very existence, are received as a *gift*. So receptivity could be defined as a pervasive stance in which one regards the world as a gift. Because of the meaning of the word "gift," this stance implies a conviction that the existence of nature and people and oneself is *good* and that this existence is neither one's own *creation* nor something one deserves, because of some prior status or service rendered or sheer need. Rather the existence of the world is a pure, gratuitous gift, and is to be received as such. This is not a matter of merely acknowledging the obvious— that the world exists and that I am not its creator.[6] It is not like merely noticing that a parcel has been left at one's front door which one did not put there oneself. For me to receive the world or the parcel as a gift, I must also regard each as good and as undeserved. Wariness, as the opposite of receptivity, involves refusing to look on world or parcel as gratuitous gifts. For the wary person, each is likely to be evil. (Probably the parcel contains an eviction notice or a bomb!) Or if world or parcel do contain something good, the wary person feels the injustice of how little good comes to her compared with what is owed to her.

Just as wariness is best understood in terms of resentment, miserliness, and hostility, receptivity is best understood in terms of its three expressions: gratitude, generosity, and confirmation of others. The conceptual connections between receptivity and these three stances are fairly obvious. Consider receptivity and gratitude. They are linked together by the concept of "gift." Many a so-called gift is not a gift at all.

Instead it is a bribe, or a way of getting someone to feel indebted and emotionally dependent, or a way of paying off a debt. If a person regards something as a real gift, he sees it as coming with no strings attached, unsolicited and unearned. Moreover, a real gift is something which he welcomes and values and enjoys. And he responds with a generous heart to what he recognizes as the generosity of the giver. His response to the giver is gratitude. If the gift has been really a gift, there is no requirement of any gift in return. Indeed, a "gift in return" would not be really a gift. Gifts are not matters of obligation or duty or justice. Even his gift of gratitude is not felt to be a requirement. It is simply a spontaneous response which imitates the generosity of the giver. And this generous response spills over towards others besides the giver. Towards them it is not gratitude, but simply generosity, an impulse to give to others in the same undemanding way that the giver has given to him. Freely he has received, so freely he gives. As Erik Erikson[7] points out, the infant who learns how to receive from the mother by "getting" and "taking" from her as generous giver is also learning how he can become a giver, "that is, to identify with her and eventually to become a giving person." Unfortunately the same infant is usually also learning from his mother some lessons in resentment and miserliness. That is, he responds to her failure or refusal to give, her depriving him of what he most needs, with resentment and miserliness. Often she herself, usually at an unconscious level, feels resentful and miserly towards the infant, and he identifies with her attitudes toward him. She is both generous giver and callous depriver. The struggle between receptivity and wariness begins in infancy and continues throughout life. In most people there is a perpetual struggle for dominance between these two pervasive stances. Sometimes wariness is almost always dominant, sometimes receptivity. So we have the "wary person" and the "receptive person." Most people, however, are a mixture.

Let us consider the receptive person. She is an ideal, but there are elements of her in most of us. Although she still struggles from time to time against wariness, in general she continuously receives the essentials for life and the world as gift. It is true that she resists specific intrusions which would deprive her of this or that item which she needs, but she does not feel basically deprived. She feels basically blessed. Even though she may walk through a valley dark as death, and have to eat and drink in the presence of enemies, her "cup runs over." She goes on actively receiving good, incorporating it into her life with a sense of joy and wonder and appreciation. Life in general tastes sweet, not bitter. Instead of demanding that others fill up an inner emptiness, she feels a spontaneous impulse to share her inner abundance with them, and to do this freely, without concern about whether people deserve it or whether they will do something for her in return. Although she gives in this free way, she is not self-sufficient. She is always open to receive psychic nourishment from others, and she does receive it. If she never received, she could not give. But she has reserve supplies, and these somehow multiply within her as she gives. So although she sometimes receives nourishment from others, she does not demand it, or feel unjustly treated if they fail to provide it. She gives affection and receives affection, but she does not relentlessly whine for it, or complain if it is not offered. The receptive person gives gratitude to others and receives their gift of gratitude, but she regards none of this as a matter of "obligation" or "duty" or "indebtedness." Such legalistic language is inappropriate as a way of thinking about gratitude and gifts and receptivity, however appropriate it may be when applied to impersonal business transactions where the ownership of goods is transferred from one person to another. The resentful woman tends to use such language to express her pervasive stance: the world "owes" her much and has been "unjust" to her. The grateful woman does not differ from her by saying the opposite. She does not say that she "owes" the world much, or that the world has been "just" to her. The grateful woman does not think in such legalistic terms at all when she expresses her pervasive stance. Since the world has been genuinely generous to her, she does not feel indebted and she does not feel that she has been treated merely fairly; she feels grateful and generous.

The words "gift" and "gratitude" are often used to refer to something very different from what I have been describing. Many "gifts" are ways of gaining or maintaining power over others, whose "gratitude" is a felt obligation to acknowledge that power as legitimate.

Seward Hiltner[8] writes very perceptively about this:

> Our society traditionally expected gratitude from all kinds of less privileged people, just as parents tended to expect it from children. Servants, the poor, the sick, the uneducated, and many others were expected to be grateful for what society, or one of its agents, did to help them in their condition . . . The present situation with its renunciation of obligations to be grateful, makes it clear that a great deal of the gratitude previously inculcated into servants, children, the poor, the workers, and others was simply an indoctrination into the benevolence of the powerful.

Perhaps the most powerful and most destructive use of pseudo-gifts calling for pseudo-gratitude occurs in the raising of children, especially during early infancy.[9] Often the mother's "giving" is, in part at least, a way of controlling the infant. Her "giving" of what the infant needs for sheer survival of body and psyche is made conditional on the infant's behaving and feeling in the ways that she requires. What the infant learns is this, if expressed in adult language: "It is dangerous to receive 'gifts,' for I must pay for them by being a 'good' infant who does and feels and is whatever is required by the giver; receiving 'gifts' means the ultimate dependency—being totally owned by another; it means creating a false self which the giver demands, instead of being and becoming my true self." In so far as such wariness of "gifts" is learned in early infancy, it is not surprising that many adults find it difficult to receive from others even when the gifts are genuine expressions of generosity, with no pricetag whatsoever. Even when the actual motives of the giver make such wariness irrational and self-defeating, the fear of being made deeply dependent, of handing over one's being to the control of another, prevails over the deep longing to receive a pure gift. Some Christian theology reinforces such fears when it says, "God creates us and thus gives us existence, so we owe our existence to him and so we should do and be whatever he commands." This is subtly but utterly different from saying. "If a person genuinely experiences his existence as a pure gift from the generosity of God the Creator, he is spontaneously moved to respond with gratitude to God and generosity towards fellow creatures: he has received freely, so he gives freely."

We have seen how receptivity is expressed in gratitude and generosity. A third expression is confirmation of others. If the world and the essentials for life are received as gifts, then people are received as gifts, for the world includes people and people are the main way in which we receive the essentials for life. The receptive person receives people as part of a total "gift package" which is generously provided for her own good and their good alike.[10] Their existence, like her own existence, is part of a gift which is accepted and confirmed: "Yes, it is gratuitous and good that we exist. None of us deserve to exist and none of us deserve not to exist. It is not a matter of desert at all. Our existence is a precious, marvelous gift, to be welcomed, valued, and enjoyed." Moreover, the receptive person can receive much from others, if they give. She confirms them as potential givers, and they often are. But even if they themselves do not give, they are part of an interrelated whole which is a gift. It is true that not every item in a gift package can be received with enthusiasm. The receptive person may strongly dislike one person in many respects, and she may see another person as a danger to her in specific ways. But she can confirm both of these persons conveying an overall message, "It is good that you exist." She can pinpoint exactly which of the one person's characteristics she dislikes and exactly what harm the other person may do to her unless she takes steps to prevent it. She can deal realistically with specific traits and actions which are repugnant or dangerous. But her realistic discernment and realistic dealings arise, not in spite of, but because of her confirming the existence of the others as a gift. It is specially important to note that when she recognizes that another person may harm her, she does not see that person as a symbol of the void and thus does not want to destroy him. Indeed, there is no impulse to destroy others, for no one can evoke in her the sense of terrifying helplessness and utter vulnerability which is the basic source of the impulse to destroy those who might harm oneself.

In many people the receptive person discerns and evokes a capacity for receptivity, breaking through their wariness to some extent because she is so obviously not out to deprive them or harm them and is willing to give without asserting power over them. And she is able to confirm others as distinct and unique and different from herself. Since she feels fundamentally safe, unthreatened, others pose no threat by being different. Each can be a unique gift to her. As Martin Buber said:[11]

> I become aware of him, aware that he is different, essentially different from myself, in the definite, unique way which is peculiar to him, and I accept whom I thus see . . . I affirm the person I struggle with: I struggle with him as a partner, I confirm him as creature and as creation.

In so far as trust involves a receptivity which moves a person to confirm others it merges with one element in another attitude-virtue, friendliness. Later we will see that confirmation of others is the fundamental element in friendliness. Since friendliness is a species of love, Knud Logstrup[12] is right when he says, "Out of the acceptance of our life as a gift—out of living life as a gift—spring the works of love." According to Logstrup,[13] if I receive my own life and other people's lives as a gift I love other people; and if I love other people, they can infer that I have receptivity, even if I am not conscious of it. It seems to me that if what we mean by "love" is a combination of the generosity and confirmation of others which I have described in this section, what Logstrup claims is true. But I would reserve the word "love" for something which includes additional elements. These will be described in Part Two in my sketches of "friendliness" and "concern."

Chapter 4

Fidelity and Idolatry

The word "fidelity" has various shades of meaning in everyday language. The slightly technical meaning which I am giving it is indicated in the following description: fidelity is a faithful commitment to the source of the essentials for life, steadfastly recognizing and accepting these essentials as they are provided in what is at hand in one's life, both within and without. Fidelity involves persisting in one's assurance, resisting the anxiety-fostered tendency to ignore the essentials and to turn away into idolatry. Fidelity involves the courage to allow one's anxiety to emerge into consciousness instead of repressing it and replacing it by idolatry.

From this description it can readily be seen that fidelity does not differ radically from assurance. Fidelity could be defined as an assurance actively continued in spite of a tendency to idolatry which is fostered by repression of anxiety. Since we have already considered assurance, the main way in which fidelity can be explained here is by giving an account of that which it actively resists—its opposite, idolatry.

Idolatry, like any of the states which we are examining in this book, varies in degree. But we will consider idolatry where it is most obvious and intelligible: where it is relatively strong, even extreme. That is, we will consider idolatry where the intensity of assurance is very low as compared with the intensity of the anxiety which fosters the idolatry. A description of extreme idolatry may help us to recognize less extreme idolatry in ourselves, though even the most blatant idolatry is rarely acknowledged by the idolater himself. Indeed, it is possible to generalize and say that the more powerful the idolatry the less likely it is that the idolater will recognize it in himself. So if a reader finds little idolatry in himself this could be either a realistic self-appraisal or a colossal self-deception!

As I noted before, idolatry is a craving and striving for some substitute-good ("Life would be worth living if only I possessed x or achieved y"), or an addiction to a substitute-good ("z alone is what makes life worth living for me; without z I could not go on living"). I have used the variables x, y, and z as a way of emphasizing the immense variety of substitute-goods which can seem to men to be the absolute, the one thing necessary and sufficient for life to be worth living. An infant may suck his thumb or cling to a favorite blanket or imagine a fantasy figure who immediately satisfies his every desire and who prevents his every pain. Adult idolatry has many versions. For example, if we look at addictions, there are first of all the more obvious addictions to food or alcohol or sensuality,[1] where a bodily satisfaction becomes the exclusive, obsessive focus of a life. The absence of the satisfaction symbolizes the absence of meaning and reality, the absence of anyone who cares. (There is little fidelity to the source of the essentials for life, little perseverance in assurance.) And when the bodily satisfaction is available it arouses in the idolater a fantastic, idolatrous hope for a cosmic Fairy Godmother who would respond instantly and infallibly to his every need. If only she could be found, she would forestall every frustration, intercept every pain, and bestow every pleasure that he asks for. The idolater seeks a kind of comfort which could only be given to an infant by a mother, if the mother were magically omnipotent and also the slave of the infant. No such omnipotent slave exists for the idolater, whether he be an infant or an adult. And there is no equivalent source of comfort available in the present, only substitutes which are second-best. Food or drugs or sensuality can provide only a temporary approximation of the ultimate fantasy figure, a temporary easing of the anxiety and the longings.

A less obvious but common addiction is an addiction to a person. Often a spouse is idolized as an approximation to the fantasy figure of one's infantile dreams and longings, a symbol of the "mystery of life and love" which one has so fervently sought. This idolatry may have two forms: the spouse is unrealistically revered as a symbol of total satisfaction or, more frequently, the spouse is angrily reviled for *not* fulfilling the unfulfillable expectations and demands which are foisted upon him or her by the idolater. These reverential and castigating modes of idolatry are often focused on a group and its ideology. Whether the group be small (a commune), medium (a religious sect, a revolutionary party), or large (a nation) there may be the same focusing of limitless needs on a limited object, and the same possibilities for both fervent eulogy and disillusioned vituperation, both the pedestal and the whipping post. The two modes of idolatry both arise because when a person or a group is idolized each is distorted in a narcissistic way. What the idolater sees in the features of his idol is only his own satisfactions being satisfied or denied. The other person becomes a symbol of a cosmic "Good Mother" and a cosmic "Bad Mother." The Good Mother is a fairy godmother of fantasy who can provide all that one yearns for by flicking her magic wand. The Bad Mother is the same godmother whenever she arbitrarily refuses to flick her wand. The idolator is obsessed with this absolute. He cannot and will not accept the meaning and reality which are actually available in the present. He cannot and will not venture into the void. Thus he is poised between the essentials for life and the void, but he does not allow himself to feel the anxiety which this precarious position brings. Instead he becomes utterly preoccupied with his quest for the fantastic Good Mother, the absolute which seems to be superior to the essentials for life and which seems to be capable of filling up the void.

We have seen that the focus of idolatry, the incarnation of the absolute, varies greatly. Idolatry varies in other ways as well. An idolater may or may not be *conscious* that he regards such and such as the absolute. For example, an alcoholic is usually *not* aware of this until the "moment of truth" when he realizes that he *is* an alcoholic. And often a momentous insight is required if an idolatry within a marital relation is to be acknowledged. Another variation among idolaters is whether the idol is only viewed as being *necessary* for life to be worthwhile, rather than also as being *sufficient*. It is one thing to feel, "I cannot live without you"; it is another to feel, "In you I find all that I need to live." An idolater who (consciously or unconsciously) regards x as necessary for life may also crave an as yet imaginary y (drug, spouse, party) which would bring relief to his limitless longings. Obviously the more open this ambivalence is, or the more openly someone vacillates between putting his idol on a pedestal and putting it on a whipping post, the less security idolatry can provide.

Idolatry is not always focused on a single thing or person or movement. Sometimes it is a scattered, unfocused pursuit of diverse diversions, each of which brings only partial and temporary relief from the craving for an absolute which is secretly at work. A person is impelled by a frantic curiosity or an insatiable search for sensations, always restless, always on the move, always hoping for a hint of a holy grail just around the corner. This form of idolatry usually involves more anxiety in consciousness than that which is strictly focused. None of the rewards even purport to satisfy the longings which impel the idolater ever onward in his agitated quest. He is stroked by sympathy here or soothed by sensuality there; he discovers a fascinating new toy today or he is thrilled by a new adventure tomorrow—all this is tantalizing rather than gratifying. It is like having sex without love with a different woman or man every night. Indeed, sexual promiscuity *is* a form of unfocused idolatry.

Idolatry, whether focused or unfocused, is a search for a kind of security, a quest for a kind of assurance. Even when it seems to provide security, even when it is focused on only one idol, even when ambivalence and vacillation are not overt and the idol seems sufficient for life to be worthwhile, idolatry brings merely a delusion of security, a pseudo-assurance. There are three reasons for this. First, the idolater needs to be able to *control* his idol. Otherwise he cannot rely on it to provide what he so desperately desires. His obsessiveness makes him possessive, his neediness impels him to ruthless subjugation. If his idol is a thing—alcohol or heroin or money—he sometimes can feel relatively secure in his possession of it. But there is always a fear of an unexpected and unpreventable disruption of his source of supply. And if his idol is a person, his concern to control his "source of supply" is challenged by that person's freedom. He can make relentless demands and employ various forms of bribery, coercion, and manipulation, but because of human freedom he rarely can come close to *owning* the other person both externally and internally, dictating both behavior and feelings. And the closer he comes to owning the other person, the more he frustrates his deepest craving as an idolator, which is for comforts *freely* given. And the closer he comes to owning the other person the more *dependent* he becomes on his slave as the source of security and significance in his life; the slightest hint of independence by the slave is a monumental threat to the idolater's sense of selfhood. An idolater is like a parasite whose own life depends on what happens in the host plant on which it feeds. If the idolater's focus is not a person but a group, there is a similar dependence and a similar need to control the source of satisfaction supply. Unless he gains power in the group, he is subject to arbitrary changes of policy which jeopardize his place within it. But the more he gains power over others in the group the less it can be for him a home which satisfies some of his limitless yearnings to belong.

A second reason why idolatry cannot provide genuine security is that none of the idols can actually be what the idolater requires: a genuine absolute, an unlimited source of meaning and reality. The limitless cravings out of which his idolatry arises can never be satisfied by his current absolute or by another combination of absolutes to which he might turn. Rather, the cravings have to be renounced. To acknowledge this unattainability and this need for renunciation would be devastatingly difficult and painful for the idolater, so he tries desperately to convince himself concerning his absolute. But since the limitations of his absolute are evident, he cannot fully conceal the awful truth from himself: at some level, and to some extent, he knows it. So beneath the surface security of his devotion to his absolute there is a turbulent insecurity. The anxiety which gives rise to idolatry is reinforced by the inner conflict which idolatry involves. He seeks to reduce anxiety by evading it and plunging into idolatry, but instead he increases anxiety, thus undermining whatever remnants of real assurance remain. Thus, although idolatry is a pervasive stance, it is not a genuinely unifying one. It is pervasive in that it influences the idolater to some extent in every situation by affecting the nature and extent of his involvement with each particular, and in that it influences all the main aspects of his personality. But although idolatry superficially unifies self and world in its devotion to an absolute, it is profoundly divisive. Idolatry divides the person into a part which is devoted to an absolute and a part which anxiously struggles not to recognize the futility of the devotion. It also divides the world into two parts. On the one hand there is an absolute, which alone has meaning and reality. On the other hand, there is everything else, which is merely a means or an obstacle in the pursuit of the absolute.

A third reason why idolatry cannot provide genuine security is that idolatry is not an effective defense against the void. Instead of facing the terrifying emptiness which is actually part of one's existence, the idolater tries to conceal it from himself by placing a gigantic absolute in front of it. But the void is still there. No absolute is big enough to hide it. And until it is recognized and endured, its haunting, half-hidden presence mocks all one's pretensions of security.

Religion is often a form of idolatry. It is often a defense against the recognition that one's limitless longings cannot be fulfilled and must be given up. It is often a defense against the void. The idolatrous religious person imagines a limitless God, able and willing to fulfill her own limitless cravings and to fill up the limitless void. Her God is very similar to the image of the "ideal" parent, which a patient in psychoanalysis projects on his analyst as the transference relation develops. Her God is a "Good Mother" in the sense of a cosmic Fairy Godmother who could and should satisfy her infantile longings and protect her from the void. This is very different from the God of non-idolatrous religion. Even the God of the first stage of the positive way is a "Good Mother" in a different sense: a cosmic source of the meaning and reality which the person is already accepting into her life. Such a God is analogous to a genuinely good mother who conveys to her infant a life-affirming, life-giving presence. This enables the infant to bear frustration when mother is absent by drawing on strengths which have developed internally in response to her. A person who has faith in the God of the first stage of the positive way has no need to cling idolatrously in devotion to this or that particular or to imagine a divine fantasy figure who immediately satisfies her every desire and prevents her every pain. She already has reality-assurance, and in fidelity she steadfastly continues to recognize and accept the essentials for life. The God of non-idolatrous religion undermines rather than fosters false consolations, pseudo-assurances. Some people say to themselves, "If only I were in heaven, all my longings would be fulfilled, and life would become worth living" or "My religion is the one source of satisfaction in life, it alone makes life worth living." Instead of encouraging such fantastic hopes and narrow-minded addictions, the non-idolatrous God is paradoxically both austere and reassuring: "You must and you can give up your false consolations; then you will discover the essentials for life which have already been provided." Such a God is analogous to a primal therapist in his stern challenge to re-experience and to renounce unfulfillable yearnings and to turn instead to the resources for life which are actually available in the present.

A person does not stop being idolatrous by shifting his obsessive, possessive cravings from something finite and particular to something infinite and universal which he calls "God." There must be a change in basic attitude. Rejection of the essentials for life must be replaced by acceptance of them and fidelity to their source. Instead of trying to control one's own private source of significance and substance one must become open and responsive to the presence which is already present. Martin Buber's criticism of Scheler (and, implicitly, of Tillich) is very illuminating in this respect:[2]

> A modern philosopher supposes that every man believes of necessity either in God or in "idols"—which is to say, some finite good, such as his nation, his art, power, knowledge, the acquisition of money, the "every repeated triumph with women"—some good that has become an absolute value for him, taking its place between him and God; and if only one proves to a man the conditionality of this good, thus "smashing" the idol, then the diverted religious act would all by itself return to its proper object.
>
> This view presupposes that man's relation to the finite goods that he "idolizes" is essentially the same as his relationship to God,

as if only the object were different; only in that case could the mere substitution of the proper object for the wrong one save the man who has gone wrong. But a man's relation to the "particular something" that arrogates the supreme throne of his life's values, pushing eternity aside, is always directed towards the experience and use of an It, a thing, an object of enjoyment . . . Whoever is dominated by the idol whom he wants to acquire, have, and hold, possessed by his desire to possess, can find a way to God only by returning, which involves a change not only of the goal but also of the kind of movement . . .

When a man loves a woman so that her life is present in his own, the You of her eyes allows him to gaze into a ray of the eternal You. But if a man lusts after the "ever repeated triumph"—you want to dangle before his lust a phantom of the eternal? . . . And what is it supposed to mean that a man treats money, which is un-being incarnate, "as if it were God"? What does the voluptuous delight of rapacity and hoarding have in common with the joy over the presence of that which is present?*

The relevance of idolatry and fidelity to religion is obvious. As we have seen, they are fundamental alternatives. Their relevance to *morality* is only slightly less obvious. Idolatry and ruthlessness go together. The cravings of an idolater are so intense, and the anxiety about their nonfulfillment so painful, that nothing is permitted to stand in the way, and whatever is a means toward fulfillment can and must be used. Obviously this influences the idolater's way of dealing with other people, both in intimate personal relations and in impersonal political activity. The influence is sometimes subtle, sometimes stark, but always powerful. The obsessive neediness which dominates the idolater moves him to a ruthless manipulation of people. Where fidelity is strong, however, and a person perseveres in his assurance that the essentials for life are provided, other people are not caught up by him in a relentless quest for the Holy Grail. Fidelity and restraint go together. One can let others be. Obviously others may at times be obstacles or means in relation to one's particular ends, but since the ends are not absolute and are not sought because of limitless cravings, the others can be treated with restraint, with some respect for *their* ends.

* Quotation from *I and Thou* by Martin Buber, tr. by W. Kaufmann, by kind permission of New York: Scribner's and Edinburgh: T. & T. Clark.

Ruthlessness versus restraint. An analysis of idolatry thus sheds light on how idolatry and its opposite, fidelity, are morally important, for each affects the way in which a man deals with others. The analysis of idolatry has also shed light on another way in which idolatry and fidelity are morally relevant: fidelity is a necessary condition for human fulfillment, whereas idolatry works against it. We have seen that idolatry cannot provide genuine security, for it attempts to satiate insatiable cravings and to avoid the unavoidable void. The ennervating inner contradictions of idolatry seem likely to undermine any of the other attitude-virtues unless they are effectively countered by the unifying strength of fidelity. We have seen that although idolatry seems to unify the person, it is actually self-deceptive and self-divisive. One part of the person is devoted to his absolute, but the other struggles anxiously against acknowledging that this absolute cannot provide what he yearns for. In contrast with this, the perseverance in assurance which I call "fidelity" does unify the person. Whatever meaning and reality is actually at hand, within the person and outside him, is accepted as such. There is no need to deceive and divide the self in a futile search for limitless consolation. As Keen says, "sanctity is given with being," and one need only go on recognizing and accepting this gift. There is no need to divide the world into the absolute which one craves and clings to and everything else which one ignores or uses. Since whatever meaning and reality the man of fidelity finds and goes on finding in himself and in the world has the same source, he can give a unified response to a unified world. In general, if a pervasive stance genuinely unifies the person, as fidelity does, it both *promotes* a recognition of a pervasive unity in one's total environment and is *reinforced* by such a recognition.

A great deal more might be said about fidelity and idolatry, but let us now consider the fourth constituent of trust: hope, and its opposite, despair.

Chapter **5**

Hope and Despair

Trust includes a hope that the essentials for life will be provided in the future. Such hope is of two kinds. First there is the hope that the assurance which exists in the present will continue into the future. Such hope has already been considered in the section on assurance. Although the main emphasis there was on the present, on the essentials now being received, there was also a forward-looking dimension in assurance. I do not think I need say more about such hope.

The second kind of hope, with which this section will be concerned, is a hope which resists despair or the temptation to despair,[1] a hope which arises although there seems to be little assurance at the present time. At a conscious level, assurance is minimal, and at an unconscious level, it may be quite low. We have seen that when assurance fades and anxiety mounts, one outcome may be a plunge into idolatrous devotion to a false absolute which provides a pseudo-assurance. Fidelity is the resistance against such a temptation. Another possible temptation is despair: an inability or refusal to see any essentials for life, or possibilities for essentials, in oneself or anyone else. The person who despairs usually shuns any quest for substitute goods which might provide some idolatrous consolation. Like the wary person, the despairing person expects and seeks little good from the outside world. Despair differs from wariness, however, in that while the wary person locates the source of her misery outside herself, the despairing person locates it inside herself. Despair, wariness, and idolatry tend to be alternative strategies for dealing with decreasing assurance and increasing anxiety,[2] though mixtures of all three are possible.

The reader may be puzzled by my treating hope, not as a distinct attitude-virtue, but as a constituent of trust.[3] There are good reasons for this, however. Above all, there are the close connections between hope and assurance, which is the basic constituent of trust. Both the hope which is a forward-looking assurance and the hope which resists despair presuppose assurance for their intelligibility: assurance is what we hope for, either its continuation or its return. And both kinds of hope require assurance for their existence. The basis for hope as forward-looking assurance is present assurance, and the basis for hope which resists despair is, as I shall show, the memory of past assurance.

We should also note that both kinds of hope are different from other human states which can legitimately be called "hope." For example, there is *idolatrous* hope, where what one hopes for is an absolute: "If only I had x life would be beautiful, for x would bring unlimited meaning and reality to me, fulfilling my unlimited cravings." As we have seen, such hope should be renounced rather than indulged. Another kind of state is what I shall call "*specific* hope." This covers most of what we usually call "hope": I hope that the next bus will come soon or that my friend, reported missing, is still alive. Such specific hopes are often imbued with the pervasive hope which is a resistance against despair, but specific hopes are not themselves pervasive, and they need not be in opposition to despair.

From now on, unless I indicate otherwise, I will use the word "hope" to refer to the hope which resists despair or the temptation to despair, where both hope and despair are pervasive states. Such hope has two contrasting but complementary elements. Each in turn may play a leading role, and each opposes an element in despair which corresponds to it. I shall call these two elements of hope "openness to liberation" and "initiative towards encounter." Let us consider them in turn.

Openness to liberation. If a person is imprisoned in a present which lacks the meaning and reality which are essential for life,[4] hope is a willingness and eagerness to be liberated. Despair, on the other hand, is a reinforcing of the prison walls from inside, a self-imprisonment. The person who hopes is open towards past and future. She looks back to times when the essentials were received, times of steady assurance or of liberation from despair. Her remembering is not a nostalgic lamentation for a security which is irretrievably lost. It is not a pouring of salt from the past on the open wound of the present so as to provide even more reason for feeling a tragic, helpless self-pity. Rather, her memory provides a basis for envisaging a future in which the essentials will again be received. Meanwhile, she refuses to accept her present spiritual famine as final. She trusts in the source of the essentials for life to bring the renewal for which she longs. She waits, patiently and expectantly, ready and alert to receive the gift, open to being liberated. At an unconscious level, there is still some assurance within her, though anxiety is dominant. She does all that she can with her imagination and her life to make herself open to whatever will expand that assurance and stir it into consciousness.

The extreme alternative to such a hope is a despair which is a kind of imprisonment. The person who despairs is like someone who chains herself to a treadmill. Round and round it goes, in the same pointless way: unchanging, endless, relentless. She binds herself to her mode of bare existence as her inescapable doom. She does this because its inevitable certainty and fascinating repetitiveness provide a false but reassuring security. At an unconscious level assurance is weak and anxiety is intense. The anxiety is radically unsettling, so she finds a way to repress it. Clinging to the fated pattern of her life as if it were a familiar, reliable friend, she can say with grim satisfaction, "*That*'s the way life is."

Such self-imprisoning despair provides the consoling pseudo-assurance of a false absolute; it is a special form of idolatry. The person finds an illusory meaning and reality in the absence of genuine meaning and reality. She fervently believes this to be her inescapable destiny, but actually what has happened is that she has secretly surrendered to the spell of sparsity. And since there is always a danger that something worthwhile might sneak into her life, her alleged destiny has to be actively promoted by herself. She must be on her guard against any good. No light from the past can be allowed into the dark present. Memories of times when life was worth living, memories which might lead her to envisage a different, worthwhile future, are blotted out; or they are recalled only so as to accentuate the tragic contrast between the past and any possible future. Any door through which a future liberation might come is closed, bolted firmly on the inside.

Hope as openness to liberation is the alternative to such self-imprisoning despair. Both the hope and the despair occur when a person lacks the conscious assurance of present meaning and reality. But the person of hope preserves a special and genuine kind of assurance. She keeps her fidelity to past assurance, she anticipates future assurance and she tries to kindle whatever sparks of assurance still remain at an unconscious level in the present, so that a liberator who comes along can fan them into a flame. She does not seek false assurance by actively binding herself to her spiritually impoverished present as if it were her fate forever. She can wait, alert yet relaxed, open to respond to any liberating help which comes her way.

Initiative towards encounter. The second element in hope differs in that it is a very active stance. Instead of waiting for someone to help, the person takes an initiative towards encounter. And the kind of despair which hope resists is different in an opposite way: it is much more passive. Instead of an actively self-imprisoning despair, there is a paralyzing lethargy.

Hope as initiative towards encounter is the creating of a new context in which meaning and reality and life energies can be experienced. Such hope is not an openness to a liberating initiative from outside; it takes its own initiative. It seizes whatever opportunity comes along to bring about a change towards a life that is worth living. Instead of waiting for someone to help, it reaches out, seeking a response from other people. If someone responds, there is a personal encounter. In such an encounter each person is for the other person what Buber calls "a presence with a meaning," as life energies are stirred and exchanged. These essentials for life are experienced as gifts, for they are not earned or created or controlled by either person. But the gifts occur in a receptive context, and initiative is required to create that context.

Indeed, in so far as hope is an initiative towards encounter it is the most active of all the constituents of trust. Hope is active, not as an independent exercise of will power by a "self-made" man who pulls himself up by his own bootstraps, but as a movement towards a relation with another which requires the free response of the other without in any way trying to control the other. But it does involve a stern bestirring of one's own strengths, a summoning of the self to move outwards into encounter. The first initiative may be to pick up the phone to get in touch with a friend. This simple step, for someone who is in the grip of despair, may seem like climbing Everest.

It is true that some people find it relatively easy to cope with despair by moving outwards, but often their hope is idolatrous. Hope as initiative towards encounter differs from idolatrous hope in that the focus of hope is not absolutized; only a limited meaning and reality is hoped for in the particular friendship which may be the outcome of the initiative. If a person is in despair he is often tempted to distort any hope by focusing it all idolatrously on one person. If he is wise, he will turn to a variety of people. And if he is wise he will turn to people whom he can realistically regard as potential friends, people who are likely to respond positively to a clear initiative. It is folly to indulge in fantasies of a future friendship with a man who is actually a manipulative psychopath or a woman who is a remote, inaccessible celebrity. Fantastic initiatives are often unconscious strategies for confirming one's despair.

Paralyzing lethargy, the opposite of initiative towards encounter, is the most passive of all the components of distrust. A massive self-mobilization is required to stir oneself out of it, even slightly. In its most extreme form, such despair is a helpless succumbing to a state of lifeless inactivity; it is a capitulation to death. Rather than endure the anxiety which arises when assurance disappears, mustering whatever courage and energy is at one's command, it seems better to give up entirely, letting go of any hold on life, even on life viewed as fate. It seems better to let the destructive, deathward processes of nature take over. Some infants actually die of despair; it is their response to lack of assurance.

So do some adults, though the process is usually less obvious and more prolonged.

How can the process be reversed? There are limits on what any outsider can do, for the fundamental choice between life and death lies deep within the individual. The best immediate help is a combination of a life-affirming care and a firm challenge to take initiatives. Even though initiatives toward encounter seem the most remote possibility to someone who is in a state of paralyzing lethargy, small steps in that direction can reverse the trend towards death. More radically, the person often needs to be helped to feel his anger, which is blocked within himself and turned against himself: if he can express his anger his energy can begin to flow again, breaking through the paralyzing lethargy. Still more radically, the person in despair must eventually face the repressed anxiety against which the despair has protected him. The first step out of paralyzing lethargy, however, is usually initiative towards encounter.

In my presentation of the two kinds of hope I have emphasized the contrast between them. In openness to liberation a person *stops* imprisoning himself so as to be able to respond to an initiative from outside himself. In initiative towards encounter a person *starts* reaching out on his own initiative to someone who will respond. There is, however, an important similarity between the two kinds of hope, a similarity which can be discerned even in the contrast which I have just set forth. In each case there is a move away from self-isolation in the direction of a dynamic relation between the person who hopes and someone else in whom he hopes. This is so whether the person who hopes initiates the relation or responds to an initiative from the other person.

The two ways in which the relation arises are analogous to two ways of relating to the mother which an infant develops during the "oral" stage, the first year of life. According to Erik Erikson,[5] the infant first learns how to "get" what he needs, that is, how to receive and accept it for himself as a gift. ("Get" here does not mean "fetch.") Then, in the latter half of the first year, the infant also learns how to "take," which involves an initiative, an active reaching out and "grasping," whether with the mouth or the hands or the organs of sense-perception. In both cases hope is a movement away from self-isolation towards a relation in which the essentials for life can be incorporated, whether by receiving or by grasping. Without such hope for relation, the infant falls into despair. He is unresponsive (not open to receive) or lethargic (unable to reach out).

The difference between the two kinds of hope should be seen as a manifestation of a more fundamental contrast which applies not only to hope but to all the constituents of trust. Earlier I noted that acceptance is the precondition for all the constituents, since meaning and reality do not exist for me unless I accept them into my life. Now I should note that acceptance occurs in two different forms: openness and initiative. Earlier I noted that acceptance is an activity. Now I should note that the activity can be mainly internal or mainly external. When acceptance is mainly openness, the main activity is internal: a letting go of one's resistance against the presence and presents which are being offered. It is a matter of allowing a blessing to enter into one's self and one's life. After it enters all that is needed is assimilation. In the extreme case all that one needs to do is, metaphorically, to open one's mouth and to swallow. When acceptance is mainly initiative, the main activity is external: a reaching out to someone to create together a context in which one receives new substance and significance into one's life. In the extreme case, one is like Jacob, who wrestled with the stranger for a blessing.

Most of what I have said so far about trust in this book implies an acceptance which involves more openness than initiative. The one clear exception to what I have said is initiative towards encounter. But the acceptance which is the crucial precondition for all the other constituents of trust also frequently requires an element of initiative. In general, when conscious assurance is weak, one must make some initiative to help create a context in which meaning and reality can be experienced. This context is primarily communal. All the constituents of trust grow as one helps to create a network of friendships in which profound human encounters can occur. This is specially true of hope, for the most fundamental hope is hope-for-relation, and the core of despair is self-isolation. Almost any initiative can be important in breaking free from paralyzing lethargy, but the crucial initiative is an initiative towards encounter: asking another human being for help. To reach out for contact is to move out of despair.

Thus hope has a considerable *moral* significance. Hope enables a person to become involved with others, participating in human life in spite of the temptation to withdraw.[6] Such participation is necessary for human fulfillment. It is necessary as a minimal condition for survival if a person is to receive physical and psychic nourishment of any kind. And it is necessary for an abundant, flourishing life which depends on the gifts of meaning and reality which come in encounters with others. Self-isolation in despair, on the other hand, brings atrophy, decay, and death.

Hope is also morally relevant in so far as it influences our dealings with others, involving ourselves positively with them rather than withdrawing from them in morbid self-preoccupation. It is interesting to compare the influence of hope on our dealings with other people and the influence of other constituents of trust or their opposites:

Assurance —others can be ends	*Anxiety* —others merely means
Receptivity —gratitude —confirmation of others —generosity	*Wariness* —resentment —hostility —miserliness
Fidelity —restraint	*Idolatry* —ruthlessness
Hope —involvement with others	*Despair* —self-isolation

When we turn from the moral to the *religious* significance of hope we see that it depends on its being not only a pervasive but also a unifying stance. The person towards whom one stands open or takes an initiative is symbolic of a liberating or responding reality which unites the whole environment. Religious convictions are involved in hope, though a person may not be aware of these convictions or may express them in nonreligious language. James Gustafson moves back and forth between secular and religious language as he talks about the cosmic focus of hope:[7]

Hope is a disposition that correlates with trust in the goodness of God and the power of goodness in life. Hope is carried by the confidence that life is more reliable than unreliable, that the future is open, that new possibilities of life exist, that the present patterns of life are not fated by the blind god Necessity, but are susceptible to change . . . The disposition of hope is aware of the openness and newness of life, aware of the possibilities for mankind that are being made possible not only by one's own initiative, but also by the events and beings to which one responds . . . It is grounded in a confidence that the future is for man, that God enables out of his goodness new possibilities for humane life.

In my account of hope and despair there is one crucial issue which remains to be considered: the relations between hope, despair, and the experience of the void. From despair there are two ways out: a positive way, *via* hope, and a negative way, *via* the experience of the void. In the positive way, a person resists the pull of despair, faces some of the raw anxiety underlying the despair, and moves forward towards a dynamic relation (responding to an initiative or initiating a response) which brings a gift of meaning and reality and thereby a renewal of assurance. In the negative way, a person faces the full impact of the raw anxiety and goes beyond it into the experience of the void, from which he emerges with a special kind of assurance, more solid and permanent and anxiety-free than any other. Both ways, as I noted when we considered assurance, are important. But they are different. My main interest here is in reminding us that hope is not the only way out of despair.

Also, I wish to emphasize that the void and despair are different. They differ in three main ways. First, the experience of the void, unlike despair, is terrifying. As R.D. Laing says, "We are afraid to approach the fathomless and bottomless groundlessness of everything . . . the ultimate terror."[8] Second, despair, unlike the experience of the void, involves some subtle, sick satisfactions and substitute-securities, as we have seen. Self-imprisoning despair involves a masochistic pseudo-assurance: "That's the way life is and must be; I can be sure of that." And paralyzing-lethargy despair involves a helpless doom, a drifting towards death, which is perversely reassuring: "When I die there will be no more possibility of anxiety." Third, despair is a self-deceptive strategy for avoiding both anxiety and the void, and it is destructive in its effects on human life. Hence despair, though it is to some extent inevitably a part of every human life and is not to be shunned or denounced in others or in ourselves as if it were inhuman,[9] is not to be indulged or prized as if it were evidence of some special profundity or seriousness or heroism in a person.

In contrast with despair, the experience of the void is neither self-deceptive nor destructive. Rather, it is what Laing calls the "great liberation from being afraid of nothing to the realization that there is nothing to fear."[10] That is, instead of being unconsciously terrified of the void and consciously afraid of various things outside oneself and inside oneself which have come to represent the void, a person experiences the void itself, facing the ultimate fear; then he realizes that the things can no longer evoke fear in the way they once did, as symbols of the void.

The contrast between the void and hope as routes out of despair will be clearer if we examine a passage in Sam Keen which differs somewhat from the earlier one which illustrated the void. I quote only a part of his account:[11]

> The root of terror is—abandonment. I was alone in the unanswering, unlimited darkness, naked and helpless in the void. My stomach knotted, whirled, and gradually came to rest. The tension began to subside. I went back up through the darkness . . . Back in my living room, fear was still present, but its face began to change. As I realized that the acid of terror was not strong enough to dissolve my strength, fear passed over into loneliness. I felt I was alone on a raft four thousand miles at sea. But my solitude was pure and strong. It rooted in the essential aloneness I feel when I must bear the burden of my decisions without recourse to any external authority. It seems that loneliness is bearable if it is not identified with abandonment and helplessness.

This passage brings out one of the special features of the assurance which follows an experience of the void: a feeling of being alone in making one's fundamental life decisions. Although, as in other cases of assurance, there is a sense that meaning and reality are already provided (one does not feel abandoned and helpless), the stress is on acceptance of responsibility for one's own life; there is no one else to do this for me.

Positive ways to assurance run the risk of contamination by the infantile fantasy that somehow someone else (mother or God) will do this for me. After the experience of the void, I am not radically afraid of being alone. But a positive way to assurance is also needed. One positive way is *via* hope of being-in-relation, such as I have outlined in this chapter. When assurance comes *via* hope, there is a dynamic process which involves not only me but also someone else: *together* we create a context for meaning and reality, even if my part is mainly an openness. Keen himself goes on in a positive way:[12]

> Being alone I may reach out to others, build bridges, risk tenderness, confess need. And if I never learn the perfect love which is said to cast out fear, I may discover enough to allow me to withstand its periodic visits.

This section on hope and despair would be incomplete without a sketch of what Kierkegaard regards as the most extreme species of despair. What he calls "despair" includes whatever is in opposition to trust, so his study of despair is a study of all the species of distrust. But the most extreme species, in which a man defiantly wills to be himself as a passive sufferer, is similar to what I have called "despair," though it also includes a good deal of resentment and hostility. Kierkegaard depicts a man who suffers from some distress, some "thorn in the flesh" and refuses to hope that it might ever be removed. Instead, he makes use of it as an occasion to be "offended at the whole of existence."

> . . . to hope in the possibility of help . . . for God all things are possible—no, that he will not do. And as for seeking help from any other—no, that he will not do for all the world; rather than seek help he would prefer to be himself—with all the tortures of hell, if so it must be . . .
>
> Precisely upon this torment the man directs his whole passion, which at last becomes a demoniac rage. Even if at this point God in heaven and all his angels were to offer to help him out of it—no, now he doesn't want it, now it is too late, he once would have given everything to be rid of this torment but was made to wait, now that's all past, now he would rather rage against everything, he, the one man in the whole of existence who is the most unjustly treated . . .
>
> He rages most of all at the thought that eternity might get it into its head to take his misery from him! . . . [A] malignant

> objection must above all take care to hold on to that against which
> it is an objection. Revolting against the whole of existence, it thinks
> it has hold of a proof against it, against its goodness. This proof the
> despairer thinks he himself is, and that is what he wills to be,
> therefore he wills to be himself, himself with his torment, in order
> with this torment to protest against the whole of existence.[13]

Kierkegaard observes that although this extreme form of despair is
seldom seen, this is because it is kept well hidden, not because it does not
occur. It is hidden from most observers and hidden, in large part, from
the person himself. It is important to keep remembering that much of
human hope and human despair is unconscious and therefore emerges
clearly only in moments of crisis or during deep psychotherapy or under
the scrutiny of a strenuous spiritual self-examinution undertaken with
the probing courage of a Kierkegaard.

Sometimes, however, the shift from despair to hope comes when
the spell of despondency is broken, not by still more serious self-scrutiny
or by earnest exhortations from others, but by humor: gentle, playful,
loving, and ironic. Leonard McGravey tells how someone used an
allusion to an Irish folk tale to reach an apparently unreachable
Irishman:

> I was relatively new to the (therapy) group when one night Big Mike
> was on the hot seat, as it were, and people were trying to get him out
> of one of his depressions which, in those bygone days, were not
> altogether that rare. Well, people were into all kinds of
> psychological ploys and psychoanalytical speech, including the
> "big M" (psychic masochism). Mike was impervious to all these
> words. It all seemed so simple when a certain member of the group
> spoke up. He said, "Mike, I know what's the trouble with you."
> Mike grunted, "Wh-what?" Our candid friend continued, "Well, ye
> know, O'Flaherty, it's a case of the Curse of Muldoon"—all this in
> the proper Irish mocking tone of voice. "It's the Curse of Muldoon,
> O'Flaherty, that's what it is." Mike's huge arms were folded across
> his great body. He turned his dark bearded face, opened one eye,
> and cocked an ear. Grudgingly Mike asked for more information
> with, "Oh, what's that?" The man with the Irish background
> continued, "Ye know, O'Flaherty, the Curse of Muldoon—you
> were born bad, you never were any good and, further (in
> appropriate higher tones of voice), you'll never amount to
> nothing—the Curse of Muldoon." Well, O'Flaherty actually began

to shake all over his great body to the black curls of his beginning-to-bald head, his mouth opened so you could see the crowns of his teeth and he laughed and laughed a great belly laugh. He had been reached and the spell had been broken.[14]

Obviously much more could be said about the connection between humor and hope. Some kinds of humor are expressions of despair and others achieve only a partial triumph or momentary escape in relation to despair. But there is a humor which warms our humanity and draws us out of ourselves, liberating us from the heavy seriousness of sullen self-absorption.

We have looked at hope and despair as species of trust and distrust. Now let us turn to consider the fifth pair of opposites: passion and apathy.

Chapter 6

Passion and Apathy

Let us consider *apathy* first. The word "apathy" comes from the Greek word *apatheia* which means, literally, "not-feeling." What I mean by the term, however, is not a complete lack of feeling but a lack of a specific kind of feeling which I shall call "passion." A passion is a powerful, intense feeling which moves the whole body. I also use the word "passion" to refer to the pervasive stance which is a trustful openness to these feelings. In sharp contrast with this, apathy is the pervasive stance which is closed to these feelings. An apathetic person has a passionless existence.[1]

Earlier I noted that each of the constituents or forms of distrust is an unconscious strategy for psychic survival. Anxiety, wariness, idolatry, despair, and apathy are alternative ways of responding to painful crises in life, whether these occur in infancy or in adult life. The responses are most vivid when they occur in infancy. The differences between the five distrustful stances can be observed in a nursery or relived in primal therapy. Let us imagine a primal scene. A mother begins to nurse her baby. He has been craving the milk in her breast, the warmth of her eyes, the gentleness of her touch, the reassurance of her arms around him. She begins, but immediately she stops. She puts the baby down in a cold and angry way and leaves the room, slamming the door. There are at least five different ways in which the baby may respond. Each of these I have seen relived and re-enacted in primal therapy. *First*, he may go into a state of chaotic agitation, thrashing about in panic, trembling in insecurity, scattering his energies in all directions. It is as if he dare not relax and let the mattress of his crib support him, for nothing is reliable. *Second*, he may whine in resentful protest at the cruel, depriving mother. Then he cowers in a corner of the crib, bristling against any intrusion, whether it brings pain or pleasure. If mother returns and offers him her breast, he spits out the milk, for it now tastes bitter. *Third*, he may reach upwards with pursed lips and imploring hands, pathetically pleading for the comforts which have disappeared. Then he finds a substitute; he seizes his blanket and holds it in his mouth. *Fourth*, he may roll over on to his face, seeking a dark place in which to mourn his loss and to begin to die. If mother returns, he remains motionless, unable or unwilling even to suck on her breast. *Fifth*, he may reveal for a fleeting moment some feelings of yearning and anger, but immediately he becomes cool, quiet, and dispassionate. His face becomes an expressionless mask. He makes himself go rigid in his shoulders, his diaphragm, and his lower abdomen. These bodily constrictions enable him to repress strong feelings from consciousness. He says nothing, but his posture conveys a message: "I don't want it anyway, and I really don't mind her leaving like that." Actually, he has buried his most intense feelings in his body. In order to survive, he has switched them off: forlorn loneliness, overwhelming helplessness, desperate yearning, immeasurable grief, and murderous rage.

Apathy in adult everyday life is analogous to what I have just described, though less obvious. Typically an apathetic person has a vague sense that her life lacks profound significance and vital substance, but she prefers to play it cool. In extreme cases, she lacks feelings of any kind, but this is rare. Usually she is conscious of feelings, but her feelings are restrained by being disembodied. She does not feel warmth towards others in her guts and her heart and she does not feel anger towards others in her shoulders and her neck. If her feelings seem to have any location at all it is in her head. She lacks emotion and passion. By "emotion" I mean a feeling which is in motion in the body and which is expressed through the body to others so that it stirs them. Emotions are "passions" in that they are uninhibited feelings which flow as powerful movements of energy through the body and out into the outside world. The feelings which I call "emotions" and "passions" involve intense kinaesthetic sensations, and there is an acute awareness of bodily pleasure and pain, warmth and coldness, and movements of energy.

Lack of passion is associated with a split between mind or self and body. The apathetic man distinguishes himself from his body, sometimes to the extent of dissociating himself from what goes on in it. The mind-body split is often manifested in a bodily way. A person whose feelings are detached from his body typically has a head which is visibly "detached" from the rest of his body: a discerning observer can see that there is no unimpeded, graceful flow of movement and energy between the two.[2] There are various forms of mind-body split. One is a split between self and sexuality. In many apathetic persons the self seems to be "spiritual" or "artistic" or "intellectual" or "scientific." Sexual feelings seem alien to this self: they do not seem to belong to him. At the very least he distinguishes himself from them. Usually he dissociates himself from them when he is aware of them or he represses them so as not to be aware of them. This split between self and sexuality is manifested in a bodily way. A discerning observer can usually detect rigidities and tensions in diaphragm and pelvis which disconnect feelings in head and heart from feelings in the genital area. Such bodily manifestations of apathy remind us that apathy is a "stance" not only metaphorically but literally. This is true of all the constituents of trust and distrust. For example, the bodily manifestations of distrust which infants display (and which I described earlier in this section) are analogous to what can be seen in adults. But the bodily dimension of pervasive stances is specially evident and important in the cases of apathy and passion.

The bodily dimension of apathy is most clearly understood when we realize that for an apathetic man the most alien and dangerous forces seem to be within himself. His internal bodily defenses enable him not only to stop consciously fearing the threat but to ignore its very existence. Tensions and rigidities in various parts of the body provide a "body-armoring" which blocks access between passions and consciousness. Yearning and rage which are too hot and tumultuous to be felt can be cooled and pacified by the armoring before they reach consciousness. Passions can thus be repressed. This means that the hidden volcano of emotion is covered by a glacier in consciousness, and the suppressed shouts of grief and protest are so muffled that the apathetic man hears within himself only a still, small voice of calm. This cool and quiet stance towards one's own hidden, passionate self is also the stance which he has towards other people and towards his environment generally. Such pervasive detachment provides a sense of security and of internal and external unity. He acknowledges as real only that which is experienced when one is in this stance. A cool and quiet person inhabits a cool and quiet world. But the security is precarious and the unity is spurious. Reality, whether it be inside or outside oneself, is not limited in the way that the apathetic man would like it to be. There are vital energies within self and world which call for passionate participation and which are disruptive when they are denied or repudiated. These energies seem to be nonexistent or alien to the apathetic person, but this is because of his detachment from himself and his world. He does not dare to risk exposure to elemental forces, which seem too dangerous and too painful to be allowed access to the secret self. But these forces are part of reality, and cannot be eliminated simply by being ignored.

It is important to distinguish what I am calling "apathy" from other states to which the term is sometimes applied.[3] In extreme cases an apathetic person may be almost insensible to feelings, but this is not typical of what I mean by apathy. An apathetic person may well have many feelings, including strong, secret feelings about himself and other people; but the feelings are disembodied. Another meaning of "apathy" which needs to be set aside is one which refers to a state of indolence or aversion to exertion and involvement. In extreme cases such indolence leads to immobility. This is not what I mean by "apathy." An apathetic person is often very active, involving himself in work or art or sport in a very absorbed, intensive way. Indeed, apathetic people are sometimes very creative and original because they can concentrate attention on something with all the focused energy of a lazer beam. The involvement, however, is not of the whole self. The body is an obstacle rather than a medium for contact with the springs of life within oneself and other people.

It is interesting to compare apathy with modern stoicism and with the life-stance advocated by the ancient Stoics. Apathy is obviously not the same as what people usually mean by "stoicism." An apathetic man is not usually impassive, indifferent to suffering and completely detached from the triumphs and tragedies of life, trying to eliminate all feeling. Such "stoicism" is not what the ancient Stoics taught.[4] But apathy is similar to ancient Stoicism in that the only feelings which are permitted are those which are *rational*, that is, those which can be kept under the strict control of reason. Like the ancient Stoics the apathetic man also tries to *distinguish* and *detach* himself from the "violent flutterings"[5] of feeling which might undermine his security and sully his self-image. Like them he tries to get rid of passions by repressing them, or, failing that, to control them by observing them as if they belonged to somebody else. Since the "irrational" feelings have not been integrated as sources of creative energy for the whole personality they seem very dangerous. To the apathetic man it seems necessary to maintain strict Apollonian law and order within the psyche, lest there be a sudden Dionysian orgy or uncontrollable violence and sexual excess.[6] There is some basis for this fear, for bottled-up passion which has been fermenting for many years can be explosive. Apathetic man thus resembles the ancient Stoics in being detached from his passions. He resembles them also in being detached from his fellow human beings. Since intimate relations with others can disturb the calm security which apathy provides, it seems wise to seek a basic independence from others. It is not necessarily a matter of self-isolation: one can be magnanimous and generous and just in one's dealings with others. But it seems wise to acknowledge neither neediness nor hostility, neither yearnings nor resentment, neither fascination nor fear. When such a detachment from one's fellows is combined with a detachment from one's passions, it is possible to live a life of minimal anxiety, wariness, idolatry, and despair. Obviously this has many advantages, which make apathy a plausible and popular pervasive stance: the price, however, is high. The price is a loss of embodied passion and embodied encounter with other human beings. By suppressing raw, primitive emotions rather than acknowledging them and integrating them into his life, the apathetic man splits himself in two and lives only half a life. At best he can love like an angel or calculate like a computer or sculpt like a god, but he can not feel as a fully incarnate human being whose whole self is in creative contact with other human beings.

Apathy, like other constituents of distrust, is part of the human condition. In some people it is the dominant form of distrust, whereas in others it is the weakest form, but it is always a possible option. Apathy begins as an unconscious strategy in infancy, and if it was dominant then it is likely to be dominant in adult life. But there are also cultural influences. It is possible that apathy may be more common in modern Western culture, which is often described as "schizoid,"[7] especially because of the emergence of "technological man."[8] Yet apathy is not a purely modern cultural product. In Western culture we can go back not only to the Stoics but to Socrates. His detached stance in the face of death—so different from the passion of Jesus—has been a major inspiration for an apathetic way of life. A good deal of Western philosophy has reflected and encouraged an apathetic life-stance. More recently, tendencies to apathy which already exist in individuals because of infantile experiences have been reinforced by a dedication to scientific method not only as a useful way of acquiring certain kinds of knowledge but as a total life-stance. Not only in experimental research but in life generally one is urged not to be influenced by feelings which might bias one's judgment or distract one's focus of attention. As a technological man I might, like an ancient Stoic, allow myself to feel some joy at discovering some new connection in nature. Or I might tolerate a craving for more knowledge. "Irrational" feelings, however, are taboo. As a technological man I acknowledge as my self only the detached observer of what goes on "out there," where "out there" includes not only the behavior of other people and the events in nature but also my own behavior and my own stream of consciousness. I view all this as if I were a disinterested spectator, dispassionately discerning regularities which will enable me to predict what happens and, perhaps, to control it. This is a sophisticated, "scientific" form of apathy.

Apathy, in its various forms, is a constituent of basic distrust, which is a vice. So it, too, is a vice, like the other constituents. But in each case the vice does not consist in *having* the distrustful, pervasive stance but in *consenting* to it. Consent means letting it dominate one's life rather than resisting it. Realistic guilt arises, not from having the stance, but from being its accomplice rather than struggling against it. What is required of each of us is not success, but struggle, not perfection but perseverance. If apathy has been one's characteristic life-stance for many years, it is unrealistic to try to eliminate it. At best it can be reduced. Indeed, even if I commit myself to a vigorous struggle against the domination of apathy I need to have a kind of self-tolerance which is based on a fundamental self-affirmation. The main way out of apathy opens up when I can accept, however cautiously at first, another person's affirmation of my being—someone who says, in effect, "I accept and cherish you as you are, with all your blocked-up feeling and detachment from me and from yourself." And even if a person who struggles against apathy remains more apathetic than passionate, her life can be very creative, as I noted above. Her pent-up passions may not become fully embodied, but her efforts to be open to them allows their energy to be released in her work or her art. Although apathy is often only "half a life," this is not true of her. Her life is richer than that of most people. The bane of her life is also a boon. But many forms of apathy involve no such benefits. And if there is no struggle against apathy, the outcome can be very destructive to self and others.

Usually apathy is a major obstacle to one's own personal fulfillment and an immoral influence on one's dealings with others. The immorality is of three kinds. *First*, there is a kind of cold detachment which thinks of itself as "amoral" (neither moral nor immoral) but which is actually immoral. A striking example of this is research on human beings which ignores their emotional needs and which ignores the dehumanizing effects of treating them as objects during the research.[9] But there are many less blatant ways in which apathy leads us to treat another person as an "It" rather than a "Thou," thus denying and subverting his humanity. Immoral "amorality" is very common in our society. *Second*, apathy may lead to immoral conduct, not because of its "amoral" detachment from other people's passions, but because of its repression of their passions, which seem to the apathetic man to be almost as dangerous as his own. Sometimes he is so moved by his fear of Dionysian eruptions that he relies on a ruthless imposition of "law and order" to suppress the vital, spontaneous forces in society. Not only does he try to restrain passionate behavior, he also tries to crush the spirit of passionate people. Worst of all, he sometimes does this to children.

A *third* way in which apathy leads to immoral conduct occurs, not when apathetic man imposes his own detachment and repression on others, but when his own detachment and repression break down, unleashing wild forces of destruction within him. He had split his body and his passions off from what he took to be his true self, imposing on them what they regarded as an alien, authoritarian regime. Now they rebel. The self, which disowned them long ago, now abdicates from all responsibility for them. Like a deposed king, the self flees the country. What remains is a demonic rabble of feelings which rush out into the streets to act out their revengeful fury in an orgy of rape, mayhem, and murder. When this happens in one person it can often touch off a similar outburst in others, leading cumulatively to mob violence. A skillful demagogue such as Hitler can foment a revolt of the demonic and use it for his own horrendous purposes. Only if passions are acknowledged and integrated within the whole personality is there a third alternative to successful apathy (detachment and repression) and unsuccessful apathy (unrestrained violence).

The relevance of apathy to morality is thus obvious. Its relevance to religion is also clear. Since apathy is a pervasive stance which seems to unify the self and the world, it involves a cosmic conviction: whatever pervasive reality unifies the world is neither benevolent nor malevolent but neutral. This neutral reality is conceived as being analogous to either personal or nonpersonal entities. In the former case the ultimate reality is a cosmic mirror image of a perfect apathetic person: detached and dispassionate, unmixed with matter, unsullied by sex, so independent from human beings as to be impassible and totally unresponsive, so attentive and disinterested as to be an Ideal World Observer. Thus apathetic man is the symbol of the ultimate. This ultimate is aptly called "the god of the philosophers," though many philosophers (especially existentialists) do not endorse it.

If the ultimate reality is conceived as being analogous to a *non*personal entity, there is a different symbol of the ultimate: not an apathetic man, but some item or aspect of the cosmos as it appears when viewed from an apathetic stance. Then the neutral, ultimate reality is conceived as "Energy" or "Matter" or "Substance." Sometimes this ultimate reality is regarded as the ultimate for scientific explanation of the universe, but the crucial point is that it is regarded as the ultimate *from* a basic life-stance: the reality reflects and reinforces the stance of apathetic man. Whatever unifies and pervades the whole cosmos is allegedly like what he observes when he perceives particulars in a dispassionate way.

Apathetic man's Ideal Observer or Matter is an alternative Deity of Distrust alongside resentful man's Grand Depriver, idolatrous man's omnipotent Fairy Godmother, and despairing man's Wheel of Fate. For each of the constituents of distrust except anxiety there is a typical way of conceiving the pervasive reality which seems to unify the world. Anxiety does not even purport to unify the world and the self, so it is not associated with a conviction concerning a unifying reality. Nor is it the case that the other constituents *always* involve such convictions. For example, idolatry is sometimes a scattered, unfocused pursuit of diverse diversions, and despair is sometimes so narcissistic that the world is simply what the self experiences, so the world has no *independent* reality to be unified by some pervasive ultimate. But in general, distrust does involve convictions which obviously compete against the convictions associated with trust. The kind of convictions which a pervasive stance involves depends on the kind of unity which it provides for self and world. In this respect apathy is a major modern rival to trust.

Passion is the aspect of trust which enables distrust to come out into the open. Perhaps the most profound example of this is Jesus' cry of dereliction from the cross: "My God, my God, why hast thou forsaken me?" (Mark 15:34; RSV). In a little while Jesus feels serenely confident, and says, "Father, into thy hands I commend my spirit" (Luke 23:46; RSV). But at the moment he is overwhelmed by almost intolerable feelings: a terrible agony as he experiences abandonment, a heavy, helpless despair, a bewildered resentment at being deprived of all consolation. Jesus is able to feel and to express his distrust, because at a deeper level he can still trust. He is not afraid that he will drive God still further away by blurting out what he feels. He appeals to a God who is still *there*, though not near. He is assured that his whole self has been affirmed and accepted by God, so he need hide nothing from himself and God. The most trusting of men can acknowledge the depths of his own distrust.

Often passionate people are not as explicitly religious as Jesus and usually they are far less profound, but the same kind of passionate trust is at work in them, enabling them to acknowledge their distrust. Their cry of dereliction need not be addressed explicitly to God. A person may feel forsaken and scream out his forlornness and despair and resentment, while being quite unclear as to who it is that has forsaken him. But he can feel and express his distrust, rather than escaping into apathy, because he has an underlying trust which involves a religious conviction: "The pervasive reality which unifies my world accepts the whole of me, including my distrust." Thus when Sartre[10] claims that there is an atheistic forlornness which is inescapably part of human consciousness if it is free of self-deception, he fails to see that the forlornness will be repressed unless there is an implicitly religious trust which enables us to overcome the self-deception. Similarly the Tillichian[11] despair which is a state of being bereft of all meaning in life is not only *overcome* by what Tillich calls "absolute faith"; it cannot even *emerge* into consciousness unless there is some absolute faith, some passionate trust which can sustain a cry of dereliction.

Passion is the form of trust which resists the temptation to apathy. Instead of dissociating myself from primitive feelings which are acutely painful and repugnant, instead of repressing these feelings, I acknowledge them as my own. I allow myself to feel them and to express them. They are *human* feelings, and in so far as I have passion as my pervasive stance, nothing human is alien to me. They are *my* feelings, and it is my need and my responsibility to own up to them. They are *elemental* feelings, which relate me to the animal kingdom from which human beings have evolved, and which relate me to the womb and the breast of the mother from whom I emerged as a man. They are passions which I feel in my heart and my gut and my groin, in my head and my hands and my feet. I *am* these passions, these embodied feelings, though I am also more than these.

In so far as I am a passionate person, I acknowledge not only distrustful feelings but also the almost intolerable feelings from which these arise. I acknowledge not only anxiety, resentment, hostility, idolatrous obsession, and masochistic despair, but also forlorn loneliness, overwhelming helplessness, desperate yearning, immeasurable grief, and murderous rage. And I also acknowledge trustful feelings. These too can emerge and find expression. In a passionate person trustful feelings are not mainly a superficial consolation to which one clings instead of facing some of the hidden horrors of the psyche. They are not like the voice of Pollyanna distracting me from opening Pandora's box. Instead, in so far as I am passionate I feel assurance and generosity and gratitude and hope springing up from the very depths of my being. Passion is not merely a reaction to apathy. Indeed, more generally, trust is not merely a reaction to distrust. The *raison d'être* of trust does not consist solely in its waging war against distrust. Trust has its own positive place at the core of human nature. This is especially true of trust in so far as it is passionate.

Thus although passion is a resistance against the temptation to apathy, it is more than this. Passion is not only a refusal to disassociate oneself from largely infantile forbidden feelings and a refusal to repress such feelings. It is not only a matter of allowing these passions access into consciousness and room to move in the body. It also is a channelling and shaping of these passions so that they energize and vitalize a whole range of adult activities in the present. And many other passions are felt and expressed in these activities, especially the passions associated with adult trust. These mature, positive emotions are not purely "mental" or "spiritual": they are embodied. Consider, for example, the feelings which spring from a pervasive stance of generosity. These have a bodily dimension which can be experienced in oneself and observed in others. The heart of a generous person feels at times as if it were filled to overflowing with a warmth and well-being which flow out to others. The face of a generous person is sometimes radiant with a brilliant, life-giving energy which radiates outward in all directions—a momentary transfiguration. And in addition to the passions which express trust there are other embodied feelings which animate the creative activities of the passionate person, feelings which go out from the self towards whomever or whatever the self is involved with. The graceful total involvement of a passionate person is powerful and beautiful. The movements of energy in the body and the structures of consciousness in the mind blend to form an indissoluble unity. This total involvement can occur when making love or writing a book or playing tennis or preparing a meal or digging a ditch or playing the piano or talking with a friend or contemplating the divine. Some of these activities are more obviously mental than physical and some are more obviously physical than mental, but all can involve letting oneself go in a total way which is both structured and passionate. In order to let oneself go one must be confident that there is a fundamental kinship between self and surroundings. One must trust that when the whole self is risked by being expressed and exposed and inserted into the world in activities which are permeated with passion and shaped by spirit, the world will receive this self-offering graciously. There are many people who will be indifferent or hostile, but the ultimate reality which pervades the world will be receptive and will confirm the creativity.

This confidence concerning surroundings is linked with a confidence concerning the self. In so far as I am passionate, I believe I can trust the passions which are most fundamental and all-inclusive in myself. I must be rigorously honest with myself, setting aside the desires which arise from the false self which I have constructed out of distrust. But when I discover what I want with the whole of my authentic self, I can trust this whole-hearted wanting.[12] It is safe and right for me to seek its fulfillment. I should follow these passions. Rigorous honesty is only possible, however, if I trust the context in which I live. I must be convinced that the ultimate is not alien to what is most genuine in me, and that instead it accepts and affirms me. Most important, I must believe that since I am integral to my environment, what I give with passion is truly needed. I must trust that the more deeply I am in touch with myself and express this in my life, the more warmly I am accepted and affirmed by the ultimate. In trust I receive the ultimate meaning and reality of my life from a source beyond myself, and in trust I offer my passionate life to be received by that source as a significant and substantial contribution to the whole. Life is like a dance for which the music is already provided, and in which many others are already creating their own patterns as they respond to the rhythms of the cosmos. To have passionate trust is to join in the dance of life with a confidence that I can express my own most deeply felt rhythms in a way which contributes a special beauty to the overall pattern.

Trusting one's passions implies a belief that human nature is not rotten at the core. If, as Freud maintained, there is an independent destructive drive or "death instinct" in human beings, then I and all human beings require an authoritarian superego to restrain and repress an alien, dangerous drive which is deep within the self. It is then folly to try to strip away all my defenses against negative, elemental feelings which society in its wisdom has helped me to repress. If part of what I most deeply want is death and destruction for myself and others it is better not to open Pandora's box, or only to open it halfway. In contrast with this, passionate man's pervasive stance implies a conviction that the only *inherent* fundamental impulse is towards life. He does not deny that there are immensely powerful destructive impulses in everyone, or that in many people these impulses are dominant. It would be foolish to underestimate their power. When Cain killed Abel he was in the grip of murderous passion. Since his day many millions have been gripped in the same way. But rage and other destructive feelings are not the most fundamental passions. They are derivative.[13] They are the result of inhibition and frustration and repression of feelings which are not in themselves destructive—above all, a yearning for an intimate relation of trust which brings the comfort of closeness, like a parental blessing. Violence is a substitute for gentle contact, rage is an expression of helpless neediness, hate is frozen and distorted love. This does not mean that destructive impulses can be totally eradicated, for the nondestructive feelings from which they arise are inherent in human beings, and centuries of conditioning move human beings to deal with them in the repressive ways which produce the dreadful distortions. But if the destructive impulses are not independent but derivative, there can be a realistic movement in individuals and communities *towards* complete de-repression, *towards* a fully passionate life. The process which leads to destructive distortions of innocent yearnings can be challenged and considerably changed. Much wisdom and caution is needed in exposing the life-denying impulses which are at work in every person. The de-repression must occur in a well-boundaried context, among people who are firmly in touch with life-affirming forces. Otherwise the previously controlled destructive inclinations may be "acted out" against self or society or both. But the dangers involved in universal repression are far greater. Society is like a giant pressure cooker which is being continually heated. Eventually there is a gigantic explosion such as the rise of Nazism. Apathy is not a viable form of life for society as a whole. Unless there is some movement from apathy towards passion, the very destructiveness which apathy tries to suppress will erupt like a volcano in individuals and groups.

The most important reason for a movement towards passion, however, is a positive one. Passion is necessary if human beings are to fufill their destiny as *participants in the life-affirming energy which pervades the cosmos.* This participation is an extremely important part of passion. A passionate person participates in a flow of energy or spirit or life force which enters his body and his psyche from outside, moves through, and moves out again. He can actually feel this happening at times. His own rhythms pulsate with the rhythms of other people and with the basic life rhythm of the cosmos which they share together. This is specially evident in sexual intercourse. In passionate orgasm waves of uninhibited movement and feeling are released which throb in unison with the orgasm of the beloved and with a flow of cosmic energy which pulsates through them both. But passionate participation is not confined to sexual intercourse. In many other kinds of encounter with other human beings and in many solitary activities such as artistic creation or scientific speculation or contemplative prayer the passionate person may be "possessed" by forces beyond his control. These mysterious forces arise from beyond himself and from his own inner depths. He seems passive and helpless in that he cannot control them. But it is actually up to him to decide whether to let them into his life. And in the moment of "possession" he is most active and energetic, most powerful and expansive, most truly himself. He is active because he is receptive, energetic because he is being energized, powerful because he is soft and open, expansive because he is given so much. Passionate participation is above all a *generous* state. The wine of life overflows to others from someone whose "cup runs over" because it is continuously being filled from a limitless source.

Passionate participation must be clearly distinguished from three other "enthusiasms" which are also states of heightened consciousness and might be confused with it. I shall call these enthusiasms "angelic," "megalomaniac," and "daimonic." *Angelic* enthusiasm is disembodied. The cosmic reality in which one participates is not experienced as immanent in nature and incarnate in human life. It is remote from matter and split off from flesh and blood. Angelic enthusiasm is a form of apathy. Instead of acknowledging and channelling elemental and infantile passions, shaping them with spirit, angelic enthusiasm flies off to heaven, refusing to acknowledge any earthly origins. Instead of integrating sexual passion with love of the divine it tries to transcend sexuality. Instead of letting go of the whole self, both mind and body, so that both may be permeated by the divine, the angelic enthusiast dissociates himself from his body and opens up only his mind or spirit. At best only part of himself can participate in the divine. But angelic enthusiasm may bring considerable peace and power and a sense of participating in an ultimate spiritual reality. It can be one of the relatively successful forms of apathy to which I previously referred. But since it depends on a self-deception and a split within the self, it cannot be as secure or as rich or as all-encompassing as passionate enthusiasm. And sometimes the movement towards participation scarcely begins, for instead of letting go of his spirit the enthusiast clings to it. That is, he savors his own spirituality, feeling excited not about God but about his own angelic love for God, and congratulating himself on his own godlike purity and power.[14] Such enthusiasm verges on megalomania, to which we now turn.

Megalomaniac enthusiasm is a mad self-inflation, a crazy delusion of divine grandeur: I alone, of all the individuals in the universe, am the center of power and insight and significance. I am like a balloon which has been so immensely inflated (miraculously, without breaking) that it now fills the entire cosmos. The secret divine powers which enter me seem to be my possession. They literally "go to my head," like the bubbles in a global glass of champagne! Instead of being possessed by the divine, I own it and control it. In my manic excitement I lose touch with the earth not only figuratively but literally: I no longer stand firmly on the ground. And in my narcissistic self-absorption I have no sense of the equal and independent reality of other people; they are merely my experiences. In some versions of megalomaniac enthusiasm I identify myself with a mob or a mass movement which revels in its own throbbing power and unique significance. I am part of a "We" which possesses the divine. The rest of the world is a nonentity.

Whether the megalomania be individual or group, it clearly differs from genuine passion. The man of passion does not single out himself or his group from the rest of mankind and the rest of cosmos as the one locus of meaning and reality. He is at the third stage of the positive way towards assurance, which was described earlier: "I include myself among the many who participate in and reveal the meaning and reality and acceptance which pervade the universe." As a *passionate* man of trust, he also participates in cosmic energy. He does not possess or monopolize this energy. And it does not literally or figuratively "go to his head." It enters his whole body and flows through his whole body and moves out of his whole body. He feels elated, but his feet are firmly grounded.

What I call *daimonic* enthusiasm involves some of the repression of painful passions which is typical of angelic enthusiasm and some of the narcissistic self-inflation which is typical of megalomaniac enthusiasm, but it has a distinctively *destructive* emphasis. It is a matter of tuning in on the life-denying forces which are at work in human beings and in the cosmos so that one is possessed by them. A person who is in the cold grip of paralyzing despair and helpless resentment can momentarily feel alive and vigorous by calling forth whatever violent anger he can find within himself. If he can feel that the hot-blooded, destructive energies are not only his but those of the universe itself, his thrill of triumph knows no bounds. Daimonic enthusiasm is a device for evading and delaying a deathward movement within oneself by participating in the contagious violence which lurks just below the surface in most human beings. If you have ever caught yourself evading a feeling of helplessness and despair by getting worked up into an orgy of anger concerning something trivial you will not find it difficult to understand the throbbing excitement of a Nazi torch-light hate rally. The fact that one can understand it does not, of course, make it any less hideous. Some of the worst atrocities in human history have been perpetrated by people in the grip of daimonic enthusiasm. It is as if a whole community were to go berserk on speed, indiscriminately dealing out death in order to feel alive. Passionate enthusiasm, in stark contrast with this, generously enhances life because it is already alive, overflowing with life force.

So far I have described four main characteristics of the passionate person, who has passion as a pervasive stance in her life:

(1)   She resists the temptation to apathy, in which painful negative feelings are observed in detachment or are repressed or are disembodied.

(2)   She permeates all her creative activities with passion as she shapes them with spirit.

(3)   She trusts in herself and her surroundings in such a way that she can confidently act on the basis of her most whole-hearted and fundamental wants.

(4)   She participates in the life energies of the cosmos, which has rhythms which resound in her body and her consciousness.

There is a fifth aspect of passion which we have not yet considered. Passion means being in close touch not only with one's own pain and aspiration but also with the pain and aspiration of other people. The passionate person is very sensitive to the intense feelings of others, whether these be openly expressed or deeply repressed. She "tunes in" not only on the vital energies of the universe but also on the inner life of other human beings. Her antennae pick up the vibrations which each person gives off from his or her inner space. She responds perceptively and powerfully to suffering and joy, moods of life denial and movements towards abundant life, distrustful "downs" and trustful "ups," cowardly self-perceptions and courageous self-confrontations, hurts and triumphs. In short, she has a profound and wide-ranging *em*pathy. She is painfully aware of the destructive forces which she sees at work in people and she feels impelled to do everything she can to help them struggle towards a more positive existence. She is joyfully aware of the creative forces which she sees at work in people and she draws them forth, celebrating every breakthrough towards a more truly human life. And, finally, she is deeply distressed and indignant whenever she sees individuals or groups dehumanizing their fellows, either by nurturing whatever is destructive or smothering whatever is creative.

The empathy of a passionate person depends on her openness towards herself. Since she is in touch with the most powerful positive and negative impulses within herself, she is in touch with these in others. Her intuition often enables her to discern what others are not yet fully aware of in themselves. Since she can discern hidden longings and hidden strengths and can help to draw these forth she is often a "charismatic figure," both disturbing people and drawing them towards herself by her very presence. Her passionate empathy is very different from the responses which some people have when they intuit the inner space of another person. One woman may use her insight in a malicious way to manipulate the other person or even to destroy him. A second woman may identify with the other person in a narcissistic way, adding the other's pain to her own so she can feel more sorry for herself; passionate empathy, however, is focused on the other, not on oneself. A third woman may be overwhelmed by the other's pain, which dominates her own consciousness because it touches on previously repressed pain within herself. But a passionate person has already faced her own pain, so the pain she is aware of is clearly not her own, but the other's. In her empathy she remains a separate person, clearly distinguishing her own state of mind from that of the other person. But although she is separate, she is not distant. Her life energies pour out generously to the other and she mercifully absorbs much of the other's soul sickness into herself. Active empathy with many people can leave her drained and spent unless, like Jesus, she retreats for spiritual refreshment in solitude or with people who can give to her and not merely receive from her. There is a saying concerning the Buddha which applies to all passionate people: "Man's real sickness springs from foolish love; Buddha's responding sickness arises from great mercy."[15] Destructive urges spring from a longing which is misdirected and perverted; the pain and weakness of a passionate person arise from her response of generous empathy.

The religious relevance of passion as a constituent of trust is related to the last three aspects of passion which we have considered: whole-heartedness, enthusiasm, and empathy. Whole-heartedness, or trusting one's deepest passions, is possible only if one has confidence that this is accepted and encouraged by the ultimate context of one's existence. It must seem all right to be doing one's own thing. This may seem incompatible with the religious conviction that one ought to be doing the will of God. But obedience to the will of God need not be interpreted as a matter of always doing what God says rather than what I want to do. It can be interpreted in a non-authoritarian way. As William Lynch [16] maintains, what God wills is that I do what I whole-heartedly want to do. The only restrictions are that I go on accepting his acceptance of me, which enables me to be honest concerning what I really want, and that I help rather than hinder others in their attempt to be true to themselves. The process of discovering what one can want with complete integrity is usually quite arduous: a great many false selves are demolished in me on the way. The process requires considerable trust in the ultimate context and the most basic self. On this approach, God is symbolized by a person in whose presence we are liberated to discover and to express our true selves. Neither the person nor God need be always present once we are to some extent liberated from false selves. If a friend or a parent has helped us to find and follow our passions, we do not need to go on being in constant I-Thou encounter with him. I can be on my own most of the time. Nor do I only find myself in the moments when I am responding to the divine presence in what I do. I have been delivered to myself.

Passionate participation implies a somewhat different conviction concerning the relation between man and God. The emphasis is not on expressing my true self as I contribute my own distinctive creative pattern to the cosmos, but on allowing myself to be moved by the pulsating energies of the cosmos. The transition can be seen in the image of the dancer whose own deeply personal rhythms will, he trusts, blend creatively with the fundamental cosmic rhythm. It will blend, in so far as he is participating in the same throbbing power that pervades the universe. God is here not conceived as the receptive context in which I dare to expose and express my inmost being—though this is not denied. God is here conceived as the immanent source of the pervasive energy which invades and possesses my whole self if I am open. God is the origin of the overflow of generous, abundant life which wells up within me and which is poured down upon me like a refreshing mountain stream. What is called "obeying the will of God" is here interpreted as being open to passionate enthusiasm, allowing God's vibrant gift to flow into my life. In so far as I am receptive to life energy in my own body and mind I am more able to discern it and to rejoice in it as I look at other people and at things in nature. I come to celebrate the pervasive presence of God as life-giving Spirit. I begin to praise God as the intimate origin of the mysterious power at work in human beings, inspiring their most creative passions, transfiguring their faces with generous radiance, animating their movements with the graceful dance of life, uniting them with me and with all creatures, breaking down our isolation from one another, and liberating each of us to be truly ourselves. Such worship can be the most intense and powerful passion a person ever experiences: an ecstatic, joyful celebration of life and its divine source, cherishing the gift and fervently thanking the Giver.

It is one thing to worship God with passionate enthusiasm. It is a different thing to worship God with passionate empathy. There is a shift from participation in the divine life to participation in the divine pain. As Gregory Baum has said, "God is not only the life of our life but also the abiding pain we experience in the face of a suffering, oppressed and hungry humanity."[17] The passionate man participates in the divine passion, the divine pain. During the last days of his life, the days of his "Passion," Jesus was acutely conscious of human suffering and sin. He felt a deep distress in every fiber of his being. One example is his anguish and grief over Jerusalem:

When he came in sight of the city, he wept over it and said, "If only you had known, on this great day, the way that leads to peace! But no, it is hid from your sight" (Luke 19:41; NEB).

"O Jerusalem, Jerusalem, the city that murders the prophets and stones the messengers sent to her. How often have I longed to gather your children, as a hen gathers her brood under her wings, but you would not let me" (Matthew 23:27; NEB).

Jesus discerned the agony and the evil which lurk just below the surface in the human heart. Since he himself had already known great sorrow and faced great temptations he responded with great compassion and concern to the struggles of others, like a good parent he longs to help his children find the way that leads to peace and love. When Jesus saw the terrible things which people do to the best of human beings, he was overwhelmed with sorrow and anger. Once, in an outburst of indignation, he had even said that those who cause children to stumble from the way should go out and drown themselves (Matthew 18:6).

In his compassion and concern and indignation Jesus participated in a divine compassion and concern and indignation. His pain at the plight and perversity of man was a participation in a divine pain. His "Passion" was a participation in a divine Passion. Before his death he invited his disciples to break bread and drink wine in remembrance of him and his Passion, and as a symbol of their participation in the divine Passion. He warned that this invitation is not an easy one to accept. In the Garden of Gethsemane Jesus himself prayed that he be spared the cup of sorrows. He had lived life in such a passionate, embodied way he did not want to give it up. He had so joyfully revelled in the acceptance of God and so enthusiastically participated in the life of God that he did not want to participate to the full in the pain of God. This "will of God" was the most difficult for him to accept.

There does not seem to be much in common between the reassuring God who encourages us to "do our thing," the energizing God who possesses us with spirit and life, and the suffering God whose pain we share when we are deeply disturbed by the ill and evil in humanity. Perhaps these different concepts of God cannot be rendered entirely consistent so that we can clearly understand how such different characteristics can be united in the same God. But the concepts reflect different modes of passion which *can* be unified in the same passionate human life. I know it can happen not only because I see it in the records of the life of Jesus, but also because I see it in passionate people today. And when such people associate the three modes of passion with explicit religious beliefs, the unity which they experience moves them to try to reconcile these beliefs. Christians, in particular, try to make conceptual sense of their worship of God as Trinity: God the Father, by whose acceptance they flourish, God the Spirit, in whose power they participate, and God the Son, whose Passion they share — one indivisible God, in three Persons.

When I began to write this section on passion I had no idea that I would end up with a reference to the Christian doctrine of the Trinity. I did not even anticipate that three major kinds of passion would emerge. What I have written reveals the influence of distinctively Christian thought and experience. But in so far as it fits and illuminates the experience of non-Christians, it also shows that Christian theology concerning a Trinitarian God is at least to some extent an interpretation of universal human experience, and is not exclusively an interpretation of events in the history of Israel, Jesus, and the Church. There are of course passionate people who do not profess any religious beliefs and who are not committed to any particular religious community or tradition. But their experience is very open to being understood by them in religious terms.

The *moral* significance of passion is threefold. Each moral aspect corresponds to one of the three modes of passion and each is in contrast with one of the ways in which apathy may be immoral. First, the person who trusts his own deepest passions gets below the layer of derivative, destructive urges to his fundamental creative impulses; the danger of explosive, violent outburst is radically reduced. Second, his own participation in life energies provides the fuel for friendship and intimate love; it moves him to encourage rather than repress the life energies in others. Third, his empathetic compassion is in stark contrast with the coldly "amoral" detachment which apathy may promote. Indeed, we will see that passionate empathy is the element in trust which culminates in the seventh attitude-virtue, concern.

This section on apathy and passion concludes my account of the struggle between trust and distrust.

Part TWO

Human Fulfillment

Trust is the fundamental stance in the way of life which I describe and commend, but there are also seven other attitude-virtues. Each of these depends on trust and yet goes beyond trust. Each, like trust, is a constituent of genuine religion and morality, and the last three are not only constituents but also goals. Together, the eight attitude-virtues constitute a religious-moral way of life which moves towards human fulfillment. In this way of life there is a struggle against eight attitude-vices. Human fulfillment occurs when the attitude-virtues, in their mature forms, predominate steadily over the attitude-vices. Few people enjoy this state, but many find authenticity and partial fulfillment because they persist in their struggle to nurture the attitude-virtues and to resist the attitude-vices.

Part Two consists of three chapters. In chapter 7 I will sketch four attitude-virtues and their opposites, and in chapter 8 I will deal with three more. In chapter 9 I will discuss the overall way of life which then emerges.

Four Attitude-Virtues and Their Opposites

After trust comes *humility*, the second attitude-virtue. It has two interrelated opposites: pride and self-humiliation. Each attitude-virtue deals with a different issue in human life. Where trust deals with the tendency to feel abandoned because of the insecurities of life, humility deals with the tendency to feel ashamed because my power and my status are limited, my freedom and my importance are finite. Some limits come from outside me, from nature and society. Others come from inside me, from my own constitution. Some limits, such as mortality, are strictly inescapable and unalterable. Others, such as my power and status in society, involve a range of possibilities; but the range is limited. My strength and significance are inherently finite. Finitude is part of the human condition. Humility is a stance of realistic, unashamed acceptance of my finitude. But it is not a fatalistic resignation, a passive acquiescence in whatever happens, like being a doormat for every creature to wipe its feet on. It includes an active exercise of the limited power which I actually have, changing the world and myself as I am able. Humility is a realistic discernment and acceptance of both what I cannot do and what I can do. It is a responsive adjustment and exercise of my finite freedom in relation to the constraints of my own constitution, the necessities of nature, and the freedom of other people. Humility is a pervasive stance of the whole personality. Since it is an internally unifying stance, it is also externally unifying. It is focused not only on all the particulars within me and outside me which limit me but also on God, conceived as the unifying reality which pervades my world, the source of all the limits on what I can do and can be. Humility is a stance of realistic, unashamed acceptance of my finitude in relation to God, the pervasive cosmic Limiter—who is also the cosmic Enabler and Encourager, for God is also present in whatever helps me to exercise the limited power which I actually have. A humble person need not necessarily have conscious, explicit convictions concerning God, but his stance involves such convictions. Humility is expressed in all three parts of a fourteenth-century prayer:

> Almighty God, our heavenly Father, give us Serenity to accept what cannot be changed, Courage to change what should be changed, and Wisdom to know the one from the other.[1]

As a religious attitude, humility is often focused first on another person. Someone who helps me both to accept my limits and to expand the exercise of my powers is viewed as a symbol of an ultimate Limiter and Enabler who pervades my environment. But, as in the case of trust, there are more mature versions of the attitude-virtue in which many people, including myself, manifest the divine Limiter and Enabler.

Humility is usually contrasted with pride: the self-deceptive attempt to act out my fantasies of infinitude, of divinity, of unlimited power and status. The proud man feels a secret shame which he cannot bear to allow into full consciousness: he feels humiliated by his limitations and his dependencies. He cannot realistically accept and appreciate the powers which he actually has. He is so afraid of littleness and lowliness that he has delusions of divine grandeur. Each particular limitation on his life, especially death, symbolizes a cosmic "put-down" which must somehow be defied, though in reality it cannot. Each particular exercise of authority over him is a symbol of a cosmic authoritarianism to which he can not submit; yet even if he rebels, he is caught up in a pointless power struggle with God.

Sometimes humility is depicted as a total submission,[2] a capitulation in the power struggle: a man gives up and tries no more to do and be. This is not humility, however. It is self-humiliation, a self-destructive kind of fatalism. It is like a little boy who first fantasizes being big and powerful like his parents and then, ignoring his own real though modest powers and achievements, gives up and reverts to infantile helplessness. Where the proud man deals with the shame of smallness by trying to deny it, the self-humiliating man succumbs to it. In either case, the person who lacks humility regards his relative smallness and subordination as a shame rather than as a simple fact. He is perpetually preoccupied with whether he is being defiant or conformist in what he does. When he is deciding what to do he must first find out what someone else who has power and authority is doing or demanding; then he can either go against it or submit to it. He is not free to do what he wants in cooperation with others. His own wants are secondary to the pervasive conflictual stance which he brings to each situation of choice: either he resists or he complies, either he subjugates or he is subjugated, either he is superior or he is inferior.[3] His great fear is to lose face, to be exposed to contempt and derision, to be "caught with his pants down." Rather than endure the complete demoralization that such shame would bring, he opts for either self-humiliation or pride. Either he accepts a subservient role and status in advance so that he cannot be put down any further, or he strives for a castle in the sky where no scorn can reach him and from which he can descend for forays of ridicule and humiliation against anyone who presumes to draw near his position of preeminence.

In contrast with this, the humble man seeks neither a gutter nor a throne but rather a place which is appropriate to his actual limitations and powers. This is not a matter of "knowing one's place" in the sense of resigning oneself to the place of subservience and exploitation which one has at the moment as a member of an oppressed class. In such a situation the humble person may well press for radical social change. But this is not because she has a private conflictual stance which he brings to any and every situation, but because the situation itself involves genuine conflicts of interest between oppressor and oppressed.

Humility is clearly a moral virtue in interpersonal relations. In so far as I am humble I respect the finitude and the freedom both of myself and of others, accepting what cannot be changed and fostering the growth of human powers. (Such respect is closely related to an element in friendliness, as we shall see later.) The humble person does not need to subjugate others so as to assure herself of sufficient power and status. And she does not need to let others subjugate her so that she can enjoy the masochistic consolations of fatalism.[4] She seeks neither absolute autonomy nor absolute dependency, but rather a combination of autonomy and dependency which transcends the conflict between them. She realizes that the freedom which matters most is not "willful" but "responsive."[5] Willful freedom is the autonomous power an individual has over capacities which are her own to exercise at will, and over people or things which are at her disposal to control. Responsive freedom is a power which arises and continues in a process of mutual responsiveness between people whose mutual influence is creative rather than constraining. When two people meet in willful freedom they are protagonists in a frantic fight for freedom as a power over and against each other. When two people meet in responsive freedom they mutually encourage and enable each other to discover new strengths and abilities.

Humility, like trust, begins early in life. In my account of trust, I noted that the struggle between trust and distrust begins in the first year of life, when what matters is mother and milk and warmth and security and tender contact. We saw how the various "strategies" for avoiding anxiety which then begin tend to persist throughout life. As people grow up, the issues of trust and distrust change, and more mature forms of trust become possible, but patterns from infancy continue to have much influence. The syndrome of pride and self-humiliation also begins in the first year, when the infant tends to alternate between a sense of being the all-powerful center of the world and being absolutely dependent on mother. But the struggle between humility and the syndrome is more clearly manifested in mid-infancy.[6] As Erikson points out, the infant becomes acutely aware at that time both of his new powers (to walk and talk and control his bowels and choose what he eats and manipulate things) and of the limitations on those powers as compared with his parents and as constrained by them. In his interactions with them he develops various "strategies," humble or otherwise, for dealing with these new problems of power and status and shame. These characteristic ways of coping with his freedom tend to persist throughout the rest of his life. Later on the issues of freedom and finitude are of course different. As an adult he typically grapples with the authority of the state or of his boss and with the inevitability of death. If he is a humble adult he can be more realistic and wise than he was as an infant, for he has a much clearer discernment of what he and others can be and do, but his humility is a development from an infantile humility. This does not mean that a person who learned mainly pride or self-humiliation in infancy is doomed and determined to remain that way all his life. With help he can learn how to change patterns of reaction which have come to seem almost instinctive and inescapable. But the shape and emphasis of his adult struggle are greatly influenced by what happened when he was very small.

Some theologians focus so exclusively and obsessively on issues of finitude and freedom that it is tempting to attribute this narrow concern to unresolved problems in mid-infancy. Such a temptation should be resisted, however, for in general such an inference is dubious and even presumptuous. Preoccupations in intellectual life can be due more to academic-cultural influences than to psychological influences. A particular tradition in academic theology may ignore vast areas of religious and moral life. Thus Reinhold Niebuhr draws on Kierkegaardian tradition when he depicts the central human problem as one of accepting or rejecting our finitude.[7] And Gordon Kaufman draws on a Schleiermachian tradition when he derives a concept of God from our various experiences of being limited.[8] But whatever may be the individual psychologies of these various thinkers, what they write about is a struggle which is common to human beings generally, beginning in infancy and continuing in new forms throughout our adult lives.

How can we struggle effectively? What is the way of liberation from being dominated by either pride or self-humiliation in our responses to people and situations? Sometimes what is needed is not "struggle" in the sense of intensely serious effort, but humor. Sometimes humor can expose the fantasies which underlie my pride or my self-humiliation, rendering them vulnerable to an insight in which they lose their power over me—for a crucial moment at least. The fantasies are ludicrous, and I can see this if they are described in a witty way. I am seated neither on a celestial throne at the center of the universe nor on a "one-holer" in an outhouse at the edge of the universe. A sharp, penetrating joke can prick my pompous pretensions, bringing me down to earth. Or, alternatively, it can pierce through the prison walls of my somber self-abasement, jolting me into an initiative towards freedom. But the humor must be gentle and humane, generating a kindly chuckle at another of the funny foibles of humanity. If the exposure is too stark and savage, it may destroy me along with my pride, or shame me into deeper self-humiliation. And usually if the joke is on me it had better come from me. Some people, however, can draw forth my own sense of the ridiculous without ridiculing me. They can get me to laugh at myself without making fun of me. This requires delicacy and sensitivity on their part, and a sense of sharing a common human condition. Together we can laugh at our common crazy fantasies. This mutuality is crucial, for the root of the pride self-humiliation syndrome is self-isolation. At its best, humor can liberate our humanity, freeing us from our obsession with comparative power and status. Together we mock the obsession so that it loses its spell.

But humor is not enough. Even more important is a passionate, positive participation in life energies which are freely available to all of us, and which each of us can channel and focus in his or her own unique way. This is the real alternative to megalomaniac enthusiasm (as we saw in the section on "passion") and to life-constricting self-humiliation. The participation in divine powers and divine significance is noncompetitive and noncomparative, for it can be shared by everyone and it comes as a gift. And each of us can nevertheless contribute our own distinct melody to the music of the world symphony, our own special expression of the cosmic creativity in a shape which conforms to our own special limits. Mature humility is not a mere mean between two extremes, halfway between divinity and nothingness, fullness and emptiness. That is merely a cautious mediocrity, a "common-sense" rejection of the extremes while remaining caught in the syndrome of comparative power and status, like a business executive settling for a middle-management position. Mature humility transforms and transcends the two extremes. We let ourselves experience the nothingness of a self-isolated existence, emptying ourselves of our proud pretensions, and we open ourselves to participate in the divine life, though in our own particular, limited way.

An adequate exploration of humility would take another book—which I am currently writing. But here I am merely sketching attitude-virtues, so we must turn our attention to the third.

Self-acceptance is included in both trust and humility, but the third attitude-virtue involves a particular kind of self-acceptance at its core: *self-acceptance in spite of feeling guilty.* The opposite stance, the attitude-vice, is *self-rejection because of feeling guilty.* The issues here differ from those which concern trust and humility. They have to do, not with insecurity and the fear of abandonment or with finitude and the fear of shame, but with aggression and the fear of feeling guilty. This problem may begin in early infancy, but usually the crucial stage is late infancy, with its new passions of attraction for the parent of the opposite sex and rivalry with the parent of the same sex. New energies are received which can either become enmeshed in self-destructive obsession concerning the parents or liberated for creative involvement in the outside world. Patterns established in late infancy deeply influence us for the rest of our lives, though once again it is not a matter of rigid determinism or mere repetition in later life.

In adult life a person who is caught up in a pervasive stance of self-rejection asks himself some agonizing questions: "How can I go on living with myself when there is so much evil passion and destructive anger within me? Is there any way to be accepted, forgiven, liberated? Can I somehow atone for my sin by sufferings which I can view as a punishment? Or by diligent service, one of mankind's hired servants rather than a member of the human family? Or by scrupulous observance of the external requirements of the moral law?"

If I have the attitude-virtue of self-acceptance I do not seek a way out through self-punishment or onerous dutifulness or scrupulosity. Rather, I accept the acceptance of another. It is as if I were told, "Yes, you do have these destructive lusts and rages within you. Acknowledge them fully to yourself in my presence. I do not condemn you. I accept you, even though much of your hostility is towards me. Identify with me in my acceptance of you. Let this liberate you so that you can turn away from being preoccupied with the burden of guilt. You don't have to impose suffering or service or scrupulosity on yourself in order to feel acceptable, justifiable in existing. Let the energies which are now trapped in conflict within you be released in you so that you begin a new life. freely taking up tasks which express your sense of new life within and a new life of active involvement in the world outside. Allow yourself to feel your new love for me and my caring for you. Let this liberate you to find and follow your own way in life."

The most primitive form of self-acceptance involves accepting the acceptance of another person who is like what one's parent was in late infancy, or, more frequently, what one's parent should have been. With more maturity, I can accept the acceptance offered by many people, Finally, I may so interiorize acceptance that I need little reinforcement from other people. In this mature form I can authentically offer acceptance to others.

Since self-acceptance unifies the whole personality it is focused on whatever reality unifies the whole environment. Each particular acceptor symbolizes and represents this cosmic Acceptor. Self-acceptance is a religious attitude, though it is not necessarily accompanied by conscious religious convictions. For some people, however, the whole struggle between self-rejection and self-acceptance is understood in explicitly religious terms. The issue is whether an accusing, condemning voice of an alleged God pervades my life, crushing me or impelling me to futile and destructive attempts at atonement, or whether I hear and identify with the accepting voice of God so that I am continuously liberated and converted and renewed.

Self-rejection and self-acceptance are alternative responses to guilt. In its pure, raw form, guilt is a state of quivering paralysis. It is felt as a dreadful terror in face of imminent destruction. A person is over-whelmed by fear and finds that he cannot flee. He feels that he is about to be annihilated, or that he is about to lash out with a lethal blow at something or someone who matters most to him. His body quivers and trembles in agonized anticipation of a *coup de grace*, or in hysterical restraint of his own murderous impulses. Usually guilt is not experienced in such a raw form. Instead, one is conscious of a nameless dread and despondency and heaviness, coupled with self-loathing. Self-rejection is an active complicity in pervasive guilt, allowing its totalitarian terror and veiled destructiveness to have full control over one's life. Self-acceptance, accepting the acceptance of others and eventually of oneself, brings liberation from this tyrany. Self-acceptance brings a radical change in body and mind. Energies which have been conscripted and consumed in defence against external and internal forces of destruction, energies which have been blocked and turned against the self, are released for creative expression in the world.

Self-acceptance has considerable moral significance. In the first place, it is obviously a constituent of human fulfillment, and its opposite is obviously an obstacle. In the second place, it deeply influences my dealings with others. Only in so far as I can accept myself in spite of my guilt can I accept others in spite of their guilt, and *vice versa*. A stance of condemnation and rejection is pervasive. It is not directed only towards oneself or only towards others. Sometimes one person may be only conscious of his own guilt and another person may be only conscious of the guilt of others, but at an unconscious level there is a pervasive posture towards both self and others, a posture which is accusatory and punitive.

Not all guilt is a pervasive and undiscriminating rejection. There is a very different kind of guilt which occurs when I inflict specific wrongs on others. This realistic guilt is not a pervasive dread and condemnation which I unconsciously and consciously carry everywhere until I am released from it by acceptance. It is a discriminating discernment of harm done which makes me feel an acute distress until I have undone the harm and restored the damaged relationship. If this is not now possible the distress can be dealt with to some extent by doing something which is relevantly helpful and constructive. Often the discernment of harm done is not even possible unless a person has been to a considerable extent released from the indiscriminate, pervasive kind of guilt. This is because, adding realistic guilt to pervasive guilt is like pouring salt on an open wound. And if the discernment does take place, there is a danger that it may reinforce the paralyzing pervasive guilt rather than being a spur to rectifying action. Realistic guilt is dealt with by action.

Concerning one form of realistic guilt, however, the action which is needed is internal, in the depths of the personality. This form of realistic guilt arises, not from specific harm done to others, but from a refusal to struggle against an attitude-vice such as distrust or pride or self-rejection. I feel guilty because I am harming myself at a very deep level. I am allowing destructive forces to undermine and frustrate my humanity. Such guilt does not arise from *having* the attitude-vice, but from *consenting* to it, as Aquinas would say.[9] The issue is whether I resist the vice or acquiesce in it. The choice is made again and again in the present. It is impossible to determine exactly the extent to which I am responsible for now having the vice. The formation of the vice began in infancy when the influence of others was dominant and my own complicity was secondary and small. The vice is usually more unconscious than conscious. The freedom of my choice depends not only on how powerful were the destructive early formative influences and my responses to these but also on the extent to which I become conscious of the choice. Such consciousness does not come directly by willing it, but indirectly through a process of deep spiritual self-examination or profound psychotherapy, or something analogous to these.

A vice may be very strong in one person and relatively weak in another, but each vice is present to some extent in every person, as part of the human condition. It cannot be eliminated. It can, however, be reduced, by refusing to let it have full control in one's life and by being open to whatever fosters the opposing attitude-virtue. For example, I can refuse to go on wallowing in pervasive guilt as my inescapable destiny and I can open myself, however slightly, to the acceptance which another person offers. For some people, the scope for this interior choice is very limited; but for them, as for everyone, opting for the vice brings a realistic sense of self-betrayal, and opting for the virtue brings a realistic sense of being true to oneself.

Self-acceptance, like trust, has both primitive and mature forms. When we looked at trust we saw that a primitive religious trust involves seeing God as Good Mother rather than Bad Mother, whereas a mature religious trust involves a shift from using God as the cosmic person who meets my child-needs to appreciating God as the source of life-affirming energies in which everyone and everything participates. Self-acceptance, too, can shift to an appreciative mode. Instead of using God's acceptance of me as the basis for accepting myself, I cherish the divine life within myself and others and find myself thereby accepting myself and others. Whereas the primitive choice is between choosing an accepting person rather than a judgmental person as symbol of God, the mature choice is between participating in divine life or turning away from it. But the primitive choice should not be despised. It is the most fundamental,

The fourth attitude-virtue is *responsibility*. In everyday life a responsible person is someone who can be counted on to do a good job when tasks are assigned to her or undertaken by her. The task might be building a boat or cooking a meal or answering the telephone or baby-sitting a child or leading an expedition or planting a crop. A responsible person conscientiously learns how to be competent in performing tasks within and for the community. She learns how to apply traditional rules of skill (what works best) and traditional rules of practice (what is required). She also learns how and when to take initiative herself.

Where responsibility is a person's pervasive life-stance, she accepts responsibility not only for what she does in specific jobs but more generally for what she does with her life. Responsibility is then a stance in which the practical orientation which is appropriate to jobs is extended over life as a whole. The responsible person looks on her life as a task or calling. She is keen to learn how to accomplish this task, how to become what she is called to be. Her pervasive stance is that of an apprentice who enjoys learning from her master how to become an effective and worthwhile human being. This involves discipline and spontaneity, industry and intuition, carefulness and curiosity, diligence and delight. The responsible person has a sense that her life as a whole should somehow be a contribution not only to the community but also to the cosmos. As she gradually discovers what this contribution is by becoming increasingly competent as a human being, she feels happy because her life has a meaning which both reflects and enhances the ultimate meaning of life.

Viktor Frankl has some interesting things to say about the person who has this stance:[10]

> The more he grasps the task quality of life, the more meaningful will his life appear to him. While the man who is not conscious of his responsibility simply takes life as a given fact, existential analysis teaches people to see life as an assignment. But the following addendum must be made: There are people who go a step further. They also accept the authority from which the task comes. They experience the taskmaster who has assigned the task to them. In our opinion we have here an essential characteristic of the religious man: he is a man who interprets his existence not only in terms of being responsible *for* fulfilling his life tasks, but also as being responsible *to* the taskmaster.

It seems to me that the attitude in which one feels responsible *for* fulfilling one's life is itself religious. It involves a conviction that there is a taskmaster *to* whom one is responsible.

It is obvious, however, that if a person interprets his life in *explicitly* religious terms, "as ever in my great Taskmaster's eye,"[11] it is easier to recognize its religious quality. The questions which he asks himself as he examines his life are typically religious: "What am I doing with the talents which God has given me? Have I learned the traditions of my religious community and applied them in my life so that, like Jesus, I may 'increase in wisdom and stature and in favor with God and man'? (Luke 22:42; KJV). Have I been diligent and attentive in the school of life, trying to understand what I am being taught in each situation? Have I taken up my life in my hands like a piece of clay and tried to shape it towards a purpose which fits in with the purpose of the world in the mind of its Maker?" The imagery which the religious person uses in these questions does not depict God as a parent towards whom one has trust or humility or self-acceptance. Rather, God is depicted as the cosmic Taskmaster, School teacher, and Master Artisan. Responsibility is thus a pervasive, unifying stance towards the pervasive, unifying reality in our environment, where the reality is conceived not as trustworthy Providence or enabling Limiter or liberating Acceptor but in pedagogical terms: God is the wise Guru who knows, and is, the way. Accepting the authority of the divine Guru does not seem difficult or demeaning or burdensome because he is already the focus of one's trust and humility and self-acceptance.

A pervasive stance of responsibility is only possible if there has been considerable prior trust, humility, and self-acceptance. It is impossible if a person despairs of ever being able to trust anyone or anything and so works only in order to become as independent as possible. It is impossible if a person in his work construes every expression of authority as a demeaning power play which he must either resist in proud defiance or accept in self-humiliating subservience. It is impossible if a person works hard because he cannot accept himself and must atone for his guilt by scrupulous rule observance and self-punishing service. In each case the person may actually carry out various tasks in a competent and predictable way. Especially in the third case, he may seem at first sight to be quite responsible; but it is a *pseudo-responsibility*. The basic stance from which he works is not responsibility but an attitude-vice. Work is for him not a blessing but a curse. It is not a joyful expansion and expression of his capacities, but a bondage and a burden. He does not work as one who is at home in Eden, but as one who has been forced into exile.

Some people are not pseudo-responsible. They are blatantly *irresponsible*. They cannot be counted on to do a conscientious and competent job. Each specific task is unstarted, or botched, or unfinished, and life as a whole is an undisciplined meandering, an unboundaried drifting. Little is learned from people or situations, and little is contributed. Jesus described the irresponsible person in various images: he builds his house on sand, buries his talents, and says, "I'll go" and does not, and lets the lamp of his life go out through sheer neglect. Since he is erratic and careless he is unreliable: others cannot count on him for anything and he cannot count on himself. Often his inability to "get his life together" arises from unresolved distrust and self-humiliation and self-rejection. Where this is the case, mere exhortation will not enable him suddenly to become a responsible person. The virtues and vices are cumulative: responsibility depends on prior self-acceptance which in turn depends on prior humility which in turn depends on prior trust; irresponsibility arises from prior self-rejection which in turn arises from prior self-humiliation which in turn arises from prior distrust. These relations of priority, however, are not deterministic or rigid. For example, it is possible for someone to become more responsible through a therapy which deals directly with attitudes and actions on a work site, even though he is also still struggling against powerful "prior" vices which tend to make him pseudo-responsible or irresponsible. Indeed, the struggle against the more fundamental vices cannot succeed unless he is also struggling to get his life together in the present, becoming more responsible.

Usually the struggle between responsibility and irresponsibility begins to loom large during the so-called latency period (6-12 years), when life is largely a learning process. At that time patters of work begin to be established which tend to persist throughout life. It is also the period when human beings learn most of what is usually called "morality": rules which regulate behavior which affects human welfare. Both the rules and exceptions to the rules are meant to facilitate cooperation and to reduce conflict in society. Responsibility is the attitude-virtue which is most closely linked to such a morality and to the "ethics of doing" which is associated with it. Sometimes moral rules are understood deontologically (certain kinds of action are right or wrong by their very nature) and sometimes in a utilitarian way (certain kinds of action tend to produce overall consequences for society which are good or evil). Sometimes such "legalistic" moralities are challenged by a "situational" morality which stresses creative decision making in each unique situation. But in all these differing moralities, with their differing ways of guiding social behavior, the same attitude-virtue is presupposed. The responsible man can be counted on to be conscientious whenever his behavior impinges on the welfare of other people.

The fifth attitude-virtue is *self-commitment*. Each of the attitude-virtues which we have considered deals with a different basic human problem. Trust deals with abandonment, humility with shame, self-acceptance with guilt, responsibility with incompetence. Self-commitment deals with a lack of a sense of personal identity. This problem first arises in infancy, but it often recurs in an intense and dramatic way during adolescence and may continue far into adult life. The crucial question here, "Who am I in relation to the human community and the cosmos?" For some people the question is answered mainly in terms of responsibility, with its competent and conscientious fulfillment of an assigned life task. But for others, whom we now consider, self-discovery comes in a different way. If I am a stranger to myself and the community, an alien in the universe, I feel too much confusion to be competent, too much insecurity to be conscientious. I need a new self-commitment to a trustworthy vision of the natural world and human history and human community and of my role in relation to them. Since my present understanding of myself in relation to the cosmos and to the traditions and expectations of my community does not enable me to discover a strong sense of who I am, I must look elsewhere. I commit myself to a different community which has a different ideology or world view. Many such self-commitments are unsuccessful, for they are mainly re-enactments of infantile dramas. As I showed in the section on idolatry, a commitment can be disastrous if it arises from a futile attempt to feel at home in the universe by clinging to some absolute as if it were the perfect Mother one never had. And sometimes the commitment to a community is mainly a perpetuation of infantile behavior patterns concerning problems of authority (I'm either a god or a slave in this community) or problems of guilt (I can atone by means of self-punishing service to the community). All such commitments are internally divisive and eventually disillusioning.

An *integrating* self-commitment is possible, however, if three conditions are fulfilled. *First*, the commitment should permit all elements in the self to be included: not only idealistic aspirations but also realistic judgments, not only personal sensitivity but also political consciousness, not only what Maslow calls "deficiency-needs"[12] but also needs for growth and creativity, not only the intellectual and the spiritual but also the bodily and the sexual. *Second*, the self-commitment requires a rigorous honesty. I need to be true not only to others (loyal, faithful, devoted) but also to myself (sincere, genuine, authentic). This second condition is closely related to the first, for what leads a person to ignore and exclude part of himself from his commitment is self-deception. Instead of acknowledging various passions which seem alien, he represses them and then commits only the self of which he is aware. One example of this is an adolescent who feels a new, exciting energy invading his life and who does not let himself feel that this energy is to a great extent sexual. He may also be participating in a cosmic spiritual force which transcends the sexual though it includes it; but his completely spiritualized understanding of this force is self-deceptive. If a self-commitment is honest, the person typically experiences an élan vital not only in his mind but also in his body; the inspiration and enthusiasm are felt in head and heart and groin. Honest self-commitment integrates the whole person. *Third*, the self-commitment should have a focus which is comprehensive and unifying. A person cannot be genuinely integrated if in his commitment he is excluding a major part of the world in which he lives. There should be a place in his ideology and in the concerns of his community for the intrapersonal, the interpersonal, and the political, for the tragic, the trivial, and the triumphant, for the material, the mental, and the moral, for the past, the present, the future, and the eternal.

Where self-commitment is genuinely unifying and integrating it has as its focus a pervasive reality which unifies the whole environment. A typical Christian theology for such a pervasive stance stresses the divine Word or "Logos" as the meaning of cosmos and history, revealed in a complex, detailed pattern of concepts and images and human lives; and it stresses the divine Spirit as the inner source of a universal energy and vitality. The person is committed to this pattern of meaning and is responsive to this inspiration in all situations of life, trying to be true to the vision and the vitality as he is true to himself.

The opposite of integrating self-commitment is *dissipation*. The literal meaning of "dissipation" is "scattering." To dissipate something is to cause it to go off in all directions. Dissipation is a scattering or disintegration of the substance or energy of a thing or a person. The word has also come to mean "waste of the moral and physical powers by vicious indulgence in pleasure."[13] This is sometimes the main way in which personal disintegration is manifested, but not always. Some people, like the prodigal son, waste their substance in riotous living, but others fall apart as they dissipate their powers in an incoherent frenzy of altruistic activity. Whatever its form, dissipation characteristically arises from *alienation*. This is the pervasive stance of someone who feels he is a stranger in a strange land. Confused and lost, drifting aimlessly from one locale to another, he is in touch neither with reliable and universal meaning nor with reliable and universal life force. For alienated man, life is not like a jigsaw puzzle in which one begins to see a pattern emerging as one acts on one's commitments. Rather, it is like a series of tales told by an idiot, signifying nothing. Life is not like the sun, unceasingly shining in splendor to energize all the earth, never failing to give us life. It is like a fireworks display: some lights are big and bright, some are small and flickering, but all are soon burnt out and dead. The temptation of alienated man is to dissipate his own energies like a fireworks display, scattering them in all directions. In order to combat this he needs a steady self-commitment which is integrating and honest, which gives a comprehensive significance to a unified world, and which links his own energies to the energies of the cosmos. In some people the sense of alienation is not at all strong. They may not even be aware of any need for such a self-commitment. But in many people there is a daily struggle against a pervasive sense of alienation and aimlessness which has to be constantly challenged by recommitting themselves in an integrated way to their role in the cosmic drama.

Chapter 8

Three More Attitude-Virtues and Their Opposites

The sixth attitude-virtue is *friendliness*. By this I do not mean a mere well-wishing, but a readiness and willingness to risk the self by entering into intimate "I-Thou" relations of love,[1] giving and receiving at a very deep personal level. Entering into such friendships seems risky because it involves letting go of the self. Friendliness means venturing out of my self-isolation into the mysterious depths of another person's life, exposing myself to an influence which I cannot control and to a gaze which may penetrate to the marrow of my being. In friendship I move out of my self-preoccupation and I deeply involve myself with another person for his own sake. What happens to him now matters almost as much as what happens to me, so I am doubly vulnerable. And I am afraid that if I really give myself away to him I may completely lose myself.

This fear of self-loss is most obvious when friendship involves sexual attraction, for the culmination of this is sexual orgasm, which can be a total letting go of mind and body.[2] But friendships which involve no sexual relations can seem just as risky. I must already have a fairly firm grip on myself if I am to let go of myself. If I do not know who I am, and change like a chameleon in response to superficial changes in my surroundings, I dare not open my secret inner self to the intense influences of intimacy, for these might dominate and absorb me completely. If I am still engrossed in a search for myself, I cannot offer myself to another person as a gift with no strings attached, for I still see others mainly as obstacles of means in my quest. It seems safer to isolate myself. This self-isolation, which is the opposite of friendliness, can take either of two forms. On the one hand, I may isolate myself in an obvious way by living in solitude. On the other hand, I can mix with people, but involve myself only in impersonal, role-playing relationships and call these "friendships," thus protecting myself from the real thing.

If, however, I have a fairly strong sense of my own personal identity, a stance of real friendliness is possible. Usually a sense of personal identity comes with a stance of responsibility and self-commitment. These attitude-virtues, as we have seen, depend on prior trust, humility, and self-acceptance. But even when I feel that I know who I am there is a radical decision, a venture, when I move into a stance of friendliness. Instead of depending on others for my sense of self, I move out to others from my own independent sense of self. Instead of focusing mainly on what others can do for me, I focus at least as much on what I can do for them. Instead of seeing others mainly in relation to my own need for trust, humility, self-acceptance, responsibility, and self-commitment as conditions for discovering who I am, I see these virtues mainly as a launch pad for venture of love into the inner space of another person. I have loved myself enough to get into a position where I can love others.

There is thus a subtle but crucial difference between self-love and self-preoccupation. Self-love can stir me to develop a sense of personal identity so that eventually I can turn away from myself in love towards others. Self-preoccupation keeps me turned perpetually inwards on myself and my own requirements. It is in conflict with friendliness, and it arises from the attitude-vices which we have considered. For example one form of my distrust may move me to try to possess and devour another person so as to fill up my inner unreality. This is a "subjectivizing" of the other, allowing him no reality except in so far as I experience him, allowing him only those qualities which are relevant to my neediness. Alternatively, I may "objectivize" the other because I have an obsessive fear of being humiliated and subjugated. I set him at a distance, observing him as an uninvolved spectator, classifying him and manipulating him; I impose my will on him lest he impose his on me. In a third kind of self-preoccupation I may be moved not so much by a subjectivizing distrust or an objectifying pride as by a self-rejection which impels me to use him to assuage my guilt: either I morally condemn him for his guilt or I placate him so he will not be my judge, condemning me for my sin.

There are thus many ways in which self-preoccupation involves what Martin Buber calls an "I-It" stance, distorting my perception of the other person so that I do not deal with him as he really is. If, however, my pervasive stance is friendliness I can regard him in the "I-Thou" way which Buber advocates; I can regard him "as the very one he is." Buber goes on:[3]

> I become aware of him, aware that he is different, essentially different from myself, in the definite, unique way which is peculiar to him, and I accept whom I thus see, so that in full earnestness I can direct what I say to him as the person he is. Perhaps from time to time I must offer strict opposition to his view about the subject of our conversation. But I accept this person, the personal bearer of a conviction, in his definite being out of which his conviction has grown . . . . I *affirm* the person I struggle with; I struggle with him as his partner, I *confirm* him.

When someone confirms me, I feel *firm* on the ground, my own ground. As he stands before me, I feel that he is *with* me, *for* me. He is not going to pull the rug from under my feet. He is not going to invade my territory or draw me into his against my will. He affirms my existence in my own space and my own style in the same way that he affirms his own. His own strong sense of who he is, evokes and reinforces mine concerning myself. Nevertheless he may sometimes challenge me in ways which are profoundly disturbing if he is my friend, for friendliness includes not only *confirmation* but also *confrontation*.

When someone confronts me, she stands temporarily in my way, challenging me to acknowledge that I am being destructive towards myself or others. She says, in effect, "Before you go on, let me put in a word." She challenges me to be more honest about my motives, more realistic about the consequences of my actions, more faithful to my better self. At the deepest level she challenges me to struggle against an attitude-vice such as distrust or self-rejection or irresponsibility instead of acquiescing in it.[4] She does not *condemn* me for *having* the vice; she *urges* me to resist it. She does not simply point out a life-denying tendency within me, though she does do that. She calls on me to draw upon the life-affirming resources which are within me and around me. She asks me to face my weaknesses as she also sets before me my strengths. Confrontation varies in depth, but obviously even a moderate version requires a special context if it is to be appropriate and constructive. I must feel that I am being confirmed by the confronter, that she accepts my right to exist even if I do not respond to what she says. I must feel confident that she is trying to be honest with herself, so that she is not simply projecting her own problems and needs on to me. (One measure of her honesty is whether she herself is open to confrontation from me and others.) I must feel confident that she has an empathy with me, so that she can really get inside me and understand what is going on. And I must feel that she genuinely cares for me, respects me, and is not intruding into my life in a manipulative way. All these conditions depend both on her and on me, for even if she is genuinely friendly I may not be able to feel her friendliness because I dare not hear what she is saying. But if I can be open to her and to other friends, there is a great security in knowing that I cannot set forth on destructive paths without being challenged. In so far as I am a friend to others, I try to provide a similar security. But although confrontation can be reassuring, it is always to some extent a risk. There is always the possibility that the other may hear it as an attack, a rejection, a condemnation; then he may turn away into self-isolation. Thus if I need the other person's nearness for my very existence, I dare not tell him what I see for fear he may leave me. Instead, I acquiesce in his destructive and self-deceptive ways and do not challenge him to be true to his better self. But if I am a true friend, I am both able and willing to risk even the cherished friendship for his sake. If he is a true friend he can do the same for my sake. As mutual confidence grows, and wisdom and sensitivity in confrontation grow, the risk does not necessarily decrease, for the level of confrontation becomes deeper. Eventually, however, there may be a stage of profound mutual openness in which the risk is minimal.

Although confrontation draws on strengths and virtues, it does so in the context of the battle against weaknesses and vices. Friendliness also involves a *celebration* of the strengths[5] of another person for their own sake. Confirmation, confrontation, celebration, these three; but the greatest of these is celebration. If I look on someone as a close friend, I celebrate his very existence. His unique way of expressing the life and creativity which are given to us all evokes feelings of praise and thanksgiving in me. His breakthroughs toward a life of even greater creativity and happiness are occasions of great rejoicing. I feel intense admiration[6] when I see him rigorously confronting himself and vigorously struggling against destructive forces which are still at work within him. And just as his "lows" can draw me out of self-preoccupation into a concern with him, his "highs" can draw me out into a celebration with him. Celebration, however, is not only an attitude which friends have towards each other. It is also an attitude which they have *together* towards other people or works or art or wonders of nature. Friends enjoy being together to "concelebrate" the many manifestations of life and creativity which surround them: the disciplined grace of an athlete, or the ecstatic rhythm of a dance, or the vibrant serenity of a saint, or the imaginative passion of a painting, or the extravagant splendor of a sunset.

Another important element in friendliness is *devotion*, which is a self-commitment, not to an ideology or a community, but to a person. The whole self is involved in a generous pouring out of energy and care. There is an implicit vow that I will be loyal and consistent in my self-giving through all kinds of unfavorable circumstances: "for better, for worse, for richer for poorer, in sickness and in health." At times, if my friend seems to be disappearing into a destructive self-isolation (which is very different from a creative retreat for revitalizing reflection), I will pursue him, both for his own sake and for the sake of our friendship. In addition to this active, persistent fidelity, devotion also involves many moments of "selfless"[7] concentration on the other. My narcissism and self-consciousness often disappear in the presence of my friend. This is partly because I feel relaxed with him: I am not anxious concerning what he thinks about me. But it is mainly because my awareness is focused outside myself, on him. This does not mean that I lose myself in my empathy with him, or confuse his feelings with mine; I feel real and distinct. But I give up my self-preoccupation and give him my total attention. It is like the self-forgetfulness which occurs when a person is completely engrossed in the appreciation of a work of art. It is the stance for which St. Francis prayed:

> Grant that I may not so much seek to be consoled as to console; to be understood as to understand; to be loved as to love.

Devotion thus involves both a long-term, loyal commitment and many intense moments of unselfconscious giving.

Such moments, however, could be disruptive intrusions into another person's privacy unless they occur in a context of confirmation. So could the moments of confrontation. Indeed, the powerful concentration of attention in devotion and the vigorous assertion of concern in confrontation require not only confirmation but also *respect*, which allows and enables the other person to respond in his own way. Respect involves two elements: patience and permission. Patience[8] is not a matter of standing to one side, passively waiting for the other person to start moving. It means being actively present to her while granting her her own time in which to grow, her own space in which to think and feel, her own room in which to find herself, her own rhythms in which to change. Indeed, I do not "grant" her these things, for they are already her own. In so far as I am genuinely patient, I help her to *find* them and to *claim* them. Patience is not only a matter of reticence, not rushing in where angels fear to tread. It also means actively helping the friend to discover and create her own path in life. Patience is not only a matter of not being drawn into the possessiveness and the manipulative maneuvering of a symbiotic relationship. It is not only a matter of conceding to a friend the right to be a separate person.[9] It also means being a presence which encourages her to develop in her own distinctive way.

What I call *permission* is closely related to patience. It is a respect for the other's freedom, her right to make her own decisions, her responsibility for her own life. Even the ultimate choice between life and death is hers alone, not mine. So are all the penultimate choices, and the trivial ones as well. I must accept her freedom as the context in which I confront her and celebrate her and devote myself to her—even if it be the freedom to turn away from me or the freedom to destroy herself. And, more positively, permission means encouragement, helping her to discover what she most wholeheartedly wants in life and then to act accordingly. Since I am her friend, I do not always have to be consulted.[10] I hope that she will consult herself. I encourage her to be as honest and as open as she can so that she may find and follow her passions.

Friendliness thus includes a patient respect for the other's privacy and a permissive respect for her freedom. We have seen that it also includes confirmation, confrontation, celebration, devotion, and respect. The final element (at any rate in this sketch, which does not presume to be exhaustive) is *affection*. This is an embodied feeling, a passion. When I feel affection I feel it in my body and I want to express it through my body. I want to see and hear and touch and embrace. Sometimes affection involves feelings of sexual arousal and attraction. When it does, the other elements in friendship provide a context of boundaries on behavior so that the feelings can be acknowledged without necessarily being acted upon. In many attempts at friendship, however, even the desire to touch is not acknowledged and the contact is purely cerebral or "spiritual." There can be a vicious circle: the repression of affection inhibits the growth of other elements in friendship, the weakness of the other elements means that the context is not secure enough for affection to be felt and expressed. On the other hand, there can be a spiral of growth in which affection and the other elements stimulate each other. As passion becomes a pervasive stance of the whole personality it can unify the physical and mental elements in friendliness in a cumulative way. The most intense and powerful form of affection is, of course, passionate sexual love. The most profound mutual expression of affection can occur when two people give themselves away to each other, body and soul, in the ecstasy of orgasm. But there are other expressions of sexual love, and of affection generally, which are not momentous or heavy or serious. Often affection is light and frivolous, gay and playful, full of fun and delight. Affection often merges with celebration in a laughter which is vibrant with the sheer joy of being together.

Friendliness includes not only the six elements which I have described but also an openness to the friendliness of others. For example, a friendly person cannot only give confirmation to others, he can also receive it. Thus since friendship is a relation of mutual friendliness between two people, my part in it is not only to be friendly to the other person but also to accept his friendliness towards me. I not only confront and celebrate and respect him; I also accept these and other elements of friendliness from him. If he is not friendly towards me, or if I do not accept a friendliness which he offers me, then we are not friends. We have at best a potential friendship. For our relation to deserve the title "friendship" all six elements of friendliness should be present and accepted on both sides; but they need not be present in greath depth. Some friendships are profound, but others are relatively superficial. One can have only a few deep friendships, but other friendships involve less time and energy and passion. Some individuals have genuine but rudimentary friendships with a great many people.

Friendliness depends on *trust*. This is specially obvious in the aspect of friendliness which is an openness to receive friendliness from others, but the more mature, outgoing forms of trust are also the main basis for the outgoing forms of friendliness. Each of the constituents of trust is related to friendliness. Assurance is mainly an openness to confirmation. Receptivity includes a readiness to confirm others. Fidelity includes a steadfast openness to what people can actually give me in the present, instead of straying into idolatrous obsessions. Hope involves a venturing out of self-isolation to receive another person's friendliness, especially his confirmation, devotion, and respect. Passion is relevant in two main ways. First, it includes much giving and receiving of friendliness, especially confrontation, celebration, and affection. Second, the active element in permissive respect is an invitation to the other to find and follow his passions. Such an invitation is authentic and effective only to the extent that the person who expresses it is already living it, already finding and following his own passions. In general, trust and friendliness are closely related because the movement into what I called the second and third "stages" in the positive way towards mature trust involves a movement from self-preoccupation into friendliness. Indeed, no sharp line can be drawn between advanced forms of trust and elementary forms of friendliness because both involve a change from childish dependency on others into a mutuality of giving and receiving. In this chapter I am considering friendliness at greater length than the other attitude-virtues because of its close relation to trust, which is the main topic in this book.

But I have digressed. Let us turn back to the exposition of friendliness. It is important to notice that friendliness is not confined to contexts of friendship, even rudimentary friendship. Some of the elements in friendliness are appropriate in dealing with anyone, whether or not the friendliness is accepted or returned. It is arguable, for example, that I ought to offer confirmation to anyone whom I encounter, even an enemy. And in so far as respect is a restraint on intrusions into the privacy and the freedom of another person it seems appropriate as a stance towards anyone. But in so far as respect is an active encouragement of the other to find his own space and his own freedom, its scope is more limited, for practical reasons. The two aspects of devotion differ in a similar way. On the one hand, if I am for a short time in one-to-one encounter with another person, that person may well need and deserve my total attention, whatever his stance towards me. But long-range loyalty cannot be given to more than a few people—I have only so much time and energy. Also, if such loyalty is not returned or even accepted, its continuation is sometimes foolish rather than heroic. Confrontation, too, has a limited scope, for it is only appropriate if it has a fair chance of being constructive; with many people it is counterproductive. Affection is obviously not felt towards everyone, even by the saints; and it is difficult to sustain unless it is reciprocated by at least some of the people towards whom it is felt. Celebration, too, though it may be my stance toward people who do not even know me, requires reciprocation from some people; otherwise it atrophies, or it degenerates into adulation.

Friendliness is a pervasive stance of the whole personality which is focused initially on anyone whom I encounter. That is, a genuinely friendly person is ready and willing to move into at least a rudimentary friendship with anyone if that person is ready and willing to respond positively. And, as we have seen, some elements of friendliness are offered unconditionally to anyone, regardless of whether they are accepted or returned. Thus friendliness is a stance towards anyone whom I may encounter which includes both a conditional friendship-readiness and an unconditional confirmation, respectful restraint and devoted attention. Obviously it is a moral virtue. But is it also a religious attitude?

It is, but if we are to understand this we must see that our friendliness can extend beyond people to the nonhuman world—to animals and trees and stones and works of art. We can confirm and celebrate the existence of particulars which are not persons, though the confirmation and celebration are only *analogous* to what is present when we focus on persons. And in relation to nature we can have a caring and concentration which is analogous to devotion, and a letting be which is analogous to respect. Affection, too, has its analogous form when we desire to caress a thing with our hands and our eyes. Friendliness is thus an expansive, appreciative, life-affirming stance which may be focused intensively on only a few people, but which spreads out pervasively in various forms to other people and beyond this to things in nature. And since the various forms of friendliness reinforce each other, the less intensive involvements enhance the special friendships, and vice versa.

Thus friendliness, as a readiness for various kinds of "moral" intimacy with people and "aesthetic" intimacy with things, is a unifying stance towards the whole of the environment. The stance unifies not only the person but also the environment, so it is focused not only on particulars but also on God, conceived as the pervasive unifying reality which is immanent in all the particulars and which transcends them all. And in so far as pervasive trust is a constituent in my own friendliness I also look on the friendliness of each other person towards me as an expression of a divine friendliness. Friendliness is thus a religious attitude which involves a belief in a mutual friendship between man and God. The belief need not be explicit or conscious, but the attitude is clearly religious.

Being friends with God is of course not the same as being friends with a human being. But each of the six elements of friendliness is present in an analogous form on each side of the divine-human encounter. I trust that God confirms, confronts, and celebrates his human friends, treating each with devotion, respect, and affection. In so far as I am friendly towards God I am open to all these elements in his friendliness towards me. This openness differs from a childlike trust in God's parental providence. The relation is not like that between an infant and his mother. It is more like that between two adult friends. This is what Buber said:[11]

> The relation with man is the real simile of the relation with God; in it true address receives true response; except that in God's response everything, the universe, is made manifest as language.

The divine friendliness differs from human friendliness in that it is expressed in and through everything; it pervades and unifies the universe. But human friendliness towards God can have all six elements. In so far as I am friendly towards God I confirm his existence, acknowledging that he is distinct from me—indeed he is the very "ground" on which I stand. I confront God, calling him to task for many of the injustices and tragedies of human life. (Jewish tradition includes more confrontation than Christian tradition.) I celebrate God's existence in worship, devote myself to him in loyalty and attention, respectfully refrain from trying to manipulate his power, and affectionately seek closeness with him by being close to his creatures. In practice, of course, I also isolate myself from God in self-preoccupation. Whether my relations are with people or with things or with God the ongoing struggle is between friendliness and self-isolation. In that struggle the question is, "Which will predominate?"

The seventh attitude-virtue is *concern*. This is a pervasive stance of readiness and willingness to help others in response to their needs. The concerned person is acutely aware of these needs because she is a passionate person and has a profound empathy with people. Their physical and psychological and spiritual needs are very real to her because nothing human is alien to her. She rejoices in whatever helps people to grow toward fulfillment as human beings and she is distressed by whatever impedes this. If what she perceives is not merely an impediment but something which dehumanizes people she feels deep sorrow and indignation. Concern moves her to take care of people, to look after them, to encourage their growth, to defend them against destructive forces.

At first sight it may seem that concern is not a distinct attitude-virtue but merely one element in friendliness. Friendliness includes a concern for my friend when he is in need of my help, and a willingness to accept his help when I am in need of it. And, as we saw, some of the elements in friendliness are expressed not only to friends but also to anyone whom I encounter. Concern could have been considered as one of these elements: a desire to help people who are likely to reciprocate is extended to people generally, regardless of their potential as helpful friends. And genuine concern is necessarily linked with the other elements in friendliness which are appropriate towards anyone, elements such as confirmation and concentrated attention. Genuine concern is thus embedded in friendliness as an outgoing, altruistic stance. It differs radically from bogus kinds of concern which seem to be focused on others but which are actually disguised forms of self-preoccupation. For example, a youth might become actively involved in a reform movement *solely* as a way of trying to discover his own identity. Genuine concern is fairly easy to detect, for it is grounded in pervasive trust and it is accompanied by other outgoing elements of friendliness. Bogus concern is permeated by anxiety: other people's troubles stir up my own worries about my own troubles and accentuate my own pervasive distrust.

But in spite of its close links with friendliness, genuine concern is a distinct attitude-virtue. Although the two attitude-virtues can be viewed as species of a more inclusive stance, love, there are important differences between them. The differences are important in practice, for it is possible for me or anyone to have considerable friendliness but little concern except for my friends. Concern goes beyond friendliness: it adds a new basis, a new emphasis and a new dimension to love. The new *basis* is an aspect of trust which was not conspicuous as a basis for friendliness: passion as empathy, a sensitive "tuning in" on other people's sufferings and aspirations, not as occasions for brooding narcissistically on one's own, but as occasions for helping in practical ways. The new *emphasis* is on helping people who are not able to help me in return, except perhaps in some lesser way: infants and children, the sick and the helpless, the underprivileged and the oppressed. The paradigm case of friendliness occurs in the context of friendship, with reciprocal giving and receiving; the giving is not based on the prospect of receiving, but it is nourished by the actual receiving. The paradigm case of concern, however, is a giving where there is little receiving or prospect of receiving. In contrast with friendliness, concern is inherently altruistic. The new *dimension* which concern adds is a concern about people whom I do not meet face to face, but know almost entirely as collectivities: "the children in our public school system" or "the native peoples in northen Canada." Concern for them is often appropriately expressed in activities which are, in a broad sense of the word, "political." The ills which many people suffer are not due solely to the villainy of powerful individuals or to their own vices and weaknesses; rather, they are caused to a great extent by society, its power structures and ideologies. So concern is expressed not only in attempts to help individuals in face-to-face encounters but also in attempts to change institutions. The political, economic, educational, and religious institutions of a society usually include both constructive structures of cooperation and destructive structures of domination. Any significant change in these structures or in the ideologies which support them can radically affect individuals for good or ill, promoting happiness and justice, or suffering and oppression. And any such change can help or hurt individuals in their struggles against the vices which dehumanize their lives.

Concern thus has two expressions, which I will call "pastoral" and "prophetic." Pastoral concern is like the caring of a good shepherd. Its typical expression is direct personal encounter with people who need help. Prophetic concern is so called, not because it includes a power to make prediction, but because it resembles the Old Testament prophet's indignation at social injustice. Its typical expression is radical reform of corrupt and corrupting institutions and trenchant criticism of thinking which sanctions these institutions.

There are two kinds of pastoral concern, "parental" and "remedial." The most common form of *parental*[12] concern is evident in a good parent who is caring for his own children, trying to pass along to them the traditions and the attitudes which are most conducive to their fulfillment as human beings. People who have no children can express a concern for other people's children in activities which are analogous to those of a parent, especially in education. *Remedial* concern is directed towards adults rather than children. It resembles parental concern, however, for the adults are those whose need and relative powerlessness places them in a position of dependence and helplessness analogous to that of children, indeed, children in distress—the destitute, the prisoner, the outcast, the sick, the mentally disturbed, the hopeless. In modern society, service professions such as social work, medicine, nursing, and ministry are supposed to express this kind of pastoral concern by the responsible application of special skills to remedy various ills. Often, however, the concern gets lost in the skills, and the childlike helplessness of the needy is accentuated by an authoritarian, "paternalistic" kind of concern. In contrast with this, genuine pastoral concern draws out the other person's strengths, helping him to decrease his dependency and to move as quickly as possible towards a position not only of equal power but of reciprocal giving and receiving. Often complete equality and reciprocity are not possible, but the movement is in that direction. Pastoral concern means being a "good shepherd" in dedicated kindness and care for each individual, but it does not mean treating people like stupid sheep.

Prophetic concern is a critical stance towards social institutions, passionately probing them in terms of their humanizing and dehumanizing effects on people, especially the needy and the powerless. Such concern involves a scrutiny of the power structures of society and the ideologies which legitimate them. While some of the power structures may be just and beneficial, usually there is much that is unjust and harmful. Because of this, and because powerful groups can usually look after their own interests all too effectively, prophetic concern has a bias in favor of the powerless. Although it is interested in conserving what is good, its dominant emphasis is on radical reform in favor of the underprivileged and the oppressed. Prophetic concern does not arise easily in me if I am someone who enjoys the privileges of a dominant group in society. I find it difficult to question the ideology which sanctions these privileges and to perceive the gross injustices and avoidable suffering which are to a great extent attributable to the kind of dominance which my own group enjoys. Even if I have considerable pastoral concern I may be almost blind to the way in which institutions produce much of the misery and degradation which I am attempting to reduce in parental or remedial activity. Just as there has to be a radical conversion from self-preoccupation to outgoing friendliness, so there has to be a radical conversion from a concern which is restricted by the interests of my social group or class to a concern which questions and transcends these interests, identifying itself with the cause of the underdog. Without this second conversion, even a person who is virtuous in terms of the previous six attitude-virtues and who has a pastoral kind of concern is falling short of what he should be. The beneficial influence which he has on many individuals in society may in some cases even be outweighed by the implicit sanction which he gives to a social order which has devastating, dehumanizing effects on people. And in terms of his own growth towards human fulfillment, he will be insufficiently aware of the *communal* dimension of his existence, restricting himself too exclusively to the intrapersonal and the interpersonal. His perception of himself and society will be distorted by largely unconscious self-deceptions which arise from the collective interests of dominant groups in society. Previously, in his struggles against other attitude-vices, he was battling against his own narcissism and against destructive forces within himself which first arose in childhood, within his family. Now the inner struggle is against a collective narcissism and against destructive forces which come mainly from society. The field of battle has shifted from the "familial" unconscious to the "social" unconscious. But the communal dimension of prophetic concern is not only a matter of overcoming self-deceptions which arise from the social unconscious. There is also a new commitment to a community, not in order to find oneself, but in order to build with others a social framework which is genuinely human. Prophetic concern brings a new awareness of oneself as a member of a group: not only the group whose privileges and powers make one partly responsible for the plight of the poor, or the group which lacks privileges and powers and is itself oppressed, but the group which bands together to combat injustice. As an isolated individual a person is ineffective against structures of domination in society, but in solidarity with a group he can do much. Prophetic concerns moves him to identify himself with the oppressed and with a movement which takes up their cause.[13]

The attitude-vice which corresponds to concern is *self-indulgence*. There are two kinds, which correspond to the two kinds of concern, pastoral and prophetic. The first kind involves turning a sentimentalized pastoral concern back in on myself as if I were my own child, my own "infant and pet," as Erikson puts it.[14] This is different from having a legitimate concern for the child within oneself as part of the struggle by which I grow towards a life of outgoing friendliness and concern. Such a self-concern is important, especially for people who try to ignore their own painful neediness by hurling themselves into frenetic activity similar to that which arises from genuine pastoral or prophetic concern. But self-indulgence is a different matter. I indulge the child within me, fussing over his frustrations, pandering to his whims and fantasies, pitying myself because his infantile longings can never be satisfied, rather than dealing with his need—which is my need—to learn how to love. When two self-indulgent people attempt a friendship, it becomes at best a contract of mutual protection against any challenge to struggle towards greater maturity. In general, if my main interest is in dealing with my own neediness, there is little room for a pastoral concern which moves out in a parental or remedial way to help other people in their neediness. When self-indulgence is contrasted with *prophetic* concern, it takes a different form. Here it is a matter of taking for granted certain rights and privileges in society which ought to be questioned. The opposite of prophetic concern is "I'm all right, Jack": a comfortable acceptance of affluence and influence which depend on my favorable position in the power structures of an unjust and oppressive society. Or, if one belongs to an oppressed group, self-indulgence is a preoccupation with one's own individual plight, refusing to work with others towards a common liberation.

The struggle between concern and self-indulgence is an inner one which goes on in the hearts and minds of individuals. But the more concern predominates in that struggle the more the essential human struggle becomes *external*. It becomes a struggle against destructive and dehumanizing forces out there in individuals and in society. Success in the inner struggle frees a person from being preoccupied with his own human fulfillment to work for the fulfillment of others. But in so far as he is focused on their fulfillment he is also furthering his own. As the range and depth of his concern develops his own self expands and grows. Indeed, one of the things he wants for others in his concern for their fulfillment is that *they* may learn concern. As Milton Mayeroff has said, "To help another person grow is at least to help him to care for something or someone apart from himself."[15] But even if concern were not a constituent for human fulfillment in individuals it would be desirable, for the welfare of society as a whole requires such a virtue in its individuals.[16] And, even more fundamentally, concern, like the other attitude-virtues which together constitute human fulfillment, is not a private achievement or possession but a way of being appropriately *related* to the whole environment. Concern is an appropriate way of being related to the social environment, with its oncoming generation, its needs, and its inhumanity.

Concern is also an appropriate way of being related to the *natural* environment. In my sketch of concern I have described two kinds—pastoral and prophetic. But actually there is a third kind which ought to be at least mentioned, even in a brief outline such as this: *ecological* concern. When we considered friendliness we saw that one can feel towards things in nature a friendliness analogous to what one feels towards people. Similarly there can be a concern, analogous to concern for people, which is directed at animals and plants and the earth. In some societies this ecological concern is one of the attitudes which is passed along from generation to generation as part of the culture; but in many contemporary technological societies it is a new, difficult stance. A third radical conversion may be needed, not to outgoing friendliness and not to politicized prophetic concern as part of a community, but to a new ecological vision and a new ecological conscience. The new vision is of myself as part of nature, and of nature as a complex system of mutual influences which includes everything: the human and the nonhuman, the animate and the inanimate, the earthly and the celestial, all depending on each other. The new conscience is an active sensitivity concerning the needs of all forms of life instead of being only concerned with people.[17]

Each kind of concern is often associated with a religious conviction:

> *Pastoral* concern: I believe that the God whom I already believe to be *my* Helper (Provider, Encourager, Liberator, Teacher, etc.) is the Helper of *all* people, especially the powerless and the needy, the children and the poor.

> *Prophetic* concern: I believe that this God is a God of reform and revolution who struggles against oppression, and a God of judgment who exposes the guilt of the oppressor.

> *Ecological* concern: I believe that this God cares for all creatures great and small, not only a fallen man but also a fallen sparrow. He is concerned not only about the scales of justice but also about the balance of nature.

The beliefs associated with each kind of concern presuppose a belief in a God who is already conceived in relation to the first six attitude-virtues, for example, as the providential God of basic trust. One believes that *such* a God has the additional characteristic of having a pastoral or prophetic or ecological concern, indeed, a concern which is a paradigm example for us to emulate.

The sense of being challenged to emulate the divine concern may be accompanied by the belief that one is being enabled to *participate* in the divine concern. When one is moved to passionate concern one is being inspired by God, participating in a divine "Passion." For example, when Bonhoeffer in a Nazi concentration camp was in anguish over human suffering and sin he realized that he was sharing in God's anguish, and he wrote, "Christians stand by God in his hour of grieving (when He is sore bestead)."[18] It is as if Bonhoeffer were standing by a grief-stricken friend, helping him by being present, as together they mourn the loss of humanity in human life.

Indeed, for Christians God is not only the paradigm of passionate concern, in whose "Passion" we may participate; he is also a *focus* of human concern. God is not only the Helper of the helpless, Provider for the needy, and Liberator of the oppressed; he is also the One who is helpless, needy, and oppressed. Christians point to Jesus, who taught and supremely exemplified the *identification* of God with those whom society despises, neglects, or exploits. Because of this identification, concern for such people is also concern for God. To feed the hungry, give drink to the thirsty, clothe the naked, visit the sick, and seek out the prisoner is not only to do these things to these people but also to do these things to Jesus and to God (Matthew 25:35-40). In this mysterious and paradoxical way God can be a focus of human concern. God empties himself of cosmic power and status, taking on the form of a child, a servant, an outcast, while still somehow remaining God. Attempts to escape the paradox take two forms. One the one hand, religious believers may deny the humanity of God, the radical identification with the poor and powerless, thus turning religion into a private and vertical piety. On the other hand, secular humanitarians may deny the divinity of man, that is, the transcendent source and focus of their human concern for humanity.

The eighth attitude-virtue is *contemplation*. In trying to describe it I am wading into deep waters, going even further beyond my depth than I did in some of my explorations of friendliness and concern. There are serious limits on any attempt to describe what one has only just begun to experience, even if one draws on the experience of others who are more mature. But I think I can describe the bare essentials of contemplation. It is an active, outgoing stance in which I view each particular — myself, another person, a bird, a branch, a snowflake—as an expression of a loving creativity which pervades and unifies the universe. It is also an inner serenity and a joyful appreciation and a oneness with the cosmos.

Contemplation involves *detachment*. By this I do not mean a lack of interest in what is going on outside or a dissociation of myself from emotions which disturb my inner life. Detachment does not mean the absence of friendliness or concern or passion. Rather, it means a detachment from my own self-preoccupation, self-isolation, self-indulgence and, above all, self-consciousness. It is a disengagement from the impulse to see and use others mainly in relation to my own unresolved personal problems. It is a liberation from the domination of a strident inner neediness and a pervasive anxiety concerning my own survival as a self. In contemplation a person can forget and abandon the self which he has constructed in distrust and pride as a private bastion of security in an alien world. He can find and express his own true self as he joins with others in the dance of life and as he ventures through the void to discover the ultimate.

Such a stance presupposes a considerable degree of resolution of struggles against the earlier vices, expecially distrust. The self must already have matured into a quite solid sense of identity. It must already have turned outwards in friendliness and concern. Already in friendliness there have been many moments in which one's total attention has been focused selflessly on another person in confirmation or confrontation or celebration or concern. And concern itself has involved a further shift away from egoism into altruism, for concern is a self-giving which does not depend on receiving anything from the other. Contemplation is the flowering of friendliness and concern, especially friendliness as confirmation and celebration and concentrated devotion, and concern as ecological awareness. Also, contemplation can be thought of as a third species of love because of its roots in the other two species and its similarities to them. But contemplation goes beyond friendliness and concern because of its intimate association with meditation, which moves it into a love of the divine.

By "meditation" I mean any discipline of the attention which does one or more of three things which I shall now describe. *First,* "preparatory" meditation helps to reduce the distortion in our perception of reality which comes from self-preoccupation and self-isolation. Not all disciplines of attention do this. If a discipline is not based on friendliness and if it is contrary to concern, it leads to a kind of detachment which may claim to be "objective," but which limits reality to whatever can be perceived from the stance of a self-isolating spectator. (We considered such detachment in the chapter on apathy.) But where meditation is grounded in friendliness and concern it can help these virtues to grow. By means of meditation a person learns how to focus his energy and attention on whatever it is that matters to him. As a tool it can be used in a selfish and narcissistic way, but it can also be used so that love may flourish and so that I may perceive things and people as they really are. Such a form of meditation is a preparation for the second and third forms.

Second, meditation is a cultivation of a capacity to celebrate the sheer existence of people and things in their uniqueness and their togetherness. Friendliness has involved occasions of celebration beyond the circle of one's friends, but through meditation this celebration can become a steady, contemplative stance which is brought to every situation. Various practices can help a person to integrate and focus his mind and his body so that he can concentrate a loving, joyful attention on a leaf or a candle flame or a human face, seeing each as an expression of a rich reality which pervades and unifies the cosmos. Such meditation is often associated with a feeling of "merging oneness" and with the kind of participation in life energies which I described in the section on passion. There is a sense of oneness and participation in a cosmic creativity which expresses itself with lavish generosity in countless ways throughout the universe.

Third, meditation promotes an awareness of a still center within, which cannot be destroyed by anything that happens in body or mind or outside world. This calm, peaceful, substantial center is me, yet it is not exclusively me. It is more real than anything else I know, but it does not exist in distinctive contrast or competitive comparison with anyone or anything. It is the core of my real self, yet it is also part of a universal reality; it somehow *is* that reality. The way to this still center is strenuous. It involves a stripping away not only of my false, distrustful self but also of what seems to be my real self, for all specific contents of consciousness are abandoned—all thoughts, images, and feelings. There is a "dark night of the soul," an experience of the void, when self and God disappear, and there is no solid ground on which to stand. At the bottom of the void, however, there is the "still point of the turning world."[19] To arrive there is to find both self and God in a new way. At this point meditation brings contemplation to a trust which cannot be undermined since it has endured the worst: contemplation and trust here coincide. This point is not an escape from everyday involvements. From it one can launch forth into a sea of troubles, whether they be one's own or other people's. But the "still point" can also provide a quiet haven of retreat to which a person can retire to replenish his resources.

The third kind of meditation is sometimes called "introvertive" in contrast with the second, which is called "extrovertive."[20] Since introvertive meditation tends to be more emotionally austere and dispassionate than extrovertive meditation is, it often risks being merely a sophisticated form of apathy, a way of repressing passions rather than acknowledging them as part of the self. For this reason it should generally be preceded by a process of "de-repression" which can be facilitated by disciplines as varied as expressive mantra chanting and primal therapy. Another danger, common to both forms of meditation, is that they become merely sophisticated forms of self-preoccupation. The first, preparatory kind of meditation can be helpful in avoiding this, in so far as it expresses and reinforces friendliness. But at their worst, extrovertive meditation is merely a self-conscious sensuality, and introvertive meditation merely a glorified narcissism. At their best, both forms of meditation draw us out of self-preoccupation so that we appreciate reality for its own sake. Above all, we become able to revere and value God for his own sake, rather than merely as a source of gratifying experiences.

Meditation is not necessarily an explicitly religious discipline, carried out in a context of religious practices and beliefs. It often is,[21] but sometimes it is quite secular. Moreover, there are aesthetic or artistic disciplines of attention which resemble meditation and which can be powerful elements in contemplation. And both deep psychotherapy and a conversion to politicized concern can expose many self-deceptions and thereby aid meditation by clearing our vision of reality. Indeed, they may be regarded as versions of what I called the "preparatory" form of meditation. It may surprise some people to think of Freud and Marx as guides on the contemplative way, but the idea is not at all fantastic.[22]

Contemplation itself, however, is clearly a religious attitude, a unifying stance of the whole personality towards a unifying cosmic reality. The attitude involves beliefs, some of which I have already indicated in my description of it. But conceptualizing of contemplative experience involves special difficulties. I suspect that if my contemplative experience were more mature, I would be willing and able to say much less about it! Some of the difficulties are discussed in the philosophical writings concerning mysticism.[23] But we can at least say that God is understood in relation to contemplative experience in a very different way from the God of primitive trust, who is like a "Good Mother who provides for me." God is not conceived as a cosmic person who comforts the child in me, but as cosmic creativity and inner peace which pervade all people and all things.

The opposite of contemplation is *self-consciousness*.[24] This is a pervasive stance in which I do not let my attention turn away from myself. It is a form of narcissism: whatever I perceive is perceived in relation to *my* needs or *my* achievements. What seems most real and important is not the person or the thing but *my experience* of person or thing. Even if I seem to be aware of ultimate reality my interest is not in it but in my awareness of it.[25] The sublest perversions of contemplation occur when self-consciousness retains an inconspicuous but decisive place: "Look at me, everyone, having these self-forgetful experiences during meditation!" The perversions can occur even though a person also has a good deal of genuine self-forgetfulness. Many people, however, are far from both genuine contemplation and its perversions. Their self-consciousness is very strong because it is the culmination of a whole series of unresolved attitude-vices, beginning with distrust and its chief constituent, pervasive anxiety. For such people there are serious limits on what meditation can do. They need to come to grips more directly with their own destructive and self-deceptive tendencies so they can consciously struggle against them.

The three species of love are successively wider in their scope. The main scope of friendliness, we saw, is friends, though it extends universally in forms which are potential or analogous or less complete; here the "We" is mainly "My friends and I." The main scope of concern is needy individuals and groups. It also extends universally, but in forms which are potential or analogous or less complete. The "We" of concern is the group or movement which takes up the cause of the underdog. The main external scope of contemplation, however, is anything and everything, and its internal scope is the self as participant in universal reality. The positive "We" is cosmic, all-inclusive. In this and other ways contemplation can be seen as a culmination of friendliness and concern, though it never authentically becomes a replacement for them.

Contemplation is a culmination not only of friendliness and concern but also of the other attitude-virtues, which find their finest form in it. *Trust* becomes a participation in a pervasive reality which pours out its creative abundance in both the outer world of people and things and the inner world of the still-centered self; and it becomes an unshakable assurance which arises at dawn after the dark night of the soul. *Humility* becomes a full acknowledgement and acceptance of the universal life, both around me and within me, in which I participate. *Self-acceptance* no longer depends on being accepted by another in spite of a destructive, condemning super-ego. If I am genuinely contemplative, I can observe my own weakness and vices (and those of others) without anxiety or hostility, accepting the fact of their existence as part of the way the world now is, while not ceasing to struggle against them. *Responsibility* becomes a learning and practicing of the highest discipline of all, beyond any skills of technology or language: meditation. Other disciplines become subordinate to this. If I practice meditation on the basis of love I can learn how to become a responsible member of the widest community —not only the human community but the cosmos. *Self-commitment* becomes a commitment not only to a view of the universe, but to the universe. It becomes a commitment to an *élan vital*, not only in so far as it helps *me* to feel alive and important, but in so far as it is the creative energy which sustains and vitalizes everything I encounter.

Chapter 9

Reflections Concerning the Attitude-Virtues

In this book I am proposing that growth in the eight attitude-virtues and struggles against the eight attitude-vices constitute a religious-moral way of life which leads towards human fulfillment. It is up to each reader to test my proposal by reflecting on it in relation to his or her own experience. What I have said raises many issues, which could fill many volumes. In this concluding part of the book, however, I will only consider four different questions: (1) Which of the attitude-virtues should have priority? (2) According to what criteria are the attitude-virtues selected? (3) How are the religious and moral aspects of the attitude-virtues related? (4) How are the attitude-virtues related to belief in God?

(1) Priorities among the attitude-virtues

I am going to begin my discussion of priorities by an excursion into intellectual autobiography. During the decade 1962-72 I was frequently preoccupied with the problem of how to find a basis for choosing among alternative life-styles, each with its dominant basic attitude, its associated depth-experiences, and its characteristic way of dealing with the world. Although for many people these life-styles are not explicitly religious, for me each was linked with a different kind of Christian conviction concerning God. I found myself intellectually and personally attracted to a variety of life-styles. In one, the focus is on I-Thou encounters; in another, politicized concern and radical activism. In a third, the dominant attitude is extrospective or introspective contemplation; in a fourth, trust or hope or courage in spite of distrust or despair or meaninglessness. A different kind of God seemed to be involved in each case: Buber's Eternal Thou, political theology's Liberator of the oppressed, Underhill's mystical One, Tillich's Power of Being which overcomes meaningless non-Being. And there were other important life-styles, each with a dominant basic attitude and a relation to a different kind of God. The choice between life-styles and related theologies seemed momentous, yet arbitrary. And a choice between them, or at least a decision of priority, seemed necessary because of the tensions and conflicts which arise in one's life and one's thought if one tries to combine them all on an equal basis.

The problem could not be settled by an appeal to the authority of Christian scripture and tradition, even if one respects that authority, for the same varieties of life-style and theology could be found there. When Christians claim such authority for, say, a dominantly political commitment and conviction, they merely select one strand in scripture and tradition and refuse to draw on others. Indeed, if scripture and tradition are properly used as authorities, one of their values is as a check against a narrowing of religious commitment and conviction to one kind which excludes or overly dominates the others. Even the New Testament teachings of Jesus and about Jesus, to which Christians often appeal in narrowly partisan ways, sanction a wide variety of emphases in life and belief. The real problem is how these differing emphases can be reconciled and ordered in some overall pattern for living and believing. A similar problem arises in a purely secular context, although issues concerning explicit religious belief are then set aside. The alternative life-styles have a relevance to human needs and aspirations quite apart from any appeal to the alleged authority of Jesus and Christian tradition. What overall pattern can be found?

The answer came to me one morning in June, 1972. I was thinking about the various basic attitudes which seemed most important to me. Suddenly I realized that the pattern is cumulative and sequential. If I arranged the attitudes in a certain order they corresponded to the succession of eight life-stages which Erik Erikson has distinguished.[1]

(1) Trust (early infancy)
(2) Humility (mid-infancy)
(3) Self-Acceptance (late infancy)
(4) Responsibility (childhood)
(5) Self-Commitment (adolescence)
(6) Friendliness or I-Thou openness (young adulthood)
(7) Concern, both parental and political (middle age)
(8) Contemplation (old age)

Moreover, the attitudes were roughly similar to the cumulative series of virtues, which Erikson has recommended, to resolve the characteristic crises of these stages. And although I had not found in Erikson an explicit exploration of the religious significance of all his eight virtues, it was at once clear to me that the virtues which seemed to me appropriate to each stage were also religious attitudes, each of which is connected with a different kind of religious belief. Erikson's overall framework thus provided the all-important initial clue for an ordering of diverse life-styles into a coherent way of life and a reconciling of diverse beliefs into a coherent theology.

From what I have said already in this book it is obvious that the connection between attitude-virtues and life-stages does not mean that, for example, trust is the religious-moral stance for early infants only, or humility for mid-infants only. One of Erikson's own main contentions is that earlier stages *recur* throughout the rest of life. They are never left behind. Crises typical of infancy recur in adults not only because adults sometimes overtly regress to infantile states during illness or psychoanalysis, not only because what happened in infancy is still part of us, influencing our present attitudes, but also because adult life goes on raising crises which are similar to those of infancy: If a loved one rejects me, can I trust anyone? If death will inevitably come, and may come tomorrow, can I face this ultimate limitation with humility rather than with pride or self-humiliation? One lesson which psychoanalysis teaches religious people is that since the earlier stages of life remain with us and life continues to raise similar crises, the kinds of religious faith which are related to them are not to be despised or discarded. For example, it is a fine thing if we have so much concern that we are mainly involved in external struggles against injustice, but the inner struggle of trust against distrust continues throughout life and ought to be supported rather than ignored. So a sermon which is a summons to share in God's liberation of the oppressed need not be embarrassed by the presence of Psalm 23 elsewhere in the service of worship. The continuity of the self from the cradle to the grave is a fact to be recognized in the way a person worships and, more generally, in the way he lives his life. The same person who now combats injustice or contemplates the eternal once sucked on his mother's breast. What happened then is still present in his nervous system. And the variety of issues in adult life should not be evaded. The person who is immersed in political activism or progressing in meditation may also be struggling against a terrible inner despair. Wise individuals, whether religious or nonreligious in their conscious convictions, have always known intuitively this breadth and depth of human life. Erikson's framework merely helps us to understand these things a little better.

Although the attitude-virtues form a sequence, this does not mean that life is like an obstacle race in which once one hurdle is cleared we never have to cope with it again. The struggle between trust and distrust, for example, recurs in adults even if it was dealt with well during infancy. Nevertheless the sequential order of the attitude-virtues is significant. The way in which an infant deals with the characteristic crisis of the first stage of life radically influences the extent to which the characteristic crisis of the second stage can be coped with in a constructive way. Without a basis of considerable trust acquired during the first stage, it is difficult to grow in humility during the second stage. Pride or self-humiliation is more likely to be dominant. Similarly a basis of considerable humility acquired during the second stage is needed if self-acceptance rather than self-rejection is to emerge as dominant in the third stage. And without a basis of considerable self-acceptance gained in the third stage, responsibility is difficult and childhood becomes a burden rather than a breakthrough. The sequential order of the attitude-virtues is important not only in processes of development during infancy and childhood but also in adult struggles to grow in the attitude-virtues. Since chronologically later crises may be difficult to resolve constructively because of inadequate resolutions of earlier ones, there is often a need to trace the difficulties back to their origins, where distrust because of inadequate resolutions of earlier ones, there is often a need to trace the difficulties back to their origins, where distrust predominated—and still predominates—over trust. For example, Erikson shows how Luther moved from a fourth-stage preoccupation with atoning works to a third-stage obsession with guilt and forgiveness to a second-stage defiance of authority figures (his father, the pope, and God) to a trust which he had lacked and on which he could henceforth base his life.[2] And when Reinhold Niebuhr finally stops describing the evils of self-deceptive pride (a second-stage issue) and asks how pride can be overcome, he sketches a kind of basic trust.[3] For Luther and Niebuhr the context for the inner struggle is explicitly religious, but a similar movement back towards trust can be discerned in many people who do not think about it in religious terms. The movement is often very obvious in the processes of deep psychotherapy. A person "regresses" in the focus of his struggle so as to establish a better "home base," and then he begins to progress through the kinds of crisis typical of each successive stage, moving from trust to humility to self-acceptance to responsibility to self-commitment and on to the three altruistic attitude-virtues. Of course the "movement" does not mean that the issues characteristic of earlier stages are completely left behind. It is not as if in January he acquires trust, in February, humility, and on to an August, devoted solely to contemplation! In any one day there may well be struggles from all the stages. The idea of a cumulative sequence and priority applies, but only in a very broad way.

Nevertheless it does apply. The attitude-virtues associated with earlier stages do have a priority as influential prerequisites. Any inadequacies in their development limit the extent to which the attitude-virtues associated with later stages can develop.[4] Trust is the most fundamental prerequisite, and has a special priority because of this. When a person gives to the struggle between trust and distrust a special priority in his life this often involves him in re-experiencing traumas from early infancy. Such a re-experiencing occurs in undisguised form when people undergo certain forms of modern psychotherapy, but it has also occurred in somewhat disguised forms when passionately religious people struggle towards a more authentic faith. But whatever its form, it is only a supplement to a struggle in the present with daily life issues of trust. The challenge is not only to combat distrust as it began in infancy in relation to one's mother but also, and more important, to combat distrust of other people (and oneself, and God) in the present. Similarly the struggle of humility against pride and self-humiliation is partly a wrestling with painful experiences from mid-infancy, but it is mainly an initiative towards greater realism concerning limits as they are now experienced.

The last three attitude-virtues, the species of love, have a different kind of priority—not as prerequisites, but as supreme *goals* in human life. The whole process of growth and struggle through the series of attitude-virtues moves towards them as the culmination. Moreover, as the other attitude-virtues mature, they tend to merge with the last three. We saw this in the case of trust. The first stage of the positive way towards assurance, when one looks to some other person as a symbol of a divine Good Mother, is very different from the third stage, when everyone, including oneself, participates in a pervasive divine life. We saw that the latter kind of trust requires a change from a childish dependency on others to the mutuality of giving and receiving which is found in friendliness. Similarly when humility matures it comes to include the kind of respect for the freedom of others which is an element in friendliness. Indeed, as each of the five earliest attitude-virtues matures it tends to become an element in the later ones. Earlier we saw how this transformation takes place in the context of contemplation. A similar transformation of all the earlier attitude-virtues can be seen when friendliness or concern have become powerfully pervasive in a person.

Thus friendliness, concern, and contemplation are the supreme goals in human life. An exclusive concentration on them, however, is self-deceptive and presumptuous. The earlier attitude-virtues, even in their relatively immature forms, have a crucial priority as prerequisites. This priority has been acknowledged in different ways by common sense, Christian tradition, and psychoanalysis, and we each need to acknowledge it realistically in our own lives. Fortunately it does not mean that we have to wait until all the problems which began in our infancies have been satisfactorily resolved before we as adults try to learn how to love. The earlier attitude-virtues and attitude-vices only provide a framework which limits and influences this learning process; they do not determine it. Indeed, a movement towards the beginning of love in present everyday life is often a prerequisite for progress in the struggle against distrust. Thus the distinction between five attitude-virtues which are prerequisites and three which are goals is not as tidy as might first appear. But it is clear that authentic human life involves two interrelated struggles. On the one hand there is a struggle in the present which looks partly backward into the past, a struggle to build foundations. On the other hand, there is a struggle in the present which looks partly forward into the future, a struggle towards a life of love.

The foundations are similar to what Christians have called "faith" (trust, humility, self-acceptance, self-commitment) and "works" (responsibility).[5] Such foundations bring a firm sense of one's own identity. This is a prerequisite for risking oneself in the venture of friendliness and, more generally, for moving out of the various kinds of self-preoccupation into friendliness, concern, and contemplation. Responsibility is specially important in establishing a sense of one's own competent reliability. If responsibility is lacking, one may want or intend to live the life of love, but actually living it will not be possible.

For various reasons it is obvious why friendliness, concern, and contemplation all come after the other attitude-virtues, which are their foundations. But what about the order of these three? Clearly friendliness must come first, for both genuine concern and genuine contemplation presuppose a basis of considerable friendliness. But it is not self-evident that concern must come second. I claimed that contemplation should not be contrary to concern, but this does not make concern, like friendliness, a prerequisite for contemplation. One reason for seeing concern as prior to contemplation might be that it is linked with middle age and contemplation is linked with old age. Here, however, I differ from Erikson, who links his last three virtues closely with three distinct life stages: young adulthood, middle age, and old age. I have two reasons for disagreeing with Erikson. One reason is that friendliness, concern, and contemplation differ considerably from the virtues commended by Erikson for these stages. His virtues, which he calls "love", "care," and "wisdom" are more plausibly linked with life stages than mine are. But, secondly, I question the link even for his virtues. I concede that Erikson's "care," as a parental kind of concern, is most obviously appropriate when a person becomes a parent, and that his "wisdom," which includes a retrospective reflection concerning one's life, is most obviously appropriate when a person has lived for a considerable period. But in some people both care and wisdom might well have strong beginnings even during young adulthood. And of course the virtues of concern and contemplation which I describe might even more plausibly begin then. And in some cases as they begin there might appropriately be more contemplation than concern.

Nevertheless I was not being merely arbitrary when I depicted contemplation as the final attitude-virtue. On the one hand, we saw that the central scope of the "We" of love expands as we move from friendliness through concern to contemplation; in this respect the order seems natural. And according to some religious traditions it is wise not to enter a life-style devoted mainly to contemplation until one has been involved in many prior years of active concern. On the other hand, sometimes a person emerges from a long period of contemplation to plunge into a life of dedicated concern. And sometimes a person combines both attitude-virtues in his way of life without having begun one before the other. There does not seem to be any universal principle concerning the ordering of concern and contemplation. Nor is there any consensus, or basis for consensus, as to which attitude-virtue is more important. When we consider the issue in individual cases, there is obviously a need for flexibility concerning both the *ordering* of concern and contemplation and the comparative *emphasis* given to each.

Differing orders and emphases may well be justified for two people who differ in temperament or life situation or political context. Even the relative emphasis given to friendliness may vary, for similar reasons. That is, although friendliness is necessary as a context for concern and contemplation, people may well differ concerning the relative amount of time and energy which they devote to the actual cultivation of friendships as compared with activities of concern or contemplation. In fact, my account of the three species of love is at best a *reminder* that all three are important and a *context* in which each individual can make his own decisions concerning practical priorities among them.

More generally, the sequence of eight attitude-virtues is not a rigid program which each person should go through in the same way, like an automobile being put together on an assembly line. There is often considerable skipping about among the stages. Each person has a unique path. What I have said about the eight attitude-virtues and the relations between them is at best a useful tool for beginning to understand the human struggle of any one person, including oneself. It is not a blueprint for designing a new humanity which might somehow be cloned as a multitude of identical specimens. In general, there is more similarity in vice than in virtue, and there is more similarity in early stage struggles than in the ways in which people can live a life of love. Although there are broad goals which can be described, and which it is helpful to bear in mind, the particular path towards them is a matter of individual discovery and decision. And the more immediate issue is the daily struggle to be open to the forces of life and resistant to the forces of destruction as these are actually at work in one's life in the present. The schema which I have presented may help us to locate where we are at in the struggle and to glimpse where we need to struggle next. A broad pattern is not a blueprint, but it is certainly better than nothing as we face practical issues of priority in daily living.

What about the theoretical issues, the conflicts between the ideas of God associated with the various attitude-virtues, and the need to order those ideas according to some criteria of priority? How, for example, do we reconcile and relate the divine providence of pervasive trust and the divine community-liberator of pervasive concern? What I have said does not provide any formula for reconciling conceptual differences. Rather, it connects these differences with differences among attitudes which do have an intelligible interconnection and a patterned ordering of priorities. Since each idea of God is associated with one of the attitude-virtues such as trust or humility or concern or contemplation, the ideas are connected indirectly, *via* the attitude-virtues. Priorities among the ideas can be understood in relation to priorities among the attitude-virtues. We will consider this again at the end of the chapter.

(2) Selection of the attitude-virtues

My reasons for selecting the eight attitude-virtues and their opposites rather than some other stances came from three sources: reflective common sense, psychoanalysis, and Christian spiritual teaching. Probably many readers will give most weight to the first source. Indeed, I have asked readers to test what I say in this book in relation to their own life experience, which may well include little from psychoanalysis or Christian tradition. But in my own thought I have given weight to all three sources. Consider, for example, my choice not only of trust and distrust as basic stances but also of the five constituents for each of these. I had three different reasons for including assurance, receptivity, fidelity, hope, and passion together as constituents of trust, and their opposites as constituents of distrust. *First*, there are intelligible conceptual connections, obvious to reflective common sense, which were displayed as I presented my analysis. For example, it is obvious that hope, as I described it, is linked to assurance, for what hope essentially hopes for is the return of assurance. Such a conceptual connection is not merely a matter of arbitrary definition on my part. I claim that I am merely making explicit a real connection between hope and assurance which can be discerned by the reader if he reflects deeply on his own experience. An example of such reflection is Gabriel Marcel's exploration of hope.[6] *Second*, in psychoanalytic descriptions of what goes on in early infancy, the main pattern which emerges is a struggle between what I call the constituents of trust and their opposites; they belong together in their origins. And the same clustering of stances is discerned in psychoanalytic accounts of adult experience where this is powerfully influenced by early infancy. My participation in the process of psychoanalysis, both my own and other people's, has confirmed this in immense detail. *Third*, in Christian spiritual teaching, beginning with Jesus and Paul, a roughly similar syndrome of virtuous and vicious stances is described. And the constituents of trust and distrust occur together in the religious experience of adult Christians. In this book I have not tried to justify my selection of attitude-virtues and their opposites on distinctively Christian grounds. I think this could be done, but I have only provided hints and allusions rather than arguments. But Christian tradition does have weight for me as a reason for selecting trust and distrust and their constituents.

The selection of the other seven attitude-virtues and their opposites had a similar threefold basis. I leave it to each reader to decide whether the selection is supported by reflective common sense. And I set aside any appeal to the authority of Christian teaching except for readers who accept such authority. But I should say a little more concerning the significance of the psychoanalytic reasons for selection. I quote Erik Erikson:[7]

> The healthy child, if halfway properly guided, merely obeys and on the whole can be trusted to obey inner laws of development, namely those laws which in his prenatal period had formed one organ after another and which now create a succession of potentialities for significant interaction with those around him.

Each virtue is a power for significant interaction with other people. According to Erikson, the development of virtues in the child is analogous to the biological development of organs in the foetus, where a particular organ must grow at an appropriate rate and in an appropriate sequence in relation to other organs if the whole organism is to develop in a healthy way. We cannot press this analogy, for an organ is different from a virtue. Each virtue, nevertheless, is linked with the person's emerging bodily needs and abilities. There is something very "natural" about the attitude-virtues, at least the first five, with their close connection to the stages of growth from infancy into adulthood. It is not that Erikson is an optimist, predicting an inevitable growth of the virtues. I do not know whether he would agree with me that few children are in fact "halfway properly guided," but he does note inescapable traumas in early infancy which no parent can prevent.[8] Yet although development of the virtues is not inevitable, it is natural. And the attitude-vices are distortions of this natural process of growth. As I see it, there are life-affirming forces within oneself and others and in the universe which a person can accept into his life and thereby grow in the virtues. In saying this I do not deny the existence and the destructive power of the attitude-vices. Moreover, I fully acknowledge both the biological origins of man and the continuity of adult life with these origins. The attitude-virtues which I describe are not angelic ideals or intellectual constructs. They are rooted in actual stages of human growth.

I should concede, however, that most of what I have just said applies more to the first five attitude-virtues than to the last three. The first five (especially the first three) are intimately related to universal processes of somatic, psychical, and social maturation which seem to be inherent in human growth from infancy into adulthood. The final three do not seem to me to be so demonstrably "natural." It seems to me that psychoanalysis as such sheds little light on the three species of love, though it does illumine the infantile origins of the corresponding vices. More light is shed by "third-force" humanistic psychologists such as Abraham Maslow. He includes among our "growth-needs" a need to love, which he describes well.[9] It is true that Erikson, a psychoanalyst, postulates a "need to be needed" as a quasi-instinctual basis for parental caring.[10] And in this book I have tried to show how growth in virtues during infancy points towards elements in the last three virtues. For example, passionate trust and respectful humility point towards elements in friendliness. But I cannot claim for friendliness, concern, and contemplation a basis in established psychological discoveries comparable to the basis which the other attitude-virtues have. My own basis has been mainly reflective common sense and Christian tradition, though my account of friendliness is also deeply influenced by experiences of friendship within a therapeutic community which shares a common psychoanalytic experience.

Thus there have been a variety of reasons for selecting the eight attitude-virtues. The selection is important, for I have described *human fulfillment* as the steady predominance of the eight attitude-virtues over the corresponding attitude-vices. Is this an adequate conception of human fulfillment? Is my list of attitude-virtues comprehensive enough? At first sight there seem to be some significant omissions, but on further examination we can see that most of the apparent omissions have actually been included or at least implied. This is true of the four traditional "natural" virtues: courage, justice, moderation, and prudence.[11] Then there is honesty, a very important virtue. It is present in each attitude-virtue as we struggle against self-deceptions caused by the corresponding attitude-vice, and it is also present in positive ways which vary according to the attitude-virtue.[12] What about creativity? Surely it is a constituent of human fulfillment. In my account I have included or implied a great deal concerning creativity, though perhaps it could be treated in part as a distinct virtue.[13] Another constituent of human fulfillment, I think, is reverence. This important religious attitude, so central in worship, is present in all the attitude-virtues in so far as they focus on a pervasive, unifying reality which is essentially mysterious.[14] But I do not include all the religious attitudes which have been commended by various people. Some of them I simply reject.[15]

Although in my own view my list of the constituents of human fulfillment is close to being comprehensive, I invite each reader to propose revisions and additions. I do not regard my proposal as the last word on the subject. Rather, it is a first word, an initial exploration. As I noted in the Introduction, my universal claims concerning human beings are made from a personal perspective which needs to be corrected by what others see from their perspectives.

(3) Relations between religious and moral aspects of attitude-virtues

In this book I have proposed a way of understanding human life which involves a new interpretation of religion and morality. I have claimed that religion and morality have a common core. Certain pervasive, unifying stances, namely the eight attitude-virtues, are both religious and moral.

This claim means that I must reject a traditional distinction between what have been called the "theological virtues" and the "moral virtues."[16] Let us consider this distinction for a moment. It has been maintained that "theological virtues" such as faith, hope, and love have God as both their immediate object and their immediate source, whereas "moral virtues" such as courage have human beings as their immediate objects and human activities as their immediate source. Where "theological virtues" are supernatural gifts from divine grace, "moral virtues" are natural developments. A "moral virtue" is a human achievement, a disposition, or a habit which is built up as we behave virtuously. Each "moral virtue" actualizes a potentiality with which human beings are naturally endowed. Although these potentialities come from God as Creator, their realization depends on our own efforts. If, however, "moral virtues" are developed in the context of the "theological virtues," the divine grace which is received for the latter spreads over, as it were, to the former, raising them to a higher level. Thus the moral courage of those who receive the supernatural gift of faith is allegedly different from the moral courage of those who have not received that gift, for it has been specially empowered by divine grace.

It is clear that the eight attitude-virtues are neither exclusively "theological" nor exclusively "moral." Each attitude-virtue has both God and people as its object or focus, and each requires an openness to accept life-affirming forces not only from within oneself and other people but also from God, who is all-pervasive. And none of the attitude-virtues are purely "natural" human achievements like the traditional "moral virtues" where these are acquired outside a context of faith. Nor are any of the attitude-virtues purely "supernatural" gifts, for they are assisted actualizations of human capacities rather than infusions from above. In my approach, traditional distinctions between "natural" and "supernatural" states in human beings break down, for the attitude-virtues which constitute human fulfillment and which are natural developments of human capacities have as their condition an openness (conscious or unconscious) to the divine.[17] And traditional distinctions between God-focused and man-focused stances break down, for each attitude-virtue has a dual focus: as a religious attitude it is focused on God and as a moral virtue it is focused on people.

This dual focus, however, requires closer scrutiny. Let us consider trust, remembering that it is a basic or pervasive stance, a way of being in the world. Suppose that I am in a room with John, James, and Mary and have this stance towards them. If Ann then comes in, and I turn to her, she is now alongside the other three persons as a focus of trust, whereas previously she was not. But for God to be a focus of trust, it is not a matter of some divine person entering the room and standing alongside the four persons who are there. God is already a conscious or unconscious focus of my trust. God is already "there" as the world-unifying, pervasive focus of my stance. I cannot "turn" to God as I turn from Mary to Ann, for God is already present in Mary and in anyone or anything I have dealings with—or, rather, they are present in God, for God includes them as God unifies them.[18] Trust directed towards them is in each case a particular expression of trust in God, the constant and primary focus of trust. Moreover, trust as a pervasive stance has an unconditional character, for it is a trust "no matter what happens," a trust sustained even though John and James and Mary and Ann and everyone may die or let me down. Such unconditional trust is not realistically focused on any fallible, variable mortal, though it can influence the specific and conditional stances which I have towards these mortals. What happens is that the pervasive, unconditional stance is *expressed* in each of the particular stances, and in this secondary way it is "focused" on persons. Since the expressions of the stance towards persons are a *moral* matter, we can say that the moral focus is in this respect secondary and the religious focus primary.

This does not mean, however, that the moral aspect of trust is a mere byproduct of its religious aspect. Both aspects develop together. Trust as a pervasive religious stance both reinforces and is reinforced by its moral expressions toward particular persons. Is the influence generally stronger in one direction than in the other? We cannot say. What we can say is that the religious and moral dimensions of trust are mutually dependent. And this is so for all the attitude-virtues. Morality, as the set of specific stances which we have towards other people, is an expression of pervasive stances which are essentially religious, focused consciously or unconsciously on God. Religion, as a set of pervasive stances focused on God, develops in mutual interaction with the moral expressions of these stances.

Which starts first, religion or morality? If we look at psychological origins in an Eriksonian way, it is plausible to claim that religion and morality begin together, when the infant first learns to trust mother. When trust begins in early infancy mother is usually its focus, and for the infant mother *is* both the pervasive, unifying reality of the whole environment and the locus of limitless value. Out of this initial way of being in the world both religion and morality emerge. Eventually there is the distinctively religious conviction that a pervasive, unifying reality transcends all particulars, including mother. And eventually there is the distinctively moral conviction that persons have value—not only mother and me but also everyone. The first experience of "god," however, is the infant's experience of his mother, and this is also his first experience of moral valuing. Thus on an Eriksonian approach religion and morality begin with an identical focus: mother. Later they transcend their origin and become distinct in their focus. Religion focuses on God and morality on people. (Whether God is a reality or an illusion is left an open question on this approach.)

But what if the infant is somehow aware of a religiously significant world which transcends mother? Some thinkers do not agree with Erikson that to the infant, "Mother *is* nature . . . all the comprehensible world."[19] Buber claims that the infant in the womb of the human mother is in the womb of the "great mother," and "knows the universe," though he forgets it at birth.[20] After birth the infant reaches out for I-Thou relation not only with mother but also with the world, longing for it to "become present"; and if mother has been truly present to the infant, he knows, even when she is absent, that he is "unceasingly addressed."[21] A mystical writer, Franklin Jones, recalls experiences of participation in life energy when he was in the womb and the crib, experiences similar to those he enjoyed much later during an advanced stage of contemplative life.[22] For both Buber and Jones these early experiences are focused on a divine reality which unifies the world. So if we acknowledge the possibility that their claims are true, we must be open to the possibility that an Eriksonian account of the infantile origins of religion is incomplete. To some extent religion would have, from the very beginning in human life, a focus distinct from morality. But morality could still be construed as beginning at the same time, and the infant's experience of the mother could still be crucial not only for morality but also for religion.

So it does not seem clear that religion is *temporally* prior to morality, or vice versa. What about *rational* priority? As I have been writing this book I have been aware of two different bases for justifying the selection of attitude-virtues. One basis is moral: stances are selected because they are moral virtues which enable us to be fulfilled as human beings. The other basis, which has not been as prominent, is religious: stances are selected because they are religious attitudes which enable us to discern the divine. The two kinds of bases are very different and might in principle give rise to very different selections. In this book, however, the selections have coincided. Nevertheless, the patterns of rational justification for the stances are very different. And the patterns of rational justification for the religious *beliefs* associated with the stances are also very different.

On the first approach, in which morality is rationally prior, I presuppose what I call a "neo-Kantian" philosophy. Certain stances are moral virtues, constituents of human fulfillment. They also happen to be attitudes which imply belief in God. Religious belief is thus justified on moral grounds.

On the second approach, in which religion is rationally prior, I presuppose what I call an "existentialist" philosophy. Certain attitudes are necessary conditions for discerning and responding to the divine. The religious experiences of discernment-response can then be conceptualized in religious beliefs, and the beliefs are justified by reference to the experiences which the atttiudes make possible. And since our fulfillment as human beings depends on rightly responding to the divine, which the attitudes make possible, the attitudes are also virtues.

Since in this book I have combined neo-Kantian and existentialist philosophies I have also been assuming two different ways in which belief in God might be rationally justified. My neo-Kantian approach to belief in God has been more evident, so we shall consider it first.

(4) Attitude-virtues and belief in God

The neo-Kantian moral approach. Where morality is rationally prior to religion, a particular conception of morality is usually dominant. We have seen that there is not only a "morality of doing" but also a "morality of being." Morality has to do not only with how we treat other people but also with what one ought to be as a person. To view a pervasive stance as a moral virtue is to consider it not only as it is expressed towards other people but also as it constitutes a part of human fulfillment. A conception of human fulfillment depends on a value-laden view of human nature, a normative anthropology in which a certain way of life is morally commended. In so far as the attitude-virtues are selected on the basis that they are the stances needed for human fulfillment, morality is prior to religion. That is, normative anthropology is prior to religious beliefs. I first ask what stances are constituents of human fulfillment and then find that these imply various religious beliefs. It is clear that if different stances had been selected as constituents of human fulfillment, different cosmic convictions would have been implied. For example, if various elements in distrust had been selected, belief in various "deities" of distrust would have been implied. Wariness has its Grand Depriver, idolatry its omnipotent Fairy Godmother, despair its Wheel of Fate, and apathy its Matter or Ideal Observer. And although someone might agree with me in selecting trust, he might describe it rather differently. If he did, the implied religious beliefs would be rather different.

In this book I have been assuming that religious beliefs are implied by attitudes which are themselves justified as constituents of human fulfillment. This approach places the book within an intellectual tradition which was initiated mainly by Immanuel Kant. He broke with an approach in which we first appeal to reason and perhaps to revelation to establish truths concerning God independently of any consideration of human fulfillment and its constituents, and then ask what implications the alleged truths concerning God may have concerning human fulfillment. Instead, Kant claimed that a certain kind of respect for the moral law is essential to being a human person[23] and then he asked what religious beliefs are presupposed by this attitude.[24] I differ from Kant in my criteria for selecting the essential attitude or attitudes. Kant explicitly set aside Christian tradition and appealed solely to practical reason. I am aware not only of nonreligious sources such as psychoanalysis and reflective common sense but also of Christian tradition.[25] Since my morality or normative anthropology depends partly on religious sources, I am not making religious belief dependent on a morality that is purely secular. Indeed, my anthropology is already theological to some extent, for I have selected moral virtues which are also religious attitudes, and as such they involve an openness to the divine. In my overall approach, as in that of Gregory Baum,[26] neither human beings nor God can be properly understood in abstraction from each other. Nevertheless it is true that in this book my theology (beliefs concerning God) depends to a great extent on my anthropology (beliefs concerning human nature). Though what then emerges is a theological anthropology or anthropological theology, I do have close affinities with Kant.

I share with Kant a common form of argument in support of religious belief. It is not the only kind of support to which I would appeal, but it is an important one. I call it an "Anthropological-Logical" argument. It can be presented in abstract form as two contentions and a conclusion:

Contention of normative anthropology: Human nature is such that attitude x is necessary for human personality or human fulfillment; therefore one ought to cultivate and live by attitude x.

Logical Contention: If anyone has attitude x he or she presupposes or implies that he or she believes in God.

Conclusion: Therefore belief in God can be justified as a presupposition or implication of an attitude which ought to be cultivated because it is necessary for human fulfillment.

In Kant's version of the argument, attitude x is respect for the moral law, which is required for being a person. Belief in God is allegedly "presupposed" by this respect in a complex way which Kant tries (unsuccessfully, I think) to demonstrate. In my own version of the argument, attitude x is any of the eight attitude-virtues which are required for human fulfillment, though pervasive trust is the most impressive candidate.

Is it possible that a religious belief could be presupposed or implied by a stance which is necessary for human fulfillment and yet be false? For Kant, since there is no other way to establish the truth or falsity of religious beliefs, such a possibility is set aside as nontestable. For me, such a possibility is genuine, so I also appeal to an "existentialist" justification of religious belief as a complement to my "neo-Kantian" way. We will consider this later.

What needs to be clarified at this point is my Logical Contention, that is my claim that the attitude-virtues imply convictions concerning God. I emphasize basic trust as the most important and most plausible instance of this. The contention can be analyzed in three steps of reasoning:

(a) *Trust implies belief that there is a focus of trust.*[27] Trust is a stance which must be directed towards some reality, usually a person. This does not mean that the focus must actually exist. The truster may be mistaken. But he must believe that the reality exists. If he does not, his state is not correctly described as "trust." It is a mood rather than a stance and should perhaps be described as "serenity" or "calmness."

In general, words which refer to stances or attitudes describe directional states which focus on a reality which is believed to exist.[28] Consider gratitude. If a person is grateful she must believe that a reality exists towards whom she is grateful. Otherwise she may be "joyful" or "ecstatic" but she is not "grateful"; her state is a mood rather than an attitude.

In so far as each of the eight attitude-virtues is genuinely an attitude, it has a focus and it implies a belief that the focus exists. Since trust is the foundation for all the others and an element in them, their focus includes at least the focus which trust has.

(b) *Since basic trust is externally pervasive and unifying, it implies a belief in a focus which is cosmic.* I defined basic trust and the other attitude-virtues as attitudes which are internally and externally pervasive and unifying. If an attitude of trust lacks any of these characteristics, it is not basic trust. The external pervasiveness of basic trust means that it is focused on anything that comes along. So its focus is not any particular, or set of particular, in contrast with other particulars. Rather, its focus is *all* particulars as an aggregate: one trusts this and this and this and so on until everything is included. Inso far as trust is externally unifying, however, it does not deal merely with an aggregate. It is focused on an x which is somehow common to all the particulars, in spite of all their difierences. In so far as one is responding in the same way to all the varied particulars one must believe that one is responding to such an x. Let us call it a "cosmic" focus. Let us also refer to any stance which is both externally pervasive and externally unifying as a "cosmic" stance. We can then see that any cosmic stance implies a conviction concerning a cosmic focus.[29]

There are two main kinds of cosmic focus: a common characteristic or an immanent-transcendent reality.[30] That is, the focus may be either a characteristic common to all particulars or a reality which, though immanent in all particulars, is not reduceable to them, but somehow transcends them. The kind of focus depends on the kind of stance. And the implied description of the characteristic or the reality also varies according to the description of the stance. For example, we have seen that the cosmic conviction implied by receptivity differs radically from that implied by wariness.

If a person has a cosmic stance he must have a cosmic conviction. But he can have the stance or the conviction without knowing that he has them. He may not be conscious of them, and even if he is conscious of them he may have articulated them in only a rudimentary way. It is not clear whether or not they are cosmic until they are articulated as such. Although we are usually at least dimly aware of a cosmic stance if we have it, considerable reflection is needed if we are to articulate it sufficiently to see that it implies a cosmic conviction of some sort. And even more reflection is needed for the next step, which involves seeing what the implied conviction is.

(c) *The cosmic focus of basic trust is God.* I have not only defined basic trust as a pervasive and unifying stance, which makes it cosmic, but I have also ascribed to it other characteristics which imply that its focus cannot be merely a characteristic common to everything. These characteristics show that it must be an immanent-transcendent reality which can be appropriately referred to as "God." Let us consider three:

First, the most primitive form of basic trust is one in which a particular person is considered as symbolic-representative of the whole environment, which then appears as "Good Mother." Clearly in this case the focus of trust is understood as a quasi-personal agency which pervades and unifies the world.

Second, as trust matures and eventually merges into contemplation, the focus of trust is far less obviously anthropomorphic, for God is conceived as the source of life energies and as the still center within the self and all things. But it is still clear that God is not merely a characteristic common to all things.

Third, I defined one form of trust, receptivity, as a stance which involves belief that the world is a gift. Since a gift implies a giver, receptivity implies belief in a world-Giver.

In my account even generosity became a religious attitude implying belief in God, for I tied it to such receptivity. As generosity is commonly understood, it does not seem to imply any religious convictions. Obviously there are people whom many would describe as "generous" because of their frequent spending on behalf of others and who are not what I call "receptive." Their "generosity" does not imply belief in a world-Giver. Only a receptive generosity does. I claimed that only a receptive generosity is both a constituent of human fulfillment and a genuinely beneficial influence on dealings with other people (since no strings are attached when a receptive person gives a gift). And I claimed that receptive generosity is an element in basic trust.

Such claims seem to me plausible, but they are certainly disputable. Here is one among many sections in my account of trust which might be questioned. Perhaps some other cosmic stance which could plausibly be called "trust" can be described and proposed as the fundamental constituent for human fulfillment. And perhaps this stance would imply cosmic convictions so remote from traditional religion that their focus could not plausibly be called "God." I cannot rule out such a possibility. Indeed, I must acknowledge that a stance *roughly similar* to basic trust might be articulated by someone else in a way which differs considerably from my account. Both descriptions could be articulations of roughly the same stance, for the stance is at core pre-linguistic and pre-reflective. After all, the primitive infantile form of trust, which continues into later life, is literally pre-linguistic. And as I have described mature forms of trust I have been conscious of trying to find words which would somehow "fit" something of which I am intuitively aware, prior to language and reflection.[31] I am convinced that people who have basic trust vary greatly in the extent to which they reflect concerning it. Such reflection is needed to articulate both its attitudinal and its convictional components. It is up to each reader to decide the extent to which my articulation rings true to his or her awareness of trust as an overall way of being in the world. The reader's reflection is the test to which I submit my account.

I am convinced, however, that some readers will need to consider the possibility that in them there is a *split* between the stance of trust as a fundamental pre-reflective way of being in the world and the appropriate articulations of the stance, especially in the matter of cosmic convictions. I think that some people who have a deep basic trust reject any religious convictions which would appropriately articulate this trust because in them there is a split in religious matters.[32] The split is between mind (intellect, articulation) and heart (will, feeling, behavior, way of being). Such a split is a different kind of thing from a contradiction[33] between an articulated description of a stance and an articulated belief or nonbelief. Such logical contradictions are in principle publicly demonstrable, but a split is something which ultimately each of us can only discover for ourselves within ourselves, through deeply personal reflection. To confirm or deny the existence of a split between a stance and its articulation one needs to become aware of the stance at a pre-linguistic, pre-reflective level. One needs to go behind the distinction between articulated stance and articulated belief so as to get in touch with the stance as a fundamental way of being in the world, out of which both kinds of articulation arise.[34] Then one is in a position to test their appropriateness.

Thus my "Logical Contention" can be contested in two different

ways:[35] On the one hand, someone may challenge the logic of the
implication from articulated stance to the articulated belief, finding
flaws in step (a) or (b) or (c). But even if she finds no logical flaws, she
may challenge my description of the stance on the ground that it is in
various ways inappropriate as an articulation of the stance in herself or
others. My hunch is that much of my description has universal
application, but this hunch is open to testing by each reader in deeply
personal ponderings.

I do not present my "Anthropological-Logical" argument in the
expectation or the hope that every reader will be convinced by it. Indeed,
I am not convinced that the most important issue in human life is
whether explicit belief in God can be rationally justified. The most
important issue is how we should live as human beings: what stances
constitute our fulfillment and what stances are needed to bring us into
right relation with God? Explicit religious belief is sometimes a blessing,
but it is sometimes a curse. I grant that sometimes it supports and
reinforces the attitude-virtues, and that in general, belief in the One who
unifies the world may help me to become one, a unity, myself.[36] But
explicit religious convictions also sometimes reinforce self-deceptions
concerning what my stances really are at a deeper level. For example,
explicit belief in divine Providence sometimes hides from me and others
my radical distrust, even if it also helps me to preserve remnants of real
trust. And such an explicit belief may reinforce distrust where this
distrust is posing as trust: we may cling idolatrously to formulations of
belief as substitutes for God. In general, explicit religious belief may be a
self-deceptive substitute for genuine openness to the divine. Instead of
using language to reflect on a mysterious human-divine relation which is
behind and beyond language, we try to grasp God in language while
abstracting ourselves from the inner dynamics of that relation. So if a
reader is "converted" by the logic of my argument instead of being
encouraged to probe his own trust and distrust he may be worse off than
a reader who remains sceptical!

Human fulfillment and vital knowledge of God matter more than
explicit belief. But if we do have explicit beliefs, it is important that we
consider whether they are rationally justifiable. Otherwise we split our

intellects off from the rest of ourselves, undermining our wholeness and integrity. So I think that my neo-Kantian argument deserves serious consideration. By itself, however, it is inadequate as a basis for belief in God. Not only is it open to challenge in the ways which I have already indicated. There are three further, and very fundamental, objections. First, the conception of human fulfillment on which the Anthropological contention depends can be challenged. A different set of stances can be proposed which do not imply belief in God. Second, my argument does not even purport to show that God exists. It only claims that belief in God is implied by attitudes which are necessary for human fulfillment and is therefore rational. It leaves wide open the possibility that the true cosmic beliefs are those which are implied by attitudes which are in conflict with human fulfillment. Maybe we have to believe what is false in order to be fulfilled. Maybe reality is not in tune with human fulfillment. Third, many people who have religious attitudes and religious convictions claim a more direct way of justifying their religious convictions. They appeal to their own religious experience. This is true in my own case. As I was writing this book my perspective was sometimes not neo-Kantian, for in so far as I was actually in the stance which I was describing (for example, passionate trust), God was not for me the conclusion of an inference but rather a real presence. I was not noting a logical connection between descriptions of passionate trust and beliefs concerning God. Rather, I was expressing an experience of a liberating life energy, which comes as a gift from a mysterious, transcendent Source. At other times, of course, God disappeared and was replaced by wariness's Grand Depriver or anxiety's Chaos, for I had a very different discernment of the ultimate. What seems ultimately true to us depends on what stance we bring to the world. This is the axiom of existentialism—an alternative to neo-Kantianism which can nevertheless be its complement.

The existentialist religious approach. There are many kinds of existentialism.[37] Some, like mine, are religious, but others are not. What they all have in common is the claim that a person's fundamental way of existing in the world is crucial in his perception of that world. In particular, existentialists claim that such-and-such nonneutral pervasive attitude is a necessary (and perhaps sufficient[38]) condition for discerning the metaphysical ultimate. Since they propose different attitudes they claim to discern different ultimates. In this book I have proposed trust and the seven other attitude-virtues as existential conditions for discerning the divine. If the opposites of these are recommended, very different ultimates are discerned. Sartre, for example, proposes a species of distrust. In a stance of forlorn, anguished, despairing dread we discern our freedom within a cosmos which has no inherent pattern.[39] For other thinkers what is discerned is divine, but since the stance they suggest is rather different from what I have proposed, their ultimate is rather different. Tillich's courage in spite of meaninglessness involves an experience of "God beyond God."[40] Otto's numinous awe is linked with a God who is distant and overwhelming.[41]

Although conclusions concerning what is ultimate vary according to what stance is selected as supreme, a common form of argument can nevertheless be abstracted. It has two contentions and a conclusion. I will call it a *Metaphysical-Reflective Argument:*

> *Metaphysical Contention.* What we discern as ultimate from attitude *x* really *is* and really is *ultimate.*
> *Reflective Contention.* What we discern as ultimate from attitude *x* is best articulated as *d* (a description).
> *Conclusion. d* is and *d* is ultimate.

In my own basic version of the Argument, *x* is basic trust and *d* is God. In the background of this book there has been the assumption that trust enables us to discern the ultimate and there has been reflection concerning this ultimate as divine.

A major objection to any Metaphysical-Reflective Argument is that there seem to be corroborating discernments for a great many different stances. This is what gives each of the different existentialist proposals its own widespread appeal. On what basis can we choose one attitude, with its associated metaphysical experiences, rather than another? When, for example, I contrasted each of the elements in trust and distrust, we saw that each brings to our experience of the environment its own different perspective concerning what is to count as real. And there is not only this selective shaping of experience in a characteristic way; each stance also usually facilitates moments of impressive metaphysical discernment which seem to crystallize the rest of experience. For the person who has the stance the discernment is often the main basis for holding the beliefs implied by the stance, for the beliefs are articulations of what is apparently discerned, whether this be God or chaos. How can we decide between the two? There is no stance-free way to settle the question. If we try to be "objective," appraising the arguments for and against the existence of God in neutral, dispassionate detachment, this too involves discernment from a stance, for such neutrality is a mode of apathy. The basic insight of existentialism is that in matters metaphysical, neutrality has no privileged position; indeed, it is an inferior stance. Neutrality is not like seeing an object through clear glasses so that we can then tell which tinted glasses distort the most and the least. Neutrality is itself selective and projective, as I have pointed out. We cannot *know* that any stance is "clear."

Since there is no stance-free way to decide between the metaphysical claims of competing stances, an existentialist warrant for religious belief is inadequate.[42] However impressive the religious experiences may be, there are also impressive experiences of a contrary nature which occur when the stance is different. The existentialist approach needs support for its selection of one stance rather than another. Here the neo-Kantian approach can help. If we seem to have to choose between competing stances as bases for discerning the ultimate, why not pick the one which most obviously promotes human fulfillment?[43] Indeed, where both approaches converge they can be mutually supportive in the selection of a stance. We can select trust not only because we believe it is a necessary condition for human fulfillment but *also* because we believe it is a necessary condition for discerning the divine. But although such a convergence of selection is significant, it is not conclusive. A similar coincidence is at least theoretically possible in the case of other stances, for example distrust, so the selection is still a matter of judgment and decision. But it seems to me that the case for distrust as a condition for human fulfillment is less plausible. Even when I view the issue from a stance of distrust it seems clear that distrust is destructive. Also, it seems to me that a world view based on trust can be more comprehensive than one based on distrust. It can include evil more successfully than the latter can include good.

These are controversial claims, however, and the second claim goes far beyond the scope of this book. Rather than pursue such issues here, I want to point out another way in which the existentialist and neo-Kantian approaches complement each other in this book. We saw that one objection to the neo-Kantian approach is that perhaps we have to believe what is false in order to be fulfilled. The existentialist approach provides experiential evidence that what we believe is true. I should now note how my existentialist approach involves a difficulty which the neo-Kantian approach can help to remedy. The difficulty arises from the fact that each of the attitude-virtues involves a discernment of God which is different, so that different beliefs are articulated. How can these various beliefs, with their different ideas of God, be reconciled? The answer to these questions lies in the attitude-virtues themselves. Even if the various ideas of God cannot be adequately reconciled in a completely consistent system by theological reasoning, we know that the attitude-virtues from which the ideas arise can be united in a human life. The lack of complete conceptual consistency is then tolerable, especially if we also remember that human language is not devised to describe the divine mystery but for much lesser tasks. But the unity of the attitude-virtues in a person does provide clues concerning how the diverse ideas of God can be brought together. And a theoretical ordering of the ideas in their relative priority can be based on a practical ordering among the corresponding attitude-virtues in relation to human fulfillment. For example, the idea of God as Providence is more basic than the idea of God as Limiter and Enabler because trust is more basic than humility. And the ideas of God as Liberator of the oppressed and mystical One have a different kind of priority from those two ideas, because concern and contemplation have priority as goals rather than as foundations or bases. Different ideas of God can be important in different ways.

Another way in which the two approaches complement each other is by bringing together an emphasis on human beings and an emphasis on God. By itself, a quest for knowledge of God may involve a flight from the human. And by itself a pursuit of human fufillment may reduce

God to a function of the human. Since such reduction was a greater danger in this book, I will say more about it. The danger was most obvious when I depicted trust in its most primitive, narcissistic form, where God exists only *for me*. But as trust matured into passion and contemplation, a non-utilizing, appreciative outlook developed, not only towards people and nature but also towards God. Nevertheless in a subtle way the neo-Kantian approach continued throughout the book to obscure the independent significance of God. In so far as this approach was dominant, I was considering attitude-virtues solely as human stances contributing to human fulfillment, abstracting them from their extra-human divine focus. So it was good that there was also a religious existentialist drive to discern the divine. On this approach the attitude-virtues are chosen because they are ways of being in the world which are conditions for vital knowledge of God. Religious beliefs are then articulations of the pre-linguistic meaning of these ways of being where we abstract from the human stance and consider only the divine focus.

So it turns out that the neo-Kantian and existentialist approaches are different ways of reflecting on the same material. They differ in their emphasis. I have noted that since it is possible to reflect concerning the fundamental ways of being so as to get behind the distinction between their attitude-dimension and their belief-dimension we can understand how both dimensions arise from their pre-linguistic core. In my neo-Kantian approach I consider the core mainly in its attitude-dimension, initially setting aside its extra-human focus. Indeed, I consider it as a moral virtue which happens also to be an attitude. Then I consider, almost incidentally, what beliefs concerning this focus are implied by the attitude which I have described. In my existentialist approach I consider the core mainly in its extra-human focus. Then I consider what beliefs arise as articulations of what is discerned.

In practice both kinds of reflection have gone on together, though the neo-Kantian has been more prominent. What matters most, however, is not whether explicit religious belief is warranted on either approach, or even whether my reflections concerning the pre-linguistic core of the attitude-virtues are accurate. What matters most for all of us is our struggle to foster the attitude-virtues and to subordinate the attitude-vices. Am I open to the forces of life and resistant to the forces of destruction as these are actually at work in my daily life?

Notes
Introduction

1. For most of this first-hand experience I am indebted to Therafields, a therapeutic community in Toronto. Some of the wisdom and insight of its chief therapist, Lea Hindley-Smith, can be seen in her novels *Ronald and Susan, Secret Places,* and *The Way It Might Have Been* (310 Dupont Street, Toronto, 1975, 1976, 1977).

2. Seward Hiltner suggests this expression in *Theological Dynamics* (Nashville: Abingdon, 1972), p.66.

3. Peter Berger, *Rumor of Angels*: (New York: Doubleday, 1969) pp.69–70.

4. Ludwig Wittgenstein, "Lecture on Ethics," *Philosophical Review*, Vol. 74, 1965.

5. For a survey of recent philosophical literature see Glenn Graber, "A Critical Bibliography of Recent Discussions of Religious Ethics by Philosophers" in *The Journal of Religious Ethics*, Vol. 2, Fall, 1974. Where religion and morality are primarily matters of belief, the main relations between religion and morality are either empirical relations between religious beliefs and moral beliefs or logical relations between statements which express these beliefs. Social scientists study the empirical relations and philosophers study the logical relations. There is thus a tidy division of labor between the two academic disciplines and each can apply its specialized technical skills in a rigorous and precise way. For example, social scientists can ask whether there are significant statistical correlations between the belief that God is our Judge and the belief that sexual intercourse outside marriage is morally wrong. And philosophers can ask whether it is possible to deduce prescriptions concerning right conduct from descriptions of God. It seems to me that such philosophizing can be illuminating, especially for the many people who do regard religion and morality primarily as sets of beliefs. But I do not regard them in this way. In this I am not alone, as I shall show.

6. Martin Buber, *Eclipse of God* (New York: Harper & Row, 1957), p. 97.

7. Cf. H. Richard Niebuhr, "Reflections on Faith, Hope and Love," *The Journal of Religious Ethics*, Vol. 2, Spring, 1974, pp. 151-3.

8. Although I am here using the word "disposition" to designate tendencies to *behave* in regular ways, I recognize that other writers use it in broader senses which are less remote from what I mean when I speak of virtues as "pervasive stances."

9. For an excellent presentation of such a conception of morality see David Little and Sumner B. Twiss Jr., "Basic Terms in the Study of Religious Ethics," in Gene Outka and John Reeder eds., *Religion and Morality* (New York: Doubleday, 1973).

10. Although a pervasive stance influences everything one does, its influence is more evident in some actions than in others. We understand more clearly what a stance is if we look at a paradigm case of its expression in an actual or imagined action, where the description of the action includes references to conscious feelings and motives and intentions as well as overt behavior. But a pervasive stance is not *merely* a disposition to such actions, and cannot be completely understood by reference to such actions. I concede that ultimately our understanding of a pervasive stance, like our understanding of any active human state, even one which is totally unconscious, depends on our experience of particular actions as observed and as consciously performed and experienced. But a pervasive stance cannot be adequately understood as a disposition to perform such-and-such a designatable *class* of actions, for it influences *all* actions (though only minimally in many cases) and it is a way of construing the relation between oneself and one's environment in an overall way. It is similar to what Maurice Natanson calls an "existential category," a "way (or mode) of being in the world," for example, desperation: "By desperation I understand a fundamental removal of the self from concrete possibilities of resolving a problem. I am desperate about this or that, I need something or somebody desperately, and these situations are solvable and so resolvable. But desperation as such, not my being desperate about this or that, but my desperation as a mode of being, a permanent possibility of human existence, is unaffected by events or persons. Events and persons, to the contrary, are seen and treated as fearful, awesome, lovable, or hateful in virtue of the self's desperation. The desperate man is not one who is desperate about this or that . . . The desperate man has a style of being; his world is structured in terms of his way of being in the world." See

"Existential Categories in Contemporary Literature," *Carolina Quarterly*, Vol.10, No.2, Spring, 1958, p.27. It would be interesting to explore the similarities between what I mean by "pervasive stance" and what is meant by various technical terms in contemporary existentialism and phenomenology such as Natanson's "existential category," George Schrader's "pre-reflective meanings" and Gabriel Marcel's "modulations" or "tonalities" of existence. For Schrader, see "The Structure of Emotion" in James M. Edie, ed., *Invitation to Phenomenology* (Chicago: Quadrangle, 1965); for Marcel, *The Mystery of Being*, Vol.1 (Chicago: Regnery, 1960), p.161.

11. See, for example, H.Richard Niebuhr, *The Responsible Self* (New York: Harper & Row, 1963), pp.118-20: "We use the word, faith, not as meaning some set of beliefs that must take the place of knowledge until knowledge is possible. The aspect of faith we have here in mind is simply that trust or distrust which is said by some psychologists to be the basic element in the development of personality in a child's first year and to which theologians, notably Luther, have pointed as the fundamental element in religion. Faith is the attitude of the self in its existence toward all the existences that surround it, as beings to be relied upon or to be suspected. It is the attitude that appears in all the wariness and confidence of life as it moves about among the living. It is fundamentally trust or distrust in being itself . . . The ways in which I shall formulate and justify and express my trust or distrust are largely dependent on the social and historical setting . . . but what is formulated and expressed in such words is individual and personal." Cf. Bibliography B, especially Ogden, Tillich, and Schleiermacher. For a discussion of epistemological and metaphysical problems which arise from starting with religious attitudes and moving to religious beliefs see Donald Evans, *Faith, Authenticity and Morality* (Toronto: University of Toronto Press, forthcoming); see also Donald Evans, "Philosophical Analysis and Religious Faith: Some Retrospective Reflections" in F. Duchesneau, ed., *Faith and Contemporary Epistemologies* (Ottawa: University of Ottawa, 1977).

12. See, for example, Stuart Hampshire, who cites Aristotle and Spinoza as background to his own position: "Some human virtues fit together as virtues to form a way of life aspired to, and some monstrous and brutal acts

are certainly vicious in the sense that they undermine and corrupt this way of life . . . What must be done is not necessary because it is a means to some independently valued end, but because the action is a necessary part of a way of life . . . A way of life is not identified and characterized by one distinct purpose, such as the increase of the general happiness, or even by a set of such distinct purposes. The connection between the injunctions, the connection upon which a reasonable man reflects, is to be found in the coherence of a single way of life, distinguished by the characteristic virtues and vices recognized within it." ("Moral and Pessimism," *The New York Review of Books*, Vol. XIX, Numbers 11, 12, January 25, 1973, p. 30.) See also Bibliography D.

13. See, for example, James Gustafson, who brings together such disparate thinkers as Karl Barth and Thomas Acquinas in his account of the Christian moral life (*Christ and the Moral Life* [New York: Harper & Row, 1968], pp. ix, 246-9): "I deal with the 'moral life' largely in terms of the personal existence of individual men, and do not develop views of men's particular moral issues . . . One need not endorse the whole of Barth's ethics in order to appreciate a perspective elucidated here . . . The good has been realized and confirmed; the power and source of life is good; it corresponds to what men know in God's goodness toward them in Christ Jesus. Human action can assume a reality and potentiality for moral good that already exists; it can attest to the fact that life and the giver of life enable humane life to be sustained and cultivated. . . . This perspective gives shape and movement to a certain disposition, or set of dispositions, in the moral lives of Christians. By disposition I wish to suggest a 'manner of life,' a 'lasting or persisting tendency,' a 'bearing toward one another and the world,' a 'readiness to act in a certain way' . . . Dispositions refer to the self's attitudes, its somewhat stable readiness to speak and to act in particular ways . . . Dispositions are 'habits' in the classical Roman Catholic usage of that term; not mechanical automatic responses to external stimuli, but persisting tendencies to act in such a way that one's action is directed in part by these lasting dispositions. Thus one can speak intelligibly about a "loving disposition,' a 'hopeful disposition,' a 'trusting disposition'; and one speaks about inner freedom, courage, temperance, justice, and prudence in a similar way . . . The traditional language of virtue pointed toward this aspect of human experience. St. Thomas wrote that "a virtue is a 'lasting disposition' that is in accord with a being's

true nature and true end." See also Bibliography C, especially Gustafson, Hauerwas, Harned, and H. Richard Niebuhr.

14. Paul Tillich, *The Courage to Be* (London: Nisbet, 1952), p.1: "Courage is an ethical reality, but it is rooted in the whole breadth of human existence and ultimately in the structure of being itself. It must be considered ontologically in order to be understood ethically." Tillich's terms "ontologically" and "ethically" correspond roughly to my terms "religiously" and "morally." I think he would have been willing to say, also, "It must be considered ethically in order to be understood ontologically."

15. Martin Buber, *I and Thou*, tr. W. Kaufmann (New York: Scribners', 1970); "Elements of the Interhuman" in *The Knowledge of God* (London: Allen & Unwin, 1965); *Between Man and Man* (Boston: Beacon, 1955), pp.13–14.

16. Gabriel Marcel, *Homo Viator* (New York: Harper, 1951), pp.7–67.

17. Erik Erikson, *Childhood and Society* (New York: Norton, 2nd. ed., 1963), ch.7. Erikson proposes a set of eight "virtues" which were the initial framework for my own proposal. The first virtue, *hope*, has to do with the dominance of basic trust over basic distrust. Erikson describes trust as a religious attitude and relates it to religious institutions but he relates the other virtues to different kinds of institution. In *Young Man Luther* (New York: Norton, 1958), however, he explores many of the religious repercussions of struggles between various virtues and vices. Although my detailed descriptions of the eight attitude-virtues are derived only minimally from Erikson's account of the eight stages and their virtues, I am deeply indebted to him for my overall framework.

18. In the history of philosophy there have been many celebrated stances which can be construed as attitude-virtues and which are very different from those which I commend, e.g. Kant's "respect for the moral law," Stoic *apatheia*, and Kierkegaard's "inwardness." See Immanuel Kant, *Religion Within the Limits of Reason Alone*, tr. R.M. Greene and H.H. Hudson (New York: Harper & Row, 1960); J.M. Rist, *Stoic Philosophy* (Cambridge: Cambridge University Press, 1969); S. Kierkegaard, *Concluding Unscientific Postscript*, tr. D.F. Swenson and W. Lowrie (Princeton: Princeton University Press, 1968), Part II, chs. 2, 3.

Part One

Chapter 2

1. Martin Buber, *I and Thou*, tr. R. G. Smith, (New York: Scribners', 1958), p.110.

2. Erik Erikson, *Childhood and Society*, 2nd ed. (New York: Norton, 1963), pp. 249-50.

3. R. D. Laing, *The Divided Self* (London: Penguin, 1965), pp. 39-43.

4. Cf. Alexander Lowen, *Depression and the Body: The Biological Basis of Faith and Reality* (Baltimore: Penguin, 1973), ch. 2, "Grounding in Reality."

5. Sam Keen, *To a Dancing God* (New York: Harper, & Row, 1970), p. 131.

6. What I here call "acceptance" I refer to as "receptivity" in "Does Religious Faith Conflict with Moral Freedom?", in Gene Outka and John Reeder, eds. *Religion and Morality* (New York: Doubleday, 1973). Here I use the word "receptivity" to refer to a constituent of trust which, like all the constituents of trust, has acceptance as a pre-condition.

7. Cf. H. Richard Niebuhr, who mentions the negative way first: "It remains questionable whether the self is led more to trust in the ultimate because it finds all the finite being about it unreliable, or more because it is led by stages from trust in the near-at-hand to trust in the ultimate. Is it because all finite powers on which we have relied for value have failed us that we turn to the ultimate or because we have seen traces of the structure of faith in the whole realm of being that we are led to confidence in Being?" *The Responsible Self* (New York: Harper & Row, 1963), p. 120. Both ways are evident in the thought of Paul Tillich. There is, for example, a version of the negative way in *The Courage to Be* (London: Nisbet, 1952) and of the positive way in *Dynamics of Faith* (New York: Harper & Row, 1957).

8. Sam Keen, *op. cit.*, pp. 100-101.

9. H. Richard Niebuhr (*op. cit.*, p. 119) considers this third option and sees it as a form of distrust: "Our primordial interpretation of the radical action by which we are is made in faith as trust or distrust. Between these two there seems to be no middle term. The inscrutable power by which we are is either for us or against us. If it is neutral, heedless of the affirmations or denials of the creatures by each other, it is against us, to be distrusted as profoundly as if it were actively inimical." Niebuhr does not distinguish, as I do, between the two meanings of "neutral"; his meaning seems closer to my first, that is, "indifference."

10. Virginia Woolf, *To the Lighthouse* (London: Penguin, 1964), pp. 19-20.

11. Sam Keen, *op. cit.*, pp. 16-17.

12. St. John of the Cross, *The Mystical Doctrine of St. John of the Cross*, selections by R. H.J. Steuart (London: Sheed and Ward, 1934 and 1974).

13. Paul Tillich, *The Courage to Be* (London: Nisbet, 1952), especially chs. 2, 6.

14. See Erik Erikson, *Young Man Luther* (New York: Norton, 1958), p. 211: "Luther abandoned theological quibbling about the cross . . . He insists on Christ's complete sense of abandonment and on his sincere and active premeditation in visiting hell. . . . It is clear that Luther rejected all arrangements by which an assortment of saints made it unnecessary for man to embrace the maximum of his own existential suffering. What he had tried, so desperately and for so long, to counteract and overcome he now accepted as his divine gift—the sense of utter abandonment . . . as if already in hell."

15. Arthur Janov, *The Primal Scream* (New York: Delta, 1970).

16. R. D. Laing, *The Politics of Experience* (Baltimore: Penguin, 1967), pp. 32-7, 46, chs. 6, 7, pp. 152-3. Laing here universalizes an experience which he first studied in schizophrenics; see *The Divided Self*, pp. 35-43.

17. Erik H. Erikson, *Insight and Responsibility* (London: Faber, 1964), pp. 153-4.

18. There are many alternative explanations of the experience, for example: (1) a re-living of a birth trauma (2) a letting go of a defensive character structure, (3) a sudden awareness of one's radical freedom to decide, completely by oneself, whether to accept or to reject life, (4) an awareness of a paradoxical nonreality which is always present but usually evaded. Each explanation, of course, may apply to a slightly different experience.

19. Even stronger support comes if one has not only experienced the void oneself but also been with many other people during their experience of it, and also sometimes correctly intuited when others are close to the experience while not yet actually conscious of it. Nevertheless, as is the case with many other claims concerning human nature which are made in this book, no decisive and universally acceptable testing is possible.

20. San Keen, *To a Dancing God* (New York: Harper & Row, 1970), p. 101.

21. *Ibid.*, p. 17.

22. Schubert Ogden argues that there is a trust which is "ineradicable" and "inescapable" in human life and that this trust somehow includes a belief in God. But only a minimal reality-assurance can be plausibly described as "ineradicable" and "inescapable." A strong reality-assurance is not a necessary condition for human life as such; one can get by with less. A strong reality-assurance is a necessary condition for human life at a high level of fulfillment. And even if such an assurance is strong at the moment, it could decrease or escape from one's life without one's ceasing to live. Ogden's main argument, however, is that when we attribute *moral* significance to our actions this implies an "original confidence in the meaning and worth of life" which is explicitly affirmed or represented as belief in God. Here the strength of assurance is not minimal and what is meant by "God" is not minimal: life has not merely enough significance for us to go on living and acting, it has *moral* significance. But Ogden cannot plausibly claim that the confidence is ineradicable and inescapable: we do not have to attribute *moral* significance to our actions in order to go on living and acting. See *The Reality of God and Other Essays* (New York: Harper & Row, 1963), pp. 34, 37.

23. Sam Keen, *Apology for Wonder* (New York: Harper & Row, 1969), pp. 204-5.

24. Erik H. Erikson, *Childhood and Society*, 2nd ed. (New York: Norton, 1963), pp. 249-50. Cf. Roy S. Lee, *Your Growing Child and Religion* (London: Penguin, 1965), pp. 50-63.

25. *Op. cit.*, p. 122.

26. Erik H. Erikson, *Young Man Luther* (New York: Norton, 1958), p. 117. Martin Buber's non-psychoanalytic account is interestingly similar: "The innateness of the longing for relation is apparent even in the earliest and dimmest stage . . . In the relationships through which we live, the innate You is realized in the You we encounter . . . In the drive for contact (originally, a drive for tactile contact, then also for optical contact with another being) the innate You comes to the fore quite soon, and it becomes ever clearer that the drive aims at reciprocity, at 'tenderness'." "What this longing aims for is the *cosmic* association of the being that has burst into spirit with its true You." *I and Thou*, tr. W. Kaufmann (New York: Scribners', 1970), pp. 76, 78-9 (italics mine).

27. See Roy S. Lee, *Your Growing Child and Religion* (London: Penguin, 1965), p. 36. Sigmund Freud, however, relates merging oneness to the first weeks of infancy when he discusses the "oceanic feeling" in *Civilization and Its Discontents* (New York: Doubleday, 1958), ch. 1. This is less plausible than a reference to the womb since birth seems to involve a *separation* trauma. It is true, however, that there are adult religious experiences which are neither pure instance of assurance nor pure instances of merging oneness, but a mixture, or something in between. It seems plausible to relate these experiences to the first weeks of infancy, when the boundaries between infant and mother are blurred, yet there is some distinction between them.

28. Paul Tillich understands faith (including both trust and hope) by means of an analysis of courage. What he calls "courage" includes not only the courage to face anxiety (which is in my account an element in all the

constituents of trust), but also the specific courage which, like what I call "hope," resists despair, and also the courage to face the void. I do not think he adequately distinguishes between these three aspects of what he calls "courage." (In my section on "hope and despair" I will show that there is a radical difference between despair and the experience of the void; I have already tried to show the difference between anxiety and the experience of the void.)

Chapter 3

1. Edmund Bergler, *The Basic Neurosis* (New York: Grune & Stratton, 1947), ch. 1.

2. "It was as if that great rush of anger had washed me clean, emptied me of hope, and gazing up at the dark sky spangled with its signs and stars, for the first time, the first, I laid my heart open to the benign indifference of the universe. To feel it so like myself, indeed, so brotherly, made me realize that I'd been happy, and that I was happy still. For all to be accomplished, for me to feel less lonely, all that remained to hope was that on the day of my execution there should be a huge crowd of spectators and that they should greet me with howls of execration." Albert Camus, *The Stranger* (New York: Vintage, 1954), p. 154, which is the last page.

3. Paul Tillich, *The Courage to Be* (London: Nisbet, 1952), p. 37.

4. R. D. Laing, *The Politics of Experience* (London: Penguin, 1967) ch. 3; (with A. Esterson) *Sanity, Madness and the Family* (London: Penguin, 1970), introduction and ch. 1.

5. It seems to me that this tendency is evident in Sigmund Freud's *The Future of an Illusion* (New York: Doubleday, 1957). In spite of his positivism ("Scientific work is our only way to the knowledge of external reality," p. 55), Freud claims to know something fundamental about the world which science could not possibly ascertain, namely that the world is *hostile*: "Man cannot remain a child forever; he must venture at last into the hostile world. This may be called '*education to reality*' " (pp. 88-9). According to Freud, nature "destroys us, coldly, cruelly, callously" (p. 22). He speaks of earthquakes, floods, storms, diseases and death and goes on, "With these

forces nature rises up before us, sublime, pitiless, inexorable; thus she brings again to mind our weakness and helplessness" (p. 23). He continues, "We know already how the individual reacts to the injuries that culture and other men inflict on him: he develops a corresponding degree of resistance against the institutions of this culture, of hostility towards it. But how does he defend himself against the supremacy of nature, of fate, which threatens him, as it threatens all?" (p. 24). Freud's criticism of religion arises partly from this basic stance of wariness towards nature and society. It seems to me that this stance is just as open to psychoanalytic investigation as the basic trust which is expressed in religion, and that whereas the latter contributes to human fulfillment, the former works against it.

6. To some people this is not obvious. As we shall see in the section on "passion and apathy," the substantial, "full-blooded" existence of environment and self is not fully felt by the apathetic man. And a person who indulges in megalomania may somehow construe the world as his own creation. In his private fantasy the world is thus not a gratuitous gift; it is his own possession, his own product. Some forms of philosophical idealism and atheistic existentialism can give these fantasies respectable intellectual status. The fantasies are a special form of idolatry: self-idolatry.

7. Erik H. Erikson, *Identity, Youth and Crisis* (New York: Norton, 1968), p. 99.

8. Seward Hiltner, *Theological Dynamics* (Nashville: Abingdon, 1972), pp. 50-1. His whole chapter on "Grace and Gratitude" is illuminating.

9. R. D. Laing, *The Politics of Experience*, chs. 4, 5; cf. Abraham Maslow, *Towards a Psychology of Being*, 2nd ed. (New York: Van Nostrand, 1968), pp. 51-2, p. 51, n.3.

10. Cf. Enda McDonagh, *Gift and Call: Towards a Christian Theology of Morality* (St. Meinrad, Indiana: Abbey Press, 1975). McDonagh contrasts the experience of others as gifts and the experience of others as threats. He sees the former as the main basis for our experience of moral "calling." He claims that when one sees the other person as a gift one sees that he calls for "recognition" and "respect." What he means by "recognition" is fairly

similar to what I mean by "confirmation" as an element in receptivity and friendliness. And what he means by "respect" is fairly similar to what I mean by "respect" as an element in friendliness. McDonagh does not provide a detailed phenomenology or a deep psychological exploration for his gift-call schema. He is more interested in using it to interpret the structure of morality, to link morality with Christian theology, and to apply to contemporary moral issues, both personal and social.

11.   Martin Buber, *The Knowledge of Man* (London: Allen & Unwin, 1965), p. 79.

12.   Knud E. Logstrup, *The Ethical Demand*, tr. Theodor Jensen (Philadelphia: Fortress, 1971), p. 150.

13.   *Ibid.*, pp. 147; cf. pp. 123-4, 130, 148, 165.

Chapter 4

1.   By "sensuality" I do not mean "sexuality." For discussions of sensuality which are interesting to compare and contrast, see Alexander Lowen, *Love and Orgasm* (New York: Signet, 1975), ch. 10; and Reinhold Niebuhr, *The Nature and Destiny of Man*, Vol. 1 (London: Nisbet, 1941), pp. 248-50.

2.   Martin Buber, *I and Thou*, tr. W. Kaufmann (New York: Scribners', 1970), pp. 153-5.

Chapter 5

1.   For other accounts of this kind of hope, see Gabriel Marcel, *Homo Viator* (New York: Harper & Row, 1962), pp. 7-67, especially pp. 32, 42; William Lynch, *Images of Hope* (New York: Mentor, 1956), Part I; James Gustafson, *Christ and the Moral Life* (New York: Harper & Row, 1968), pp. 249-54. (Gustafson's analysis of "cowardice" is included in an account of "freedom," but it seems to me that it is more aptly considered as part of the despair which *hope* resists.)

2.   Indeed, one common route to despair is *via* the collapse of an idol. Another is *via* the collapse of an enemy. When idolatry or wariness fail, we turn to despair instead of facing our anxiety.

3. When I include hope within trust, my procedure differs from that in the accounts of hope, trust, and other stances given by some writers. Gabriel Marcel provides an analysis of "absolute hope" which includes much that I include in discussing not only hope but other constituents of what I call "trust," e.g. fidelity and receptivity. He notes that absolute hope is inseparable from what he calls "absolute faith," but he does not include it in absolute faith. See *op. cit.*, pp. 7–67, especially p. 46. As I mentioned in ch. 1, Paul Tillich includes trust and hope together as elements in "faith" and elucidates faith by providing an analysis of courage. David Baily Harned holds that faith (i.e. trust and loyalty) hope and love are distinct, inseparable, and mutually dependent. What he means by "love" is partly covered by what I say about "receptivity" and "passion" as constituents of trust, but most of it is included in my accounts of three attitude-virtues which depend on trust, but which may or may not develop if there is trust: friendliness, concern for anyone in need, and contemplation. Later I shall try to show that such "love" is a goal for which trust is a foundation. For Harned, see *Faith and Virtue* (Philadelphia: Pilgrim Press, 1973), chs. 1, 2, 3, 6, especially pp. 36–7.

4. Here, as in the discussions of assurance, receptivity, and fidelity, I focus mainly on psychic needs, for reasons similar to those given when I considered the relation between reality-assurance and satisfaction-assurance. But as in the case of assurance, hope for satisfaction of bodily needs, though subordinate, is not dispensable.

5. Erik H. Erikson, *Childhood and Society*, 2nd ed. (New York: Norton, 1963), pp. 72–80.

6. Cf. James Gustafson concerning what he calls "cowardice," which seems to me to be virtually the same as paralyzed lethargy despair: "Cowardice as a disposition stems in part from fear, from the absence of fundamental confidence in the goodness of life. It is a moral paralysis that vitiates the human capacity to initiate and to act in the course of life's events . . . Cowardice cripples participation in the historical struggles and opportunities to achieve what is morally good." (*Op. cit.*, pp. 253–4.)

7. *Ibid.*, pp. 250–2.

8. R. D. Laing, *The Politics of Experience*, p. 33.

9. Cf. William Lynch, *Images of Hope* (New York: Mentor, 1966), p. 43.

10. *Op. cit.*, p. 36.

11. Sam Keen, *To a Dancing God*, pp. 120–1.

12. *Ibid.*, p. 121.

13. Søren Kierkegaard, *The Sickness Unto Death* (New York: Doubleday, 1954), pp. 205–7. (The volume also includes *Fear and Trembling*.)

14. Leonard McGravey, "Writing," in P. McKenna, ed., *Love Life* (Toronto: Therafields, 310 Dupont St., 1977), p. 55.

Chapter 6

1. "Passionless existence" is one of the phrases included in the definition provided by the *Shorter Oxford English Dictionary*, which is as follows: "1. freedom from, or insensibility to, suffering, passion, or feeling; passionless existence. 2. indolence of mind, indifference to what normally excites emotion or interest." One meaning given for "indolent" is "averse to toil or exertion." On the whole, my account of "apathy" differs from the dictionary definition, especially "indolence"; it is closer to the ancient Stoic meaning.

2. Cf. Alexander Lowen, *The Language of the Body* (New York: Collier Macmillan, 1971), pp. 327–77.

3. I should note here that apathy, as I describe it, is different not only from insensibility and indolence, but also from the vice which Acquinas called *acedia* and which one modern translation renders as "spiritual apathy." *Acedia* is a sadness or despondency concerning the divine good, especially in so far as men might participate in this spiritiual good (cf. what I call "meaning and reality provided by God"). *Acedia* is turning away from this good instead of rejoicing in it. As Aquinas describes it, *acedia* is a combination of what I call *despair* (mainly paralyzing lethargy—torpor or

cowardice) and *wariness* (mainly resentment—malice and spite). There is also some scattered, unfocused *idolatry*—a restless, curious straying after illicit things. And in Cassian's account of *acedia*, which Aquinas quotes, there is a suggestion of some pervasive *anxiety*. But Acquinas does not understand *acedia* in such a way as to include much of what I call "apathy." *Acedia* involves a good deal of indolence, lethargy, and weariness about work but this is associated with the *despair* in *acedia*. In any case, it is not a necessary element in what I call "apathy." And Aquinas contrasts *acedia*, not with embodied passion, but (explicitly) with rejoicing in spiritual good (cf. my "receptivity," with its element of "gratitude") and (implicitly) with hope for spiritual good. In general, what I describe as basic distrust towards God and man is roughly covered (except for apathy) by Aquinas's accounts of *acedia*, hatred (towards God and man) and envy (of man). Concerning all this see Thomas Aquinas, *Summa Theologiae*, Vol. 35 (2a2ae, 34-6), Blackfriars ed. (London: Eyre and Spottiswoode, 1972). T. R. Heath edited Vol. 35 and discussed *acedia* in appendix 2.

4. See J. M. Rist, *Stoic Philosophy* (Cambridge: Cambridge University Press, 1969), p. 26.

5. *Ibid.*, p. 26: cf. p. 72. Rist notes that Panaetius differs from the Old Stoa in calling for the *restraining* of a non-rational *part of the soul* rather than the *suppression* of irrational emotions which are allegedly *alien* to the soul (see *ibid.*, pp. 195-6).

6. Cf. Sam Keen, *Apology for Wonder* (New York: Harper & Row, 1969), ch. 6.

7. Cf. Rollo May, *Love and Will* (New York: Norton, 1969), ch. 1, "Our Schizoid World."

8. Cf. Sam Keen, *op. cit.*, chs. 5, 6; cf. also Theodore Roszak, *The Making of a Counter Culture* (New York: Doubleday, 1969), ch. 7.

9. Roszak (*op. cit.*, pp. 222-23) severely criticizes the following stance: "I can perceive no more than your behavioral facade. I can grant you no more reality or psychic coherence than this perception allows. I shall observe this behavior of yours and record it. I shall not enter into your life, your task,

your condition of existence. Do not turn to me or appeal to me or ask me to become involved with you. I am here only as a temporary observer whose role is to stand back and record and later to make my own sense of what you seem to be doing or intending. I assume that I can adequately understand what you are doing or intending without entering wholly into your life. I am not particularly interested in what *you* uniquely are; I am interested only in the general pattern to which you conform."

10. Jean-Paul Sartre, *Existentialism and Humanism*, tr. P.Mairet (London: Methuen, 1948), pp.32–39.

11. Paul Tillich, *The Courage to Be* (London: Nisbet, 1952), pp. 163–80.

12. Concerning this whole-hearted wanting and its dependence on a trust in one's context, see William Lynch, *Images of Hope* (New York: Mentor-Omega, 1966), Part II: chs.1—3. Cf. Donald Evans, "Does Religious Faith Conflict with Moral Freedom?", p. 367, in Gene Outka and John Reeder, eds., *Religion and Morality* (New York: Doubleday, 1973).

13. Cf. Wilhelm Reich, *Character Analysis* (New York: Noonday Press, 1949), chs. 11—13. Although empirical evidence (from psychotherapy, anthropology, etc.) is relevant to the dispute concerning an alleged inherent destructive drive in human beings, it seems to me that the conflict is ultimately between apathy and passion as pervasive life-stances rather than between rival scientific hypotheses.

14. Cf. Søren Kierkegaard concerning the "knight of infinite resignation" in *Fear and Trembling* (New York: Doubleday, 1954), a volume which also includes *The Sickness unto Death*: "He who loves God without faith reflects upon himself, he who loves God believingly reflects upon God" (p.47). "I do not trouble God with my petty sorrows, the particular does not trouble me. I gaze only at my love, and keep its virginal flame pure and clear" (p.45). "I am still able to save my soul, if only it is more to me than my earthly happiness that my love to God should triumph in me" (p. 60).

15. Kazoh Kitamori, *Theology of the Pain of God* (Richmond: John Knox, 1965), p.26. He quotes Shotoku Taishi, a seventh-century Japanese interpreter of Buddhist scriptures.

16. William Lynch, *op.cit.*, pp.129-35, 148-51.

17. Gregory Baum, *Religion and Alienation, A Theological Reading of Sociology* (New York: Paulist Press, 1975), p.292.

Part Two

Chapter 7

1. Quoted from "The General's Prayer" in Christopher Cross, ed., *A Minute of Prayer* (New York: Pocket Books, 1954), p.85.

2. Friedrich Schleiermacher is sometimes interpreted in this way, but this is not true to his thought. For him, God is the "Whence" of our "receptive and *active* existence"; *The Christian Faith* (Edinburgh: Clark, 1928), p. 16 (italics mine). His "absolute dependence" does, however, involve more resignation than I wish to commend in what I call "humility."

3. Albert Camus vividly describes a character who is caught up in this perpetual preoccupation in *The Fall*, tr. Justin O'Brien (New York: Vintage, 1956).

4. Jean-Paul Sartre gives an accurate description of a person for whom the only alternatives are "sadism" and "masochism": either he objectifies and subjugates the other person or he lets the other person objectify and subjugate him. What Sartre fails to recognize is that what he describes is an attitude-vice which varies in strength from person to person and which is challenged in many people by a powerful attitude-virtue, humility. Nor does Sartre see that his focus on issues of freedom, power, status, shame, etc. is a narrow one, so that he is ignoring and minimizing many of the other kinds of issues in human life. For Sartre see *Being and Nothingness*, tr. Hazel Barnes (New York; Washington Square Press, 1966), Part III: ch. 1, section IV, and ch. 3, sections I and II. For a useful summary of Sartre, see Mary Warnock, *The Philosophy of Sartre* (London: Hutchinson, 1965). For a criticism of Sartre's application of his conflictual model of interpersonal relations to human-divine relations, see Martin Buber, *Eclipse of God* (New York: Harper & Row, 1952), pp. 67-70.

5. I explore this distinction in "Gregory Baum's Theology of Liberation" and "Does Religious Faith Conflict with Moral Freedom?" (See Bibliography A). The distinction is influenced by Buber and Marcel.

6. I once thought, influenced by Erikson, that mid-infancy is the most *crucial* stage for this struggle. It now seems to me clear that the narcissism of early infancy is more important. In a book concerning humility and its opposites which I am currently working on, my main genetic focus is early infancy rather than mid-infancy. A focus on the latter can be illuminating, however, and I have retained it in this section of *Struggle and Fulfillment*.

7. Reinhold Niebuhr, *The Nature and Destiny of Man*, Vol.I (London: Nisbet, 1941), chs. 6–8. Niebuhr is deeply influenced by Søren Kierkegaard's *The Concept of Dread* (Princeton: Princeton University Press, 1944), and *The Sickness Unto Death* (New York: Doubleday, 1954).

8. Gordon Kaufman, *God the Problem* (Cambridge: Harvard University Press, 1972), ch. 3.

9. Thomas Aquinas, *Summa Theologiae*, Vol.35 (2a2ae, Blackfriars ed. (London: Eyre and Spottiswoode, 1972), T.R.Heath, ed.; see question 35, article 3.

10. Viktor E. Frankl, *The Doctor and the Soul* (New York: Bantam, 1967), p.47.

11. John Milton, Sonnett II, "On His Having Arrived at the Age of Twenty-Three."

12. Abraham H. Maslow, *Toward a Psychology of Being*, 2nd ed. (New York: Van Nostrand, 1968), ch.3.

13. *Shorter Oxford English Dictionary*.

Chapter 8

1. Friendliness is a species of love. I have not called the attitude-virtue "love"

because the term has so many different meanings and because the seventh attitude-virtue is also a species of love. But what I mean by "friendliness" is close to what H. Richard Niebuhr means in his classic description of "love": "Love is *rejoicing* over the existence of the beloved one; it is the desire that he be rather than not be; it is longing for his presence when he is absent; it is happiness in the thought of him; it is profound satisfaction over everything that makes him great and glorious. Love is *gratitude*: it is thankfulness for the existence of the beloved; it is the happy acceptance of everything that he gives without the jealous feeling that the self ought to be able to do as much; it is a gratitude that does not seek equality; it is wonder over the other's gift of himself in companionship. Love is *reverence*: it keeps its distance even as it draws near; it does not seek to absorb the other in the self or want to be absorbed by it; it rejoices in the otherness of the other; it desires the beloved to be what he is and does not seek to refashion him into a replica of the self or to make him a means to the self's advancement. As reverence love is and seeks knowledge of the other, not by way of curiosity nor for the sake of gaining power but in rejoicing and in wonder. In all such love there is an element of that 'holy fear' which is not a form of flight but rather deep respect for the otherness of the beloved and the profound unwillingness to violate his integrity. Love is *loyalty*; it is the willingness to let the self be destroyed rather than that the other cease to be; it is the commitment of the self by self-binding will to make the other great." *The Purpose of the Church and Its Ministry* (New York: Harper & Row, 1956), p.35 (italics mine). (I have quoted the passage in full because it is not easily accessible.)

2. Concerning the difference between genuine orgasm and what most people understand to be orgasm, and concerning the fear of self-loss in orgasm, see Alexander Lowen, *Love and Orgasm* (New York: Signet, 1965), chs.4, 11, 17.

3. Martin Buber, *The Knowledge of Man* (London: Allen & Unwin, 1965), p.79. Buber is describing the main condition for "genuine dialogue" or "I-Thou encounter." What I call "friendliness" includes many elements which are not necessarily present in an I-Thou attitude, as we shall see.

4. For a vivid description of deep-level confrontation, see Gregory Baum, *Man Becoming* (New York: Herder, 1970), pp.43-51, 155-58.

5. Erik Erikson advocates an interpretation of the Golden Rule in which we

seek a human encounter which strengthens the ego-strengths or virtues of each person. This involves a giving and receiving which are appropriate to the different needs and capacities of each person, e.g. the parent and the child. More subtly, in relations between adults, both the adult and the child within each person needs to be acknowledged. In my sketch of friendliness I have not explored these very important features of friendship, which could be considered under both "confrontation" and "celebration." For Erikson, see *Insight and Responsibility* (London: Faber, 1956), ch.6. Cf. Don Browning, *Generative Man: Psychoanalytic Perspectives* (Philadelphia: Westminster, 1973), pp.153, 212–13.

6. Milton Mayeroff makes an important distinction between admiration and adulation: "Admiration as spontaneous delight should not be confused with adulation. Admiration brings me closer to the one cared for; I see him as he is. In hero worship, however, I relate largely to a figment of my own imagination and am basically out of touch with the other. Also, admiration is not at the expense of yet another whom I necessarily disparage by comparison with the one I praise excessively. Adulation has nothing to do with caring." *On Caring* (New York: Harper & Row, 1971), p. 45.

7. Concerning "selflessness" as an unselfconscious, self-forgetful concentration of attention outside oneself, see Herbert Fingarette, *The Self in Transformation* (New York: Harper & Row, 1963), ch.7. He sees this selflessness as a possible outcome of both deep psychotherapy and (Zen-type) mysticism.

8. Concerning patience, see Mayeroff, *op.cit.*, pp.17–18. See also Gabriel Marcel, *Homo Viator* (New York: Harper & Row, 1962), pp.38–40.

9. A major theme in Arthur Miller's play *After the Fall* is the need to become, and to let others become, a separate person; but Miller indicates little that goes beyond *not* being entangled in a symbiotic relationship. Carl Rogers is more positive: "The degree to which I can create relationships which facilitate the growth of others as separate persons is a measure of the growth I have achieved in myself" (quoted at the beginning of Mayeroff, *op.cit.*).

10. Cf. William Lynch, *Images of Hope* (New York: Mentor-Omega, 1966),

pp.129–30: "What accounts for the possibility of an absolutely autonomous act of wishing that simply wishes a thing and is at peace with itself in doing so is some relationships of mutality. Let us imagine that the individual has achieved a satisfactory relationship or set of relationships of friendship or love. Granted such a relationship, the individual does whatever he wishes so long as the range of action does not put him outside the relationship . . . Love and do what you will . . . He who has a real friend need not consult him."

11. Martin Buber, *I and Thou*, tr. R.G.Smith (New York: Scribners', 1958), p.103.

12. Erik Erikson's label for parental concern is "generativity." See *Insight and Responsibility* (London: Faber, 1964), pp.130-2. He links it with a "need to be needed" which is allegedly instinctual in human beings in relation to the oncoming generation.

13. For a further discussion of prophetic concern, see Gregory Baum, *Religion and Alienation: A Theological Reading of Sociology* (New York: Paulist Press, 1975), especially chs. 4, 9—12. See also essay on Baum in Donald Evans, *Faith, Authenticity and Morality* (Toronto: University of Toronto Press, forthcoming).

14. Erik Erikson, *op.cit.*, p.130.

15. Milton Mayeroff, *On Caring* (New York: Harper & Row, 1971).

16. If the collective needs of society and the natural environment provide the *only* criteria for deciding on a life-style, this can blind us to individual needs and individual virtues which should also be recognized. Victor Ferkiss errs in this direction in *Technological Man* (New York: Braziller, 1969). Sam Keen errs in the opposite direction in *Apology for Wonder* (New York: Harper & Row, 1969), though in recent writings he brings in more communal concern. Don Browning finds middle ground in his version of Erikson's philosophy in *Generative Man: Psychoanalytic Perspectives* (Philadelphia: Westminster, 1973), introduction, chs. 6, 7. For further discussion of the tension between personal (intrapersonal and interpersonal) emphases and communal emphases, see Donald Evans, *Faith Authenticity and Morality*, chs. 3, 4, and 6.

17. Ecological concern is linked in an interesting way to Erikson's "generativity" (cf. my "parental concern") by Don Browning in *op.cit.*, chs. 6, 7.

18. Dietrich Bonhoeffer, *Letters and Papers from Prison* (New York: Macmillan, 1972), p. 174.

19. T.S.Eliot, *Four Quartets* (London: Faber, 1944), "Burnt Norton."

20. Concerning this distinction see W.T. Stace, *Mysticism and Philosophy* (London: Macmillan, 1961), ch. 2. Cf. Evelyn Underhill's first two stages of contemplation in her *Practical Mysticism* (New York: Dutton, 1943).

21. For example, J.-M. Dechanet, *Christian Yoga* (London: Burns & Oates, 1960).

22. Concerning Freudian analysis as a preparation for contemplation, see Ian Kent and William Nicholls, *I A Mness: The Discovery of the Self Beyond the Ego* (New York: Bobbs-Merrill, 1972).

23. For example, Stace, *op.cit.*, chs. 5,6; or Ninian Smart, *Reasons and Faiths* (London: Routledge, 1958), ch.2.

24. Here I am influenced by Herbert Fingarette, *The Self in Transformation* (New York: Harper & Row, 1963), ch. 7.

25. Cf. Søren Kierkegaard's knight of infinite resignation, who is very narcissistic and self-conscious about his own piety. *Fear and Trembling* (New York: Doubleday, 1954), pp.45-7.

Chapter 9

1. Erik Erikson, *Childhood and Society*, 2nd ed. (New York: Norton, 1963), chs. 2, 7; *Identity, Youth and Crisis* (New York: Norton, 1968), ch. 3; *Insight and Responsibility* (London: Faber, 1964), ch. 4; *Young Man*

Luther (New York: Norton, 1958), ch. 8; Richard I. Evans, *Dialogue with Erik Erikson* (New York: Dutton, 1969), ch. 1.

2. Erik Erikson, *Young Man Luther*. What I say is a simplification of Erikson's account, which is far more complex and far less tidy, and which includes a good deal concerning fifth-stage struggles in relation to trust and distrust. But I think I am not distorting the broad outline of Erikson on Luther.

3. Reinhold Niebuhr, *The Nature and Destiny of Man*, Vol.I (London: Nisbet, 1941), pp.267-8, 306-8.

4. Responsibility is a complex exception to this. It is true that irresponsibility can seriously limit the extent to which a person is capable of integrated commitment. But a common kind of responsibility can also limit this. If a person is responsible in a very conformist way and does not question the roles which have been assigned to him or the traditions which he has been taught, he probably will not need to be part of an innovative moment in order to discover who he is. He already knows: he is the person who contributes such-and-such skills to the community. Many people develop little beyond a snug, conformist kind of responsibility. They might, paradoxically, benefit from a little alienation to spur them on to a non-conformist self-commitment. Sometimes, however, alienation is not necessary for this. Sometimes responsibility includes a growing awareness of what one's own work and other people's work is *for*: to meet the basic needs of people in a society. And it then becomes obvious that society as it now exists is incompetent and unjust in performing this task. Responsibility can then be a stimulus to self-commitment, and complement it. Responsibility is then to a great extent an *undertaking* of new tasks, an *innovating* in response to human needs, a *creation* of new roles in new communities, But such responsibility is still far short of a radical *concern*, which presupposes responsibility but transforms and transcends it as a stance towards human need.

5. It is perhaps misleading to contrast responsibility with the other attitude-virtues in this way, for since it is a religious attitude, it could be included under "faith"; so also, for that matter, could the three species of love. But responsibility not only has a great deal to do with *work* in everyday life but

it is also close to what Christians have included under "works" as contrasted with "faith." Similarly "love" has traditionally been contrasted with "faith."

6. Gabriel Marcel, *Homo Viator* (New York: Harper & Rox, 1951), ch. 2, especially pp.63-7.

7. Erik Erikson, *Childhood and Society*, 2nd ed. (New York: Norton, 1963), p.67.i

8. See *op.cit.*, pp.79-80.

9. Abraham Maslow, *Toward a Psychology of Being*, 2nd ed. (New York: Van Nostrand, 1968), ch. 3; see also *Motivation and Personality*, 2nd. ed. (New York: Harper & Row, 1970), chs. 4, 12.

10. Erik Erikson, *Insight and Responsibility* (London: Faber, 1964), p.131.

11. *Courage* is an element in all the constituents of trust, as we have seen; and more generally it can be understood as a persistence in the struggle to be open to life-affirming forces and resistant to life-destructive forces. *Justice* as a virtue is an element in prophetic concern and also in responsibility, where it is a conscientious fairness in rule observance. *Moderation* is not always a virtue, in my opinion: immoderate concern may well be virtuous. But moderation is clearly virtuous where it is a restraint on idolatrous excess; so it comes under fidelity-trust. *Prudence* could perhaps be included in fuller accounts of humility and responsibility.

12. As an element in responsibility, honesty is a conscientious fulfillment of requirements, a reliability in word and deed. As an element in self-commitment, it means being true to oneself and to the full range of one's experience in the shape of one's commitment. As an element in friendliness, honesty is a candor in confrontation. As an element in passionate trust it means facing and following one's passions in daily life.

13. Creativity can be regarded to a considerable extent as a by-product of various attitude-virtues which provide the main conditions for its flourishing. Among the main conditions for creativity I would list the following: passionate trust, humility as an active, unashamed exercise of one's powers, self-acceptance as a liberation of energy for involvement in

the world outside the family, responsibility as a disciplined competence, friendliness as confirmation, celebration, concentration, and affection, concern as empathy, and contemplation generally. But creativity is not only a by-product of various attitude-virtues; it is also an element in all of them, for each attitude-virtue is a distinctive way of participating in a life-affirming power which is creative. But perhaps there is a case for also listing creativity as a distinct and additional constituent of human fulfillment. One possible reason for adding creativity is that it is closely associated with desirable human states which have not been adequately emphasized in my account of human fulfillment: spontaneity, exuberance, joyfulness, and imaginative fertility. But all these states might well have been emphasized, especially in the section on passion. A possible reason for *not* adding creativity is that it is ultimately a gift actively received into one's life rather than a private achievement; but this is true of all the eight attitude-virtues, in varying ways. Yet even if creativity is a virtue, it does not seem to be an attitude. There are some interesting questions here which deserve further investigation.

14. Reverence, with its associated feelings of awe and wonder, varies according to the attitude-virtue in which it is present. It arises in all of them because they focus on a mysterious reality which pervades and unifies the cosmos. This reality is mysterious not only because it transcends all particulars in the universe, but also because it transcends our intellectual understanding and practical control. God is beyond our grasp. We can only describe God as the appropriate focus of such-and-such a pervasive, unifying attitude; we can not understand how there can be such a focus.

15. For example, I omit a particular kind of reverence, namely most of what Rudolph Otto includes in his description of a "numinous" dread of the divine. I certainly accept the kind of reverence which is associated with humility, as I have described that attitude-virtue. Otto's stance, however, verges at times on self-humiliation. See his *The Idea of the Holy*, 2nd ed. (London: Oxford University Press, 1950). Another religious attitude which I reject is a Kierkegaard obedience to God which overrides and contradicts morality. In *Fear and Trembling* (New York: Doubleday, 1954) Søren Kierkegaard interprets the story of Abraham and the sacrifice of Isaac as one in which Abraham obeys God even though he believes that what God commands him to do is immoral: and Kierkegaard applauds

Abraham for this. Some hints concerning how I would construe obedience to God as a stance to be cultivated can be seen in the sections of receptivity, passion, and responsibility. I also discuss it in "Does Religious Faith Conflict with Moral Freedom?" (See Bibliography A.)

16. For a brief and brilliant criticism of this tradition, see H. Richard Niebuhr, "Reflections on Faith, Hope and Love," *The Journal of Religious Ethics*, Vol. 2, Spring, 1974.

17. On an Eriksonian view of the origins of trust it is a natural development of a human capacity. We do not need to show that trust has God as in some sense part-*cause* in order to hold plausibly that the belief in God which trust involves may be true. The origin of a belief has nothing intrinsically to do with its truth. In this book, however, I have been assuming that trust grows as we are now responsive to the divine gift of life energies. Whether this begins in infancy is a question which I note a little later in this chapter. (The idea that a statement concerning the origin or genesis of a belief can by itself disprove the belief is what philosophers call the "Genetic Fallacy." Freud's argument that religious beliefs are false does not involve this fallacy. His argument depends on his positivist philosophy, which restricts truth to scientific truth, and on his personal view of nature as so obviously hostile that distrust and unbelief are obviously rational. His psychoanalytic account of the origins of trust and religious belief is introduced as a supplementary "coup de grace" to explain why people are so irrational as to believe in God. If, with Erikson, we reject Freud's positivism and view of nature, we need not hold that the infantile origins of religious belief disproves it. On Freud and Erikson see ch. 3, note 5, and my *Faith, Authenticity and Morality*, Bibliography A.)

18. Martin Buber is illuminating in his discussion of the nature of the divine all-inclusiveness. See his *I and Thou*, tr. W. Kaufmann (New York: Scribners', 1970), pp. 127, 148, 160–61.

19. Erik Erikson, *Insight and Responsibility* (London: Faber, 1964), pp. 117, 180.

20. Martin Buber, *I and Thou*, p. 76.

21. Martin Buber, *Between Man and Man* (Boston: Beacon, 1955), pp. 88, 98; see also *I and Thou*, pp. 77–79.

22. Franklin Jones, *The Knee of Listening* (Los Angeles: Dawn Horse Press, 1972), pp. 9, 18-19. Wilhelm Reich also claims that the infant comes into the world with an awareness of life energies. See *The Murder of Christ* (New York: Noonday, 1970), p. 36.

23. "The predisposition to personality is the capacity for respect for the moral law as in itself a sufficient incentive for the will." See Immanuel Kant, *Religion Within the Limits of Reason Alone*, tr. R. M. Greene and H. H. Hudson (New York: Harper & Row, 1960), pp. 22-3. According to Silber's interpretation of Kant one must respect the moral law in order to be a person, a responsible individual acting according to the inner law of one's free nature; to reject the moral law is to forfeit personal fulfillment. See *ibid.*, pp. lxxxvii, xci, xciii, xciv, cxxxi.

24. Kant claimed that belief in God as Providence is presupposed by respect for the moral law. This presupposition is claimed on the basis of a complex analysis of various alleged elements in the moral law, so Kant's logical contention is more complex than those which move directly from attitude *x* to a religious conviction which is implied. See *Critique of Practical Reason*, tr. L. W. Beck (New York: Liberal Arts, 1956), Bk. II, ch. II.

25. Indeed, my own personal conviction is that a great deal of what Christians regard as revelation provides insight mainly concerning human nature and only indirectly and secondarily concerning the nature of God.

26. I discuss this more extensively in my essay on Baum in *Faith, Authenticity and Morality* (see Bibliography A).

27. The implication can be expressed as an *entailment*-relation between propositions: "Jones has attitude *x*" entails "Jones has belief *y*". In previous writings I construed the implication as a logical connection between a *speech-act* and a state of mind: in saying, "I have attitude *x*," I imply that I have belief *y*. A similar kind of logical connection holds between promising and intending: In saying, "I promise to do *a*," I imply that I intend to do *a*. Two features of speech-act implications should be noted: (i) The speaker is logically committed to having the state which is implied, but as a matter of fact he may not have it at all—for example when he promises insincerely. If religious attitudes "imply" religious convictions in this sense, a person might express the attitude while not having the

conviction. On my new entailment-relation analysis, he must actually have the conviction if he has the attitude. (I will consider this further in notes 28 and 34). (ii) Speech-act implications are assymetrical between first-person and third-person speakers. In saying, "*He* promises to do *a*," I do *not* imply that he intends to do *a*. But on my new analysis the proposition "He has attitude *x*" implies (entails) "He has belief *y*" in precisely the same way that the proposition, "I have attitude *x*" implies (entails) "I have belief *y*:" (I first explored speech-act implications, influenced by J. L. Austin, in my *The Logic of Self-Involvement* (London: SCM, 1963), where I showed how expressions of belief imply attitudes. My attempts to show that expressions of attitude imply beliefs can be seen in *Faith, Authenticity and Morality* (See Bibliography A).

28.   For example, "Jones trusts" entails "Jones trusts *x*" which entails "Jones believes that *x* exists." The entailment depends on the meaning of the word "trusts" as this is universally understood. It is a matter of universal definition. To trust *x* when one does not believe that *x* exists is not merely irrational; it is logically impossible. The entailment does not hold, of course, if the general context is one of make-believe, so that one is not *really* trusting *x*, but pretending to. In such a context, however, many other entailments of belief are suspended, for example, "Jones is grateful to *x*" no longer entails "Jones believes that *x* exists." A context of make-believe is precisely one in which such entailments are suspended. To have an attitude includes having the belief that its focus, *x*, exists. What characteristics of *x* are implied is a further matter, which I investigate in steps (b) and (c), where the entailments depend on *my* definitional description of "basic trust."

29.   A conviction concerning a cosmic focus is also implied in so far as a stance is *unconditional*, for example a trust "no matter what happens." Such a trust is not focused on any particular or set of particulars (or even the aggregate of all existing particulars, for these could change). The focus must be a common characteristic or a transcendent reality which continues regardless of changes in particulars. And, of course, if it is a trust "though the universe cease to be," its focus must be a transcendent reality.

30.   A third lies somewhere between the two: existence. Some philosophers deal with existence as if it were a fundamental common characteristic, a

category. Others deal with existence as if it were an immanent-transcendent reality.

31. I realize that the idea of "fitting" one's language to one's pre-verbal experience of a way of being in the world is controversial. Philosophers of the "linguistic analysis" school which recently emerged in the English-speaking world under the influence of L. Wittgenstein and J. Austin tend to repudiate such an idea. They assume that we cannot elucidate such involvements of the self except by examining the language in which the involvements are publicly expressed. They reject the claim that we can judge the appropriateness of public language concerning psychological states by intuitively introspecting some private experience or pre-verbal meaning. Although I once tended to agree with this "linguistic" approach, I now disagree. My shift in philosophical method from linguistic analysis to phenomenology is explained in "Philosophical Analysis and Religious Faith" and *Faith, Authenticity and Morality* (see Bibliography A). I have three reasons for believing that we can get "behind" or "below" language so as to understand and appraise talk about fundamental human states. First, I have myself during psychotherapy relived experiences prior to my learning of language and I have been with dozens of people who have done the same; moreover, I know what it is to be aware of the same experience in one's present daily life, saturated though that life now is with language. As I wrote many of the sections on trust and distrust I was aware of this dimension of adult experience. It is literally pre-linguistic. Second, other philosphers have shown that it is possible to philosophize in an intelligible and illuminating way concerning experience which is epistemologically prior to language and reflection. Marcel's "secondary reflection" is an example of this. Marcel argues convincingly that—to take only one of his many claims—an understanding of the expression "*my* body" by reference to the meaning of "my" in "*my* possessions" or "*my* tools" is useless, for all three depend on a primary, pre-linguistic awareness which Marcel somehow conveys through language: *The Mystery of Being*, Vol. I, chs. 5, 6 (see Bibliography A). See also George Schrader on "pre-reflective meaning" in "The Structure of Emotion" in James M. Edie, ed., *Invitation to Phenomenology* (Chicago: Quadrangle, 1965). Third, contemplative writers also successfully write about prelinguistic experience—or perhaps we should also refer to it as "post-linguistic" experience—somehow choosing appropriate (though at times paradoxical) language to fit what

they intuit. And in reflections concerning my own limited contemplative experience I have found the same process going on.

32. If a person is very apathetic the split sometimes goes beyond religious matters into a wide range of life. It is often reinforced by a technological mind-set in which religious convictions are divorced from their life context of religious attitudes. Often what a positivist disbelieves concerning "God" has little to do with what is implied by basic trust—his own or other people's.

33. The contradiction is a violation of an entailment which depends on the meaning of the attitude-word, for example on my description of basic trust in so far as this is proposed as a stipulative definition of "basic trust."

34. Earlier I said, "If a person has a cosmic stance he must have a cosmic conviction." This claim needs to be understood on two different levels, pre-linguistic and linguistic. At a pre-linguistic level there are two distinguishable but inseparable elements in a person's way of being in the world: the overall orientation of the person (later articulated as a stance which has components of behavior, emotion, and will) and the person's discernment of his overall environment (later articulated as a conviction of the mind). The orientation or inchoate stance and the discernment or inchoate conviction are linked in an indissoluble unity. At the linguistic level this unity is expressed as an entailment-relation between the description of the cosmic stance and the description of the cosmic conviction. Hence someone whose stance is appropriately articulated as, for example, basic trust, must have a belief in divine providence. But whether or not such an articulation is appropriate is essentially a matter for the person himself or herself to decide by reflection. He has the final say concerning what linguistic structure best fits the pre-linguistic structure of his way of being in the world. He may have an inchoate conviction which I think would be appropriately articulated as belief in divine providence, but I can merely propose this to him. On the linguistic level he does not have such a conviction unless and until he has articulated it as his own conviction. But since words which have generally accepted or stipulative meanings carry entailments, it can make sense for me to point out to him that he is *logically committed* to a conviction which is entailed by what he has already said about his stance, even though I am not claiming that he

already has the conviction. And if his articulation of his own trust includes an expression of religious conviction to elucidate what he means by the stance, he cannot affirm that he has the stance and deny that he has the conviction; he *must have* the conviction. The distinction between saying that someone is logically committed to a conviction which he may or may not have and saying that he must have the conviction is important. For example, it is one thing to say that someone who has basic trust is logically committed to belief in God and another to say that he must have belief in God. The difference lies in the stage he is at in articulating his own trust. Where he has not articulated it at all, I can at most propose an articulation for his consideration, for he has privileged access to his prelinguistic way of being in the world. Also, as I show in *Faith, Authenticity and Morality*, ch. 7 (see Bibliography A) the acceptance of an articulation involves a commitment to live in the world in such-and-such a linguistically structured way; the decision is his, not mine.

It is important to distinguish the claim that someone who has stance *S* is *logically committed* to conviction *C* and the claim that someone who has *S must have C* from the claim that *S* is *usually accompanied* by *C*, consciously or unconsciously. Where the first and second claims are established by logical analysis, the third is an empirical generalization and is established by compiling empirical observations, that is, by induction. Both induction and logical analysis differ from reflection. Induction involves observation of correlation between two kinds of already articulated events or states. Logical analysis involves a comparison between two linguistic structures, looking for logical consistency. Reflection involves a comparison between pre-linguistic and linguistic structures, looking for fit.

35. Another kind of objection, which I do not consider here, is that the religious convictions which are allegedly implied are not tenable because they are so internally inconsistent as to be unintelligible—like belief in a round square. For example, some philosophers have claimed that it is logically impossible for there to be a reality which is personal yet bodiless and omnipresent. Perhaps some cosmic conviction is implied by basic trust (as in step (b)) but the conviction cannot be intelligibly articulated. I am not convinced by this kind of objection, and elsewhere have attempted to deal with some of the basic philosophical issues which it raises concerning talk about God. See *Faith, Authenticity and Morality* (Bibliography A).

36. I am thinking not only of what H. Richard Niebuhr has pointed out concerning "the One" (see page 42) but also the integrating function which some ideologies can provide in self-commitment (see page 126).

37. I think of Kierkegaard, Sartre, Marcel, Buber, Tillich, Bultmann, and many others. They all agree that the best stance from which to discern the ultimate is *not* the neutral, disinterested posture of positivist science. But they disagree in their proposed alternative.

38. Some Christian theologians would deny that trust is a sufficient condition for discerning the divine. Their reason is that this would make religious experience depend entirely on man, ignoring our human dependence on God's free will in revealing himself to us. But if trust itself is as much a divine gift as it is a personal decision, this objection loses some of its power.

39. Jean-Paul Sartre, *Existentialism and Humanism* (London: Methuen, 1948).

40. Paul Tillich, *The Courage to Be* (London: Nisbet, 1952).

41. Rudolph Otto, *The Idea of the Holy*, 2nd ed. (London: Oxford University Press, 1950).

42. If there *were* a stance-free way to settle metaphysical issues, then philosophers could first try to establish the existence and nature of God and, if successful, could then ask what stances are appropriate towards God. This rationalistic approach, with its assumption of stance-freeness, is different from both a neo-Kantian and an existentialist approach.

43. There is of course all the more reason to do this if there are as yet no impressive experiences of metaphysical discernment, whether theistic or atheistic. The neo-Kantian approach is specially appropriate when religious and anti-religious experiences are both meager.

BIBLIOGRAPHIES

Bibliography A lists works which have been the most influential in writing this book, and works by the author which are directly relevant. Other bibliographies include some works which were not influential and some which conflict with the approach or the conclusions in this book.

BIBLIOGRAPHY A: GENERAL BACKGROUND

GREGORY BAUM   *Man Becoming* (New York: Herder, 1970). *Religion and Alienation: A Theological Reading of Sociology* (New York: Paulist, 1975).

MARTIN BUBER   *I and Thou*, tr. W. Kaufmann (New York: Scribners', 1970; London: T. and T. Clark, 1971). "Elements of the Interhuman," *The Knowledge of God* (London: Allen & Unwin, 1965).

ALBERT CAMUS   *The Fall*, tr. Justin O'Brien (New York: Vintage, 1956; London: Penguin, 1970).

DONALD EVANS   "Differences Between Scientific and Religious Assertions," Ian Barbour, ed., *Science and Religion* (New York: Harper & Row, 1968). "Gregory Baum's Theology of Liberation,"* *Studies in Religion*, Vol. I, No. 1, Summer, 1971. "Keen on Authentic Man,"* *Studies in Religion*, Vol. III, No. 1, Summer, 1973. "Does Religious Faith Conflict with Moral Freedom?",* Gene Outka and John Reeder, eds., *Religion and Morality* (New York: Doubleday, 1974). "Faith and Belief," *Religious Studies*, Vol. 10, Nos. 2, 3, March & June, 1974. "Philosophical Analysis and Religious Faith: Some Retrospective Reflections," F. Duchesneau, ed., *Faith and Contemporary Epistemologies* (Ottawa: University of Ottawa, 1977). *Faith, Authenticity and Morality* (Toronto: University of Toronto Press, forthcoming): this includes revised versions of essays marked with an asterisk * above.

ERIK ERIKSON   *Childhood and Society*, 2nd ed. (New York: Norton, 1963; London: Paladin, 1977). *Young Man Luther* (New York: Norton, 1958; London: Faber, 1972).

HERBERT FINGARETTE   *The Self in Transformation* (New York: Harper & Row, 1963), ch. 7.

JAMES GUSTAFSON   *Christ and the Moral Life* (New York: Harper & Row, 1968).

SAM KEEN   *Apology for Wonder* (New York: Harper & Row, 1969). *To a Dancing God* (New York: Harper & Row, 1970; London: Collins, 1971). *Voices and Visions* (New York: Harper & Row, 1974).

R. D. LAING   *The Divided Self* (London: Penguin, 1965; New York: Pantheon, 1969). *The Politics of Experience* (London: Penguin, 1967).

D. H. LAWRENCE   *The Virgin and the Gipsy* (London: Penguin, 1970).

ALEXANDER LOWEN   *Depression and the Body: The Biological Basis of Faith and Reality* (Baltimore: Penguin, 1973). *The Language of the Body* (New York and London: Collier Macmillan, 1971).

WILLIAM LYNCH   *Images of Hope* (New York: Mentor, 1956).

GABRIEL MARCEL   *Homo Viator* (New York: Harper, 1951), ch. 1, 2. *The Mystery of Being*, Vols. I, II (Chicago: Regnery: 1960).

MILTON MAYEROFF   *On Caring* (New York: Harper & Row, 1971; London: Harper, 1972).

ARTHUR MILLER   *After the Fall* (New York: Bantam, 1965).

H. RICHARD NIEBUHR   *The Responsible Self* (New York: Harper & Row, 1963; London: Harper, 1963).

PAUL TILLICH   *The Courage to Be* (London: Nisbet, 1952; New Haven: Yale University Press, 1952).

LEO TOLSTOY   *The Death of Ivan Ilych* (New York and London: American Library, 1960).

EVELYN UNDERHILL   *Practical Mysticism* (New York: Dutton, 1943).

WILHELM REICH   *The Murder of Christ* (New York: Noonday, 1970; London: Souvenir Press, 1975).

BIBLIOGRAPHY B: RELIGIOUS ATTITUDES

J.-M.DECHANET   *Christian Yoga* (London: Burns & Oates, 1960).

H. H. FARMER   *Revelation and Religion* (London: Nisbet, 1954).

F. C. HAPPOLD   *Mysticism: A Study and an Anthology* (London: Penguin, 1963).

GORDON KAUFMAN   *God the Problem* (Cambridge: Harvard University Press, 1972), ch. 3; (London: Harvard University Press, 1973).

SØREN KIERKEGAARD   *Fear and Trembling* (New York: Doubleday, 1954).

SCHUBERT OGDEN   *The Reality of God and Other Essays* (New York: Harper & Row, 1963), pp. 32–7. "The Task of Philosophical Theology," Robert A. Evans, ed., *The Future of Philosophical Theology* (Philadelphia: Westminster, 1971).

FRIEDRICH SCHLEIERMACHER   *The Christian Faith* (Edinburgh: T. and T. Clark, 1928; Philadelphia: Fortress, 1976), sections 3–5, 15–17, 29–30.

And from Bibliography A: Baum, Buber, Evans, Gustafson, Keen, Lynch, Marcel, Niebuhr, Tillich.

BIBLIOGRAPHY C: CHRISTIAN ETHICS OF VIRTUE

FREDERICK S. CARNEY   "The Virtue-Obligation Controversy," *The Journal of Religious Ethics*, Vol. I, Fall, 1973 (including extensive bibliography of both Christian and secular works concerning ethics of virtue).

RICHARD S. CROUTER   "H. Richard Niebuhr and Stoicism," *The Journal of Religious Ethics*, Vol. 2, Fall, 1974.

JAMES GUSTAFSON   *Christian Ethics and the Community* (Philadelphia: Pilgrim Press, 1971), Pt. 2. *Can Ethics Be Christian?* (Chicago and London: University of Chicago Press, 1975).

DAVID BAILY HARNED   *Faith and Virtue* (Philadelphia: Pilgrim Press, 1973; Edinburgh: St. Andrew Press, 1973).

STANLEY HAUERWAS   *Character and the Christian Life* (San Antonio, Texas: Trinity University Press, 1975). *Vision and Virtue* (Notre Dame: Fides Publishers, 1975), chs. 2-4.

SØREN KIERKEGAARD   *Concluding Unscientific Postscript* (Princeton: Princeton University Press, 1941), Pt. 2, chs. 1-3.

KNUD E. LOGSTRUP   *The Ethical Demand* (Philadelphia: Fortress, 1971).

ENDA MCDONAGH   *Gift and Call: Towards a Christian Theology of Morality* (St. Meinrad, Indiana: Abbey Press, 1975; London: Gill and McMillan, 1975).

HELEN OPPENHEIMER   "Christian Flourishing," *Religious Studies*, Vol. 5, No. 2, December, 1969.

GENE OUTKA   "Character, Conduct and the Love Commandment," Gene Outka and Paul Ramsey, eds., *Norm and Context in Christian Ethics* (New York: Scribners', 1968). *Agape* (New Haven and London: Yale University Press, 1972).

H. RICHARD NIEBUHR   "Reflections on Faith, Hope and Love," *The Journal of Religious Ethics*, Vol. 2, Spring, 1974.

REINHOLD NIEBUHR   *The Nature and Destiny of Man*, Vol. 1 (London: Nisbet, 1941), chs. 6-8; (New York: Scribners', 1949).

And from Bibliography A : Baum, Evans, Gustafson, Keen, Marcel, Niebuhr, Tillich

BIBLIOGRAPHY D: PHILOSOPHICAL ETHICS OF VIRTUE

ARISTOTLE   *Nicomachean Ethics*, in Richard McKeon, ed., *Introduction to Aristotle* (New York: Modern Library, 1947; Oxford: Oxford University Press, 1954).

WILLIAM FRANKENA   "The Ethics of Love Considered as an Ethics of Virtue," *The Journal of Religious Ethics*, Vol. 1, Fall, 1973. "Conversations with Carney and Hauerwas," *The Journal of Religious Ethics*, Vol. 3, Spring, 1975.

STUART HAMPSHIRE   "Morality and Pessimism," *The New York Review of Books*, Vol. XIX, Nos. 11, 12, Jan. 25, 1973.

IMMANUEL KANT   *Religion Within the Limits of Reason Alone*, tr. R. M. Greene and H. H. Hudson (New York: Harper & Row, 1960). *Critique of Practical Reason*, tr. L. W. Beck (New York: Liberal Arts, 1956).

JOHN MACMURRAY   *Reason and Emotion* (London: Faber, 1962).

IRIS MURDOCH   *The Sovereignty of Good* (London: Routledge, 1970).

THOMAS NAGEL   *The Possibility of Altruism* (Oxford: Clarendon, 1970).

E. PINCOFFS   "Quandary Ethics," *Mind*, Vol. LXXX, No. 320, October, 1971.

J.M. RIST   *Stoic Philosophy* (Cambridge: Cambridge University Press, 1969).

PETER STRAWSON   "Social Morality and Individual Ideal" *Philosophy* Vol. 36, 1961.

RICHARD TAYLOR   *Good and Evil: A New Direction* (London: Macmillan, 1970), chs. 15–17.

JAMES D. WALLACE   "Cowardice and Courage," *Studies in Ethics*,

American Philosophical Quarterly Monograph, No. 7 (Oxford: Blackwell, 1973).

J.R.S. WILSON   *Emotion and Object* (Cambridge: Cambridge University Press, 1972), pp. 185-7.

GEORGE HENDRIK VON WRIGHT   *The Varieties of Goodness* (London: Routledge, 1963), ch. 7.

And from Bibliography *A*: Mayeroff

BIBLIOGRAPHY E: PSYCHOTHERAPY AND HUMAN NATURE

EDMUND BERGLER   *The Basic Neurosis* (New York: Grune & Stratton, 1947).

ERIK ERIKSON   *Insight and Responsibility* (London: Faber, 1964; New York: Norton, 1964). *Identity: Youth and Crisis* (New York: Norton, 1968; London: Faber, 1971).

RICHARD I. EVANS   *Dialogue with Erik Erikson* (New York: Dutton, 1969; London: Harper, 1967).

VIKTOR E. FRANKL   *Man's Search for Meaning* (New York: Washington Square Press, 1963; London: Hodder, 1963). *The Doctor and the Soul* (New York: Bantam, 1967).

LEA HINDLEY-SMITH   *Ronald and Susan* (Toronto: Therafields Foundation, 1975); *Secret Places* (Toronto: Therafields Foundation, 1976); *The Way It Might Have Been* (Toronto: Therafields Foundation, 1977).

ARTHUR JANOV   *The Primal Scream* (New York: Delta, 1970; London: Sphere, 1973). *The Primal Revolution* (New York: Simon Schuster, 1972; London: Sphere: 1975).

ALEXANDER LOWEN   *Bioenergetics* (New York: Coward, McCann and Geoghegan, 1975).

ROLLO MAY   *Love and Will* (New York: Norton, 1969; London: Fontana, 1972).

ABRAHAM MASLOW   *Towards a Psychology of Being*, 2nd ed. (New York: Van Nostrand, 1968; London: Van Nostrand; New York: Reinhold, 1969).

WILHELM REICH   *Character Analysis* (New York: Noonday, 1949, London: Vision Press, 1976).

ROBERT WAELDER   *Basic Theory of Pyschoanalysis* (New York: Schocken, 1964).
And from Bibliography *A*: Erikson, Laing, Lowen

BIBLIOGRAPHY F: PSYCHOLOGICAL DIMENSIONS OF RELIGION & MORALITY

ERNEST BECKER   *The Denial of Death* (New York: The Free Press, 1973; London: Collier Macmillan, 1976).

DON BROWNING   *Generative Man: Psychoanalytic Perspectives* (Philadelphia: Westminster, 1973). *Atonement and Psychotherapy* (Philadelphia: Westminster, 1966).

SIGMUND FREUD   *The Future of an Illusion* (New York: Doubleday, 1957; London: Hogarth Press, 1962).

SEWARD HILTNER   *Theological Dynamics* (New York: Abingdon, 1972).

PETER HOMANS   *Theology After Freud* (New York: Bobbs-Merrill, 1970).

IAN KENT and WILLIAM NICHOLLS   *I AMness: The Discovery of the Self Beyond the Ego* (New York: Bobbs-Merrill, 1972).

SØREN KIERKEGAARD   *The Concept of Dread* (Princeton: Princeton University Press, 1944). *The Sickness Unto Death* (New York: Doubleday, 1954).

ROY S. LEE   *Freud and Christianity* (London: Clarke, 1948). *Your Growing Child and Religion* (London: Penguin, 1965).

SHARON MACISAAC   *Freud and Original Sin* (New York: Paulist, 1974).

THOMAS ODEN   *The Intensive Group Experience: The New Pietism* (Philadelphia: Westminster, 1972).

MAX SCHELER   *Ressentiment*, tr. W. Holdheim (New York: Schocken, 1961, 1972).

And from Bibliography *A*: Baum (1970), Camus, Evans (1971, 1973), Fingarette, Keen, Lawrence, Lynch, Miller, Tolstoy

AUTHOR INDEX

Aquinas, Thomas, 120; ch. 6, n. 3

Baum, Gregory, 104, 173; ch. 8, n. 4, 13
Berger, Peter, 3, 27
Bergler, Edmund, 51
Bonhoeffer, Dietrich, 147
Browning, Don, ch. 8, n. 16; 17
Buber, Martin, 12, 16, 23, 60, 67, 68, 131, 139, 156, 170; Intr. n. 15; ch. 2, n. 26; ch. 7, n. 4; ch. 8, n. 3; ch. 9, n. 18

Camus, Albert, ch. 3, n. 2; ch. 7, n. 3

Eliot, T. S., ch. 8, n. 19
Erikson, Erik, 16, 24, 35, 39, 56, 76, 114, 144, 157, 158, 159, 162, 165, 166, 170, 171; Intr., n. 17; ch. 2, n. 14; ch. 7, n. 6; ch. 8, n. 12

Ferkiss, Victor, ch. 8, n. 16
Fingarette, Herbert, ch. 8, n. 7; ch. 8, n. 24
Francis of Assisi, 134
Frankel, Viktor, 122
Freud, Sigmund, 9, 97, 151; ch. 3, n. 5; ch. 9, n. 17

Gustafson, James, 78; Intr. n. 13; ch. 5, n. 1, 6

Hampshire, Stuart, Intr. n. 12
Harned, David, ch. 5, n. 3
Hiltner, Seward, 57; Intr. n. 2
Hindley-Smith, Lea, Intr. n. 1

Janov, Arthur, 35
John of the Cross, 35
Jones, Franklin, 170

Kant, Immanuel, 172, 173, 174; Intr. n. 18; ch. 9, n. 23, 24
Kaufman, Gordon, 115
Kent, Ian, ch. 8, n. 22
Keen, Sam, 25, 27, 28, 33, 35, 36, 37, 41, 69, 80; ch. 8, n. 16
Kierkegaard, Soren, 81, 82, 115; ch. 6, n. 14; ch. 8, n. 25; ch. 9, n. 15
Kitamori, Kozoh, ch. 6, n. 15

Laing, R. D., 24, 25, 54, 79, 80

SUBJECT INDEX

Good and Bad Mother, 29
ocean waves, 31
and bodily needs, 39, 62
the void, 59
liberating presence, 103
accepting person, 119

Theological virtues, 167

Unconscious
maternal image, 29
reality-assurance, 41
womb and infancy, 43
strategies, 47
idolatry, 64–65
fear of void, 80
despair, 82
apathy, 90
accusatory stance, 119

Void
negative way, 32–34
common to all, 35
unconditional acceptance, 35–36
and anxiety, 45
and wariness, 49–50, 51, 51–52
and idolatry, 66
and despair, 79–80

Wariness
as hostility, 51–52
as miserliness, 53
as resentment, 50–51